LOU
MY WONDERFUL LIFE

Front cover: The greatest moment in football. Being carried from the MCG by adoring fans after captaining Collingwood to the 1953 premiership win over Geelong.

Back cover: Coming up 90 years and still as proud as ever to wear the most famous football jumper in the land.

The Slattery Media Group
1 Albert Street, Richmond
Victoria, Australia, 3121
visit slatterymedia.com

National Library of Australia Cataloguing-in-Publication entry
    Author: Richards, Lou.
    Title: Lou : my wonderful life / Lou Richards, Stephen Phillips.
    ISBN: 9781921778780 (pbk.)
    Subjects:
        Richards, Lou.
        Collingwood Football Club.
        Australian football players--Biography.
        Football players--Victoria--Collingwood--Biography.
        Sportscasters--Victoria--Biography.
        Australian football.
Other Authors/Contributors: Phillips, Stephen.
Dewey Number: 796.336092

Group Publisher: Geoff Slattery
Authors: Lou Richards and Stephen Phillips
Creative Director: Guy Shield
Designer: Kate Slattery
Typesetting: Stephen Lording

Printed and bound in Australia by Griffin Press

LOU RICHARDS WITH STEPHEN PHILLIPS

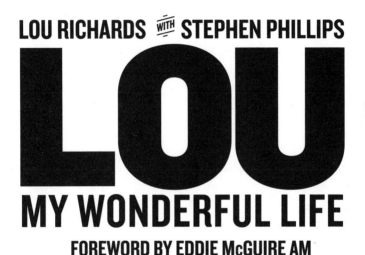

LOU
MY WONDERFUL LIFE
FOREWORD BY EDDIE McGUIRE AM

slattery
MEDIA GROUP

visit *slatterymedia.com*

CONTENTS

THE FACE OF THE GAME

There is no doubt: Lou Richards is one of the greatest names in the history of Australian sport and the media.

Walk into a pub in the bush, stroll into a footy club on the Murray or chat with folks in Alice Springs, along the beachfront on the Gold Coast or anywhere in the world where you find an Aussie, drop the name Lou Richards and you'll get a response. Everyone loves Lou.

For 50 years he has been the face of our game. A super rover who made the transition from premiership captain of Collingwood in 1953 into self-proclaimed multimedia megastar. He wasn't exaggerating.

He single-handedly took Collingwood and football, and gave it glitz and glamour. He turned average, everyday knockabouts into household names. Think of the Richards lexicon. Think of the Doormat and Slammin' Sam, Lethal Leigh, Fabulous Phil, the Macedonian Marvel and Rotten Ronnie, Bustling Billy and the Cowboy. If you didn't get a nickname from Louie you hadn't made it.

In a time when football journalism was one-dimensional, one man stood out. The *Sun News-Pictorial* became a marketing masterpiece on the crystal ball of the 'Kiss of Death'. The signs outside newsagents said it all: "Lou's Tips." That was enough.

At Collingwood he is revered. Not just because he is part of the famous Pannam that stretches back a hundred years to his grandfather Charlie. It is because at Collingwood we cherish our own.

From the backstreets he rose to become first a cheeky but super-talented rover and then a mighty leader. He is one of four living premiership captains who hold pride of place in the Collingwood family. The fact that he is the oldest living VFL premiership captain just adds a little lustre.

Sometimes we don't do enough to honour those who have gone before. At Collingwood we have made a legitimate effort to make our heritage come alive for the kids of today and for their kids and those to follow. Outside the Westpac Centre is a statue of Bobby Rose, a man regarded as the epitome of Collingwood's great heritage. In the months ahead we will be unveiling another statue. It will be of Lou Richards. It is Collingwood's way of saying thank you for a life dedicated to our club and the game.

Has any man in football history done more for the game? Through millions of words in the pages of *The Sun*, on air for a quarter of a century on radio and for half a century on television, Lou Richards has been the face of the game. More than that he gave it life and a sense of humour. He invented football as entertainment.

Generations grew up watching him deliver his verdict on the *World of Sport* panel, waited for their favourite player's name to be read out and, of course, for Lou's recipe of the week on Thursday night on *League Teams* with his great partners 'Captain Blood' Jack

Dyer and Bob 'Woofa' Davis. Others will remember listening to his commentary on so many Grand Final broadcasts and memorable highlights that were the soundtrack of our football lives.

For another two decades he was at Nine—the news-breaker, the newsmaker and a man we felt so deeply about that *The Footy Show* named its medal after him.

The football world loves Lou Richards. They love his outlook on life. They love the way he embraces our great game.

Louie—a legend, I salute you.

Eddie McGuire AM, President of Collingwood

September, 2012

THE LEGEND LIVES ON...

When it was suggested that *The Kiss of Death, Memoirs of a Sporting Legend* should be updated and reprinted, the central figure was delighted.

While not in the first bloom of youth, Lou Richards had to be dragged kicking and screaming into retirement. He frequently pointed out that his great inspiration in all things humorous was the American comedian George Burns.

The fact that they looked almost identical was one thing, they had been blessed with magnificent wives and both ambled through their 70s and 80s.

Like George, who passed away in 1996 at the age of 100, Lou always felt that the century was within his grasp, too.

To have watched and remember Lou on the football field you would need to be approaching 70. To have seen him and remembered him on *World of Sport* you'd be approaching middle age.

Yet the legend lives on...

The following pages are how I introduced him back in 1989 as yet another chapter in his remarkable life was to unfold:

The Kiss of Death: Introduction, 1989

Not many people can claim to have been crowned 'King', honoured by the Queen and classified as a living treasure by the National Trust, all in the space of a year. Pretty heady stuff for a knockabout kid reared in the back streets of one of Melbourne's toughest working-class suburbs. Those three honours emphasise just how important Lou Richards has become to the people of Melbourne.

In 1981 Lou was appointed King of Moomba, following such dignitaries as the Russian clown Oleg Popov, British actor Robert Morley, Australia's Frank Thring and an American rodent named Mickey Mouse. Lou had been court jester to John Farnham back in 1972 but few argued that Lou's crowning as representative of the city in 1981 was undeserved.

Louie the Fifteenth immediately issued his royal edict: "There will be sunshine for 10 days. I want everyone to have fun." He appointed 'Captain Blood' Jack Dyer as his court jester and announced that his four-year-old grand-daughter, Lucy Morrison, would accompany him in the yellow 1927 Rolls Royce for the Moomba parade. Mrs King, as his wife Edna was quickly dubbed, was relegated to the crowd. For Lou the 27th Moomba parade lived up to all his wishes—with just one major exception. For the first time in the history of Moomba it rained. The skies opened over Melbourne and none of its inhabitants was spared. The 'Kiss of Death' had struck again. Hurried research showed that it was indeed fine for the first 10 days of Moomba 1981. The problem was that Lou hadn't done his homework: the parade was on the 11th day!

The Queen was obviously impressed with his mock regal bearing and in her New Year's Honours in 1982 she appointed the one-time toothpaste tube-maker a Member of the British Empire. Former Australian Test vice-captain Neil Harvey, an old boy of Lou's *alma mater*, Collingwood Tech., and Ron Casey, the man who guided

Lou's radio and television career from the earliest days, were also honoured but Lou grabbed the front-page spotlight.

One reader of the *Sun* wrote:

We wondered how Liz
Could choose for our Lou
A gong to which he could really aspire.
We were all in a tizz
Till we finally knew
He's the Mouth of the British Empire.

It was little wonder that Rodney Davidson, the chairman of the National Trust, launched Heritage Week in 1982 with the announcement that Lou had been classified. There were those at *World of Sport* who had been urging the same thing for years. Mr Davidson did point out that Lou was now a person "of national importance".

Now in his 67th year, Lou Richards has come to mean a lot to many people. To the kids he's a television personality who comperes *Wide World of Sports* on Sunday mornings with a former tangle-footed fast bowler with a big grin named Max Walker.

To their parents he's the witty TV clown who called football for close to 30 years and dominated the world's longest running sports show, *World of Sport*, and hammed it up on *League Teams*.

To their grandparents he was a talented, cheeky and tough little rover who captained Collingwood to a VFL premiership, highlighting a football career which stretched from 1941 to 1955 and spanned 250 games.

To those of us who work with him day in and day out he's lots of fun. He's a bloke with a great sense of humour who plans to work into the next century and occasionally threatens beyond. As a friend and a workmate I have lived some 20 years of the story of this book with 'Louie the Lip'.

On my first day of work as a cadet reporter on the *Sun* in 1970, my chief of staff Peter Livingstone suggested that I join my new workmates over the road at Lou's pub. The man himself was there, pulling beers, cracking gags and making us feel at home. We would work together for seven years at *World of Sport* on Channel Seven and then start all over again at Nine in 1987 on *Wide World of Sports*. To me he is the consummate professional, with an unquenchable desire to make his show and his station number one. It is an end he has achieved in his 33 years at the *Sun* and in his long career at Seven.

One morning Lou was in at Bendigo Street talking to the kids in *Wide World of Sports*. He was going on about what a great footballer he was when one girl said, "Oh, you played did you?" This set Lou back a pace or two and resulted in the birth of this book. Though enriched by some of Lou's tall tales, this autobiography is a mostly true story of a genuinely unique character in Australian sport and television.

Stephen Phillips

A BLACK-AND-WHITE DYNASTY

As a kid kicking a paper footy around the backstreets of Collingwood and Abbotsford in the dark years of the depression, my future had been predestined. My blood lines on my father's side would see me go into the hotel trade. On my mother's side the black-and-white of Collingwood and its feared football team ran deep and true.

Just as I would attend Lithgow Street state school, my father and his twin brother had before me. Dad had been small but very fast. He was a champion schoolboy swimmer and runner and a pretty handy footballer and cricketer as well. He came from good hotel stock, his father being publican at the Morning Star, which stands to this day in Hoddle Street, Collingwood. They called my grandfather 'Chow Bill' because of his love of strong dark Chinese tea which he bought from a Chinese travelling salesman every week. His wife Polly was a superb tailoress and people talked of 'Chow Bill' as a very smartly dressed man about town—a bloke who would wear magnificent off-white suits made by his wife, topped off with a panama hat. In the lapel there was always a red rose. In those days around the turn of the century he and Polly would take the best dressed awards at the annual Collingwood Mayoral Ball. That was where I inherited my sartorial splendour and exquisite dress sense.

Mum was Irene Pannam and in the early years of the century her surname was a godlike moniker in our part of Collingwood and for miles around. Her father Charlie was one of the football club's greatest champions, a man who would sire a dynasty at Victoria Park. He played from 1894 until he crossed to Richmond in 1907 as captain-coach and helped take the fledgling Tigers into the VFL for the first time in 1908. Photographs show him to be a well-muscled lad with jet-black hair and the family eyebrows, dark and intimidating. With his black-and-white lace-up canvas uniform and a chest covered with best and fairest medallions, he looked a real champ. In 14 seasons with Collingwood he played 179 games (plus another 50 in the old VFA days), was a member of the side's first VFL premiership team in 1902 and captained the club into the 1905 Grand Final. That same year he was the champion goal-kicker of the League.

Like my paternal grandfather, old Charlie was in the liquor business but according to those who knew him well, he wasn't one of the hardest workers. He worked at the old Yorkshire Brewery and spent most of his days bouncing the rubber bungs from the barrels across the courtyard to his mates, or else he'd be across the street enjoying the fruits of his labour. Charlie obviously saved his energy for his home duties and here he worked overtime. He had five sons and two daughters to comfort him in his old age, and had the thrill of watching two of his boys make the big-time. His eldest son Charlie junior starred across the centre for Collingwood for six seasons and was a cornerstone of one of the club's greatest eras. From 1917, when he made his debut and walked into a premiership side, he was to play in five Grand Finals and in two premiership teams.

III

At the start of 1923, the year I was to make my debut as a squawking ankle biter, Charlie junior was making headlines with his decision to move to South Melbourne as captain-coach. He was making the princely sum of £2 a match with Collingwood and in those days it was unheard of to walk out on the club for a better offer—it was heresy, in fact. The offer of £12 a week from South Melbourne obviously swayed him and knowing our family's love of a quid it is little wonder. I would have done the same myself.

Charlie junior was disqualified for three years for leaving without the necessary clearance papers and although he took up coaching duties immediately, he was ineligible to play. Finally in 1926 he was registered as a player and although he'd lost that premiership sparkle, he continued until injury ended his career midway through 1928.

At South Melbourne Charlie junior coached some fine players but none more famous than Roy Cazaly, the high-flying ruck-rover who teamed with Mark 'Napper' Tandy and Fred 'Skeeter' Fleeter. The cry "Up there Cazaly" was born in the mid-1920s and would be adopted as a battle cry for Australian troops in the Middle East during World War II. Charlie junior ended his footballing days with Brunswick before taking the plunge and selling his house to buy property out in the bush. He moved to Vermont. Now Vermont is a densely populated suburb and a most attractive and desirable place to live, but back in the 1930s there was nothing but the odd apple orchard and farmhouse. Charlie opened a general store, which became known as 'Pannam's Corner', and with the profits kept adding to his burgeoning real estate interests.

I remember visiting him in my grandfather's T-Model Ford, and it was a full day's outing. There would be old Charlie behind the wheel, my grandmother alongside him and then Mum and Dad, my brother Ronnie and me squeezed into the back. For us a visit to Uncle Charlie's was a trek of Burke-and-Wills proportion. Halfway we'd stop for a breather at the Templestowe Hotel. Dad and Charlie enjoyed a brief lubrication at the bar and then it was on again towards the hills. Some of those hills resembled mountains and were so steep that Charlie would order us out while he turned round and reversed up them: the forward gear in the Model T was not nearly strong enough. On the way back we'd stop off again at the Templestowe pub for further replenishments. I can recall being shocked when the publican asked my grandfather for his address. "Frankston," Charlie told him. I felt like saying, "Collingwood, you mean don't you, Grandpa?" but something inside me told me to keep my mouth shut. In those days to get a drink on a Sunday in Victoria you had to be a bona fide traveller and be able to prove that you had trekked some 20 miles from home base. Obviously Collingwood wouldn't have fitted the bill.

When Charlie junior passed away at 50 (playing cricket for the local side), his beloved Vermont was a thriving suburb, his local store an institution and his property holdings worth a small fortune.

Alby was the youngest of Charlie senior's brood but quickly took pride of place as my hero. He was the model of my footballing career and the man who moulded my early years. As a schoolboy at Collingwood Tech. Alby would call in at Dad's electrical shop in Johnston Street every afternoon on his way home. He called by to see Mum, his eldest sister, and to babysit me. Alby is nine years older than me, and I remember as a 10 year old the thrill I got from his selection to play in his first senior game with Collingwood in the 1933 season. He would go on and play for Collingwood for 13 years, represent the club in 190 matches and eventually captain the club as his father had before him.

Alby was quite simply one of the best rovers I've seen to this day and miles away the smartest. In his everyday life he was just as crafty. He was a real go-getter. He worked for the Collingwood Council for most of his life and for many years was assistant curator at Victoria Park. If there was something lying around, Alby would find a new home for it, and I reckon over the years he must have accumulated hundreds of Collingwood Football Club towels. His wife Alma must have been sick to death of them. Every time I went round to their home, they'd be fluttering from the clothesline out the back. Badges were, and still are, another of Alby's specialities. He always turns up with an assortment. Be it Grand Final day at the MCG or Melbourne Cup day at Flemington, Alby sorts through his collection and wears something out of date and totally meaningless but somehow vaguely appropriate. It might be an old RSL badge or something he's picked up at the Collingwood Social Club but, with a wink and a nod to the gatekeeper, Alby will proffer the badge and walk straight in. The royal enclosure at Ascot on Gold Cup day wouldn't stop Alby; he's a marvel.

Consider the Pannam players and Lou and Ron Richards and you get some idea of the dynasty that old Charlie spawned all those years ago. Between the old bloke, his two sons and the Richards brothers, we accumulated 878 games in the Collingwood colours between 1897 and 1955, played in 17 Grand Finals and took part in eight VFL premierships, and I reckon we averaged 25 kicks a game. Our names feature on every honour board at Collingwood, and when I was named captain in 1952 we created a unique record in the Victorian Football League: three members of one family captaining a VFL club is a feat I won't see equalled in my lifetime and something that I have always been exceptionally proud of.

III

When you think of it, we could have all been lost to soccer had the round-ball code been strong in those far-off days. Evidently Mum's grandmother was a Constantine Pannamopolis, or it could have been Pannamicus, but whatever it was, it was certainly Greek. The name was anglicised to Pannam late last century and at the same time the roots of the family tree were severed. We haven't been able to find out much more. It probably explains why Greek cab drivers love me. I get into a cab and the driver says, "Hey, Louie, welcome aboard. You're one of us." At first I was mortally offended. I thought they meant I was an out-of-work cab driver but in time I got to appreciate my ethnic roots.

A few years ago I was travelling home from a European jaunt and had flown into Athens International Airport. (To this day I can't think of anything international about the building: it looked like a shearing shed.) Edna and our eldest daughter Nicole were in transit, planning to hurry across to the domestic terminal to catch an Olympic Airways flight to Rhodes. Nicole, being university educated and very intelligent, found that the going rate was 400 drachma. Outside the airport the place was crawling with cabs which all looked the same-old cars driven by men who hadn't shaved in weeks with great flowing moustaches just like Max Walker's.

I grabbed a cab and said to the driver, "How much to the domestic terminal?"

"1000 drachmas," he drawled in his best Anthony Quinn impersonation of Zorba the Greek.

"It's only 400, Dad!" chipped in Nicole.

"For goodness sake, let's pay the bloke and get going," said Edna, reserved and cool in the midst of this growing international storm.

Sanity prevailed and we packed the suitcases into the boot and headed off into the great unknown. Five minutes later the driver stopped the car in the middle of nowhere and turned to me.

"1600 drachmas!"

Once again tempers flared and again Edna quietened things down.

"Just pay the man and let's get going," Edna said.

When we finally got to the domestic terminal and unloaded the bags, I spotted a policeman and hurried across to him.

"Excuse me, sir," I said. "This bloke is trying to rob me." As the policeman remonstrated, the driver grabbed a 1000 drachma note out of my fist and bolted.

This episode made me question my Greek heritage.

III

Football was always my number-one priority and it gave me great pleasure to be able to carry on the family tradition. I can still recall my grandfather Charlie coming to watch the Magpies when I was a kid with Collingwood. He had a strange sense of humour and came out with some shockers. "You know you can pickle pork but you can't pea soup," was one of his favourite one liners. Another was, "You know Theresa Green? You know, trees are green. Get it?" I guess that's where I inherited my sense of humour.

As old-time football champions tend to believe, he was of the opinion that the kids of today are never as good as those of days gone by, and he frequently pointed this out to Charlie junior, to Alby, and in the end, to Ron and me. He died in 1952 at the age of 78 and just missed seeing me emulate his feat of leading the Magpies to a premiership. His one great hope was that I would play 15 years with the club and get my name on the honour board at Victoria Park—a feat that he had missed out on. Unfortunately he didn't see that dream come true.

Old Charlie lived the latter stages of his life with my Aunt Dorrie at her place in Greenwood Street, Collingwood. Dorrie was the family mover and shaker; a bit of a mentor for all her brothers and sisters. She could boss people around and none was bossed around more than her husband Barney. They had no kids and he became the family gopher, doing all the odd jobs. Sadly for Barney he barracked for Richmond, but that matter was never raised in this proud and defiantly Collingwood household. It wasn't until Alby took over as coach of the Tigers in the early-1950s that Barney came out of the closet to fervently follow his side. So involved did he become that he took on the duties of assistant property steward to the legendary Charlie Callendar at Punt Road.

While I was desperate to play football, little brother Ronnie was less inclined. As a 16 year old he stunned the family when he turned out with the Eureka Youth Club, or 'the Commies' as we less than affectionately called them at home. He had natural ability and was tough and talented, so I had a brotherly chat to him one night at home and talked him into trying out at Victoria Park with the seconds. I used to push up for him all the time with our coach Jock McHale, and some of the other rovers got more than a little upset about it. Kevin 'Skeeter' Coghlan, who was to be a fellow panellist on *World of Sport* in the years ahead, used to say to anyone within earshot: "Look at Lou, he'll baulk seven players to get the ball to his brother Ronnie." It wasn't true but I let him keep believing it. Ronnie was finally on the verge of senior selection after a string of outstanding performances in the seconds and I grabbed him before practice one night. "This is your big chance," I confided in him. "Just impress the pants off old Jock tonight, and you're in." Well, Ronnie looked a million quid as he weaved and turned magnificently through the quagmire in the middle of Victoria Park. All went well and godlike old Jock was standing back in his long-sleeved Collingwood guernsey, sporting those long black shorts over waxy white legs. Ronnie just overdid it, simple as that. One blind turn too many and he sent Jock sprawling into the mud. Ten minutes later he did it again. "Sorry, Mr McHale," Ronnie was heard spluttering as he helped the VFL's most famous coach to his feet. "Everything all right?" Not content with flattening the boss, Ronnie proceeded to brush him down with his hands covered in mud. Poor old Jock hadn't felt a speck of mud on his jumper in 20 years and now Ron had turned him into a human mud pie. Later in the showers I consoled Ronnie as only an older brother can. "That's put you back three bloody years," I told him. "You've done your dash now and there's nothing I can do to help." In 1953 Ronnie would be Collingwood's best player in our Grand Final win over Geelong and I would have the honour of captaining the side to its twelfth VFL flag.

III

My sporting career had a humble beginning—the only thing even vaguely humble in my sporting life. Football and cricket teams from Lithgow Street state school would play other schools in our district. I have anything but fond memories of our clashes with the hated Cromwell Street state school. Sport was a matter of survival in those days. You might win on the field but you rarely escaped unscathed. Cromwell Street boasted the local bully, a budding thug named 'Digger' Whitburn, who was an 11 year old who didn't wear shoes and was reputed to be able to crush rocks with his bare feet. One of his favourite tricks after a cricket match would be to grab a stump and try to belt you over the ear with it. He was a really sporting type whose name has remained indelibly etched on my mind for more than half a century. (If you're reading this 'Digger', my old mate, I'm only teasing.) My football ability was blossoming at Lithgow Street but I rarely felt fit enough to play against Cromwell Street. Visions of 'Digger' made me physically fragile.

My teacher in grade six was a bloke named Maurie Sheahan who coincidentally was full-back for Richmond, the reigning power of the VFL at the time. With Martin Bolger and Kevin O'Neil he formed one of the great back-lines of all time. Maurie knew I was a Pannam and knew my footballing background only too well. One particular afternoon we were drawn to play Cromwell Street and visions of 'Digger' and the ensuing beating came flooding through my young and fertile mind. "Sir, I can't play this afternoon," I explained to Mr Sheahan, "because I don't feel well." Maurie was onto me in a flash. As I turned to walk away he booted me fair up the backside. I played that afternoon and he taught me a very valuable lesson. It was to stand me in good stead for the future. In those depression years of the 1930s it hadn't quite dawned on me why kids like 'Digger' didn't wear shoes: most of the parents were out of work and those who weren't were battling to keep themselves in food and with a roof over their heads. It had also escaped my attention that Mum would often eat vegetables while Dad and I would tuck into a couple of chops. Dad was out of work by then and Mum was working at the boot factory to keep us going.

The Collingwood of the 1980s is a vastly different suburb from the area I grew up in. Sixty years ago it was traditional working class, an area that knew poverty well, where it could be very dangerous and silly to walk the streets at night. The Don mob operated from its base outside the Don billiard parlour in Johnston Street, the Dight mob ruled the area around the Cromwell Street state school, and both would be on the warpath against Bull Eddy's crowd from Richmond. These were boys of 14 or 15, and to youngsters like my mates and me, who were relatively well behaved, they were thugs who could put the fear of death into you. It was easy to tell when the Eddy mob had crossed into Collingwood: there were no fence pickets left. (Bull Eddy's brother Dolph later went on to become a member of the Victorian parliament. Dolph was a man of words, unlike his brother.) Students at Collingwood Tech. lived in fear of the walk to the railway station after night school. They were young apprentices trying to improve themselves at compulsory trade classes. Unfortunately for many of them, their way home led them past the Don billiard rooms where they would inevitably receive a beating from the louts who called that particular place home. Things became so serious that the headmaster called in the local police to sort them out.

The local copper was a bloke named Freddie Hughson. In the years to come he would captain and coach Fitzroy to the 1944 VFL premiership. He was a fine full-back, one of the best, and over the years I had nothing but the highest regard for him as a footballer and a man. Freddie and a fellow policeman lay in wait one night. They saw the kids from Collingwood Tech. making their way to the station and were there as the Don mob ambushed them. With batons flailing, Fred and his mate sent them flying. These days such action would be considered police brutality; in those far-off days it was deemed a public service. A year or two ago I visited Fred as he lay dying of cancer. This was a futile battle which he fought with all the courage of old.

To set you straight on the geography of the area where I was raised, Collingwood and Abbotsford are frequently mistaken as the same patch. Collingwood station and its famous football ground, Victoria Park, are actually located in Abbotsford and although I grew up on the wrong side of Hoddle Street, I am always referred to as a Collingwood boy. Collingwood is actually bordered by Alexandra Parade to the north, Smith Street to the west and Victoria Parade to the south. Abbotsford is east of Hoddle Street and takes up the land right through to the Yarra River which winds through in a north-south direction. Our family lived in Park Street.

Those depression days of the 1930s were a remarkable time in which to grow up. They were tough, no mistaking that, but sociologists would say they were character-building as well. There were no televisions and very few radios, and most families were struggling to put food into the mouths of their kids. You made your own fun. It's amazing how competitive you can be, even at primary-school age, and in our neighbourhood we were always out to win. We'd play Test matches against the Cappers or the Martins. There'd be a proper scorebook, a kerosene can for the wicket and a chunk of wood for the bat, and just occasionally the old worn tennis ball would be replaced by the cork and rubber 'compo' ball. When that hit you in the guts it left a nice red ring with a purple centre that stayed there as a reminder for weeks.

The Cappers were a famous sporting family in the area. The brothers, Syd, Frank and Ted, were all handy footballers and cricketers as kids and played in the district competitions for years. Ted Capper's grandson has made his own mark in Australian sporting legend. Hardly a sporting fan in the land hasn't seen or heard of the one-time Sydney Swan, now Brisbane Bear, Warwick Capper, of white-boots-and-tight-shorts fame. He's a VFL superstar and has inherited some of his grandfather's prowess, although I can't quite imagine Ted waltzing up to play footy in Studley Park with those ball-bursters hugging his hips. The boys would have beaten the tripe out of him.

III

The Martins were another sporting family who would play the lads from my street. Then, like now, it was fashionable to represent your own sporting idol in these pick-up games. If it was football you'd be a Collier or a Coventry, a Regan or, in my case, an Alby Pannam. In cricket season every kid wanted to be Don Bradman, although I hankered after the flamboyant style of the late Stan McCabe, who was my favourite. It was in the schoolyard that the Martin name was most feared. Harry Martin was another of the barefoot brigade but he was a youngster with purpose. Marbles, or alleys as we called them then, was his particular forte. We'd play big ring, a game where you would fire from the outside of the ring and try to knock another marble out of the circle drawn in the dirt. Harry could arrive without an alley to his name, walk across the ring and pick up a couple between his toes. Then he would just dominate the game. By the end of the day we'd all be cleaned out. And it was important to note that he didn't fire funnyknuckle. He was an orthodox shooter, and a beauty. When he fired the marble, it came out of his fist like a bullet and there were times I saw him hit another alley with such force that it would disintegrate.

We played sport in the streets under the lights until it was time to go to bed. It was fairly safe outside our place because you rarely saw a car and you knew the locals. In winter we'd roll up paper and make a footy unless someone knew someone who had a friend who knew someone who owned a genuine leather football. Then we'd head to Studley Park. The football would inevitably be patched up and kicked so often that it had become round and resembled a basketball. Invariably the owner would be a sonk and his best mate would wear glasses. The secret was that they would stay at one end while about 30 of us would fight it out at the other. You were very careful not to offend the owner because he could always grab the ball and go home. It was the same with the kids who owned real cricket bats. They got first-class treatment and were always invited to open the batting to very gentle medium-pace bowling. Bowl them out and frighten them off and the game was over.

Football was my love but I did play in six successive premierships for the Collingwood branch of the Irish National Foresters' cricket team. My only memories of those glory days were of our skipper Frank Kelly, who went on to play League football with the Magpies, and of our ritual of unrolling the matting, laying it out and then putting out the flags. I was an all-rounder. I did have visions of being a tearaway quickie in the Laurie Nash mould but never quite made it. One problem was my height. It was hard to hurl them down from five feet two inches. There were times when you did get up to the odd bit of mischief, and water was usually one of the key ingredients. The 'haunted' house at the corner of Mollison and Charles Streets was, in fact, a vacant house that was hidden behind a huge tree. One of our favourite pranks was to climb into the branches overhanging the footpath in the evening and drop water on the people walking home from work. They always thought we were peeing on them. Not so; that would have been far too undignified.

Another trick was to tie a piece of black cotton from a lamp post to a jam tin on a gate post, preferably head high. We would fill the jam tin with water and as the pedestrians sauntered past they collected the unseen cotton and water would splash all over them. Good gag. One night we were set up. We saw a bloke and his girl walking towards us and took cover in Brown's Reserve, giggling in the bushes and waiting for the screams. Just as we took up our hiding place we recognised the couple. The bloke was Joey Turner, very well-known man about town, for all the wrong reasons. He was definitely a man to avoid and the type of bloke who may have had more in his pocket than a handful of change. His reputation as a strong-arm man was, I can assure you, very frightening. Anyway, he walked smack into the cotton and the water poured down, all over his natty grey suit, the cotton sending his pearl-grey hat flying. If you've seen movies of Al Capone enraged, you might get the picture. "I know you little bastards are hiding in those bushes," he screamed. "I can hear you in there." We finally broke cover and took off for home. I remember to this day running straight through a barbed-wire fence, ripping my trousers from waist to knee and very nearly losing something infinitely more valuable. Only a few years ago my ghostwriter at the Sun, Tom Prior, was having a beer when he bumped into Joey Turner. He recounted the story and Joey just laughed. "So Louie was one of those little bastards, was he?" Joey said. "You know, I've never forgotten that incident."

Most of us learned to swim at the Collingwood baths as seven or eight year olds, before graduating to the Yarra River. The baths were pleasant enough, although the bottom was so slimey at the shallow end that you'd find it hard to keep your feet. In summer we'd swim in the river behind the Sisters of the Good Shepherd convent, occasionally sneaking into their vegetable garden and helping ourselves to fresh carrots, cauliflowers and peas. You started cautiously in the river, first learning the currents, then building up your confidence to swim across to Studley Park and back. As you got more daring, you'd swim downstream to the old Abbotsford Brewery and when you were a red-hot swimmer, you'd make it back against the current.

I recall with particular distaste one outing to the river. Mum had given me a new pair of shoes, and I can tell you they weren't easy to come by for us in those days. My mates had called round and we decided to go after the yabbies in Merri Creek. It was the usual rort. You dangled a piece of string in the creek with a bit of meat tied to the end and then yanked in the yabbies. This was simple and very well organised. Just when we were doing well I slipped and fell in the bloody creek, drenching my brand new shoes. That was the end of the yabbying for the day. I was in a quandary: what would I tell my mother? We went back to the place of a mate, Laurie Yates, to think it over. Now Laurie's Dad 'Jumbo' was an SP bookie, so named because of his huge schnoz. They were pretty well-off and had a billiard room with a small table. While we were enjoying a game or two of billiards, Laurie's sister Myrtle, whom I really fancied in those pre-teen years, suggested she put the shoes in the oven. This was a great idea! We continued playing billiards and about three hours later I remembered my shoes. I opened the oven and they were white. They'd shrunk. We blackened them up and I squeezed into them. For three weeks I had the biggest and nastiest blisters you have ever seen, but I couldn't say a word: my life wouldn't have been worth living.

III

It was about this time that Dad came home and announced that he'd bought a radio. We were overjoyed. Just try to imagine life at home now without the television, the radio, the stereo, the compact disc and all the other electrical things you take for granted. It was wonderful. We'd come inside at 6.30pm and huddle around the wireless listening to the Hit Parade, the Lux Radio theatre and Roy Rene. There was one minor drawback. Dad had put down a pound and was paying it off at 2/6 a week. His job had been done. He'd bought it. Now Mum had to earn the money, and I had to get on my bike and ride from Collingwood over to Maples in Sydney Road, Brunswick, every Saturday morning to make the payment. It was miles and every inch of the way I'd be cursing him for buying the bloody thing.

CHAPTER 2

STEELED FOR THE FRAY

The trouble with ruckmen is that, basically, they are dumb. Take my old mate Jack Dyer. Now, he's a classic big man. I was walking into the Melbourne Cricket Ground one day when I saw Jack chatting to a group of radio blokes.

"G'day Jack," I yelled.

There was no sign of recognition.

"Jack, it's me. Louie."

There was still no sign from the big log. Then the light dawned.

"Oh it's you," he replied. "I didn't recognise you. You're getting littler."

He drove me mad for 30 years on and off the football field by asking me if I'd always been little. Crikey, the way Jack thinks, a bloke is born a giant and spends the rest of his life shrinking. It would have been nice being two-metres tall but, to be honest, it never worried me. Look back over history and you'll see that some of the greatest men have been small in stature: Napoleon Bonaparte, Julius Ceasar, Alexander the Great and even Mickey Mouse.

In 1935 I enrolled at Collingwood Technical School in Johnston Street. It was a trade school with a fine reputation and my father had visions of me continuing the family business in the electrical field. Maths, geometry and mechanical drawing were my best subjects, but all I wanted to do was get the lessons over so I could join my mates on the football field. The school played in a regular Wednesday afternoon competition, and on Saturday afternoons provided the curtain-raiser for Collingwood at Victoria Park. Our captain Des Fothergill was on his way to being a VFL superstar even in those days and by the age of 16 had broken into a Collingwood side that had played in five League Grand Finals in a row. Those of us in our first year at the school could only hope to look on in awe.

The coach was our woodwork teacher, Les Hanger. He'd spent weeks watching me craft a copper stick for my mother. These days you throw the washing in the machine and push a button and presto, out it bobs, all clean. In those days you had to light the copper in the shed out the back, get the water nice and hot and then prod the wash with a wooden stick. I was in the process of making such a stick—an octagonal one with 13 sides—when I came to Mr Hanger's attention. I told him football was more my forte and he let me come down one afternoon for a kick with the older boys. He liked what he saw and despite being the smallest boy in the group and the youngest by miles, I was picked to play in the school side in the fourth last match of the 1935 season.

The match was against Swinburne Tech. and all my class mates trooped down to the famous Victoria Park to watch me play my first match. It was the first time I'd ever played on the ground that was to be like home for the next 20 years, and it was a dream debut. Mr Hanger started me in the forward pocket and I repaid his faith with six goals. It was the greatest thrill of my life and I still get goosebumps 50 years later as I remember my classmates carrying me from the ground on their shoulders. I was nicknamed 'the Ant', and my place in the side was secured. That's when I started to get a big head. The following week I played in the curtain-raiser at Victoria Park in front of a huge crowd and I loved it. It was the start of a love affair and the beginning of a career that was to have me centre stage for life.

Collingwood Tech. was a tough breeding ground, a sort of asphalt jungle, in the 1930s. I remember our literature teacher who was a nice old bloke named Dr Ferguson. He'd read poetry to us one moment and have the tripe belted out of us the next. I was in C2 section in my first year, which was considered up market. Down the scale a bit, quite a bit, in fact, there was C12 where Tommy Benjamin and his bike pump ruled supreme. Tommy would load his pump with peppercorns and was lethal from 20 paces.

III

In my second year I developed many of the theatrical talents that stood me in such good stead in later life. These were the formative years of Australian television and film. My English teacher back then was nicknamed 'Tubby' Crome and the old fellow seemed to enjoy lunchtime better than anyone. He had a watering hole around the corner and came back for the afternoon classes in wonderful spirits. He was generally half-whacked. That year we studied *The Merchant of Venice* and Mr Crome had given all the kids a part to learn. I was the third servant and had only one line. In fact, I had only one word to learn: "Enter!" Even then I stuffed it up. I always knew when it was my turn because the blackboard duster would whistle across the room and hit me right behind the ear. He was a deadly aim, old 'Tubby', especially after lunch, but, looking back, I have much to thank him for. It was a school that churned out honours students year after year. They were always saying, "Yes, your honour. No, your honour." One of my class mates in second year was so excited when he was promoted to third year that he cut himself shaving. He was all of 21.

There was never much of an old boys' network at Collingwood Tech. and judging by some of the rough heads who made life miserable for everyone in those days, I'm not likely to bump into many of them at Safeway in Toorak. Collingwood Tech. was a school that had the knack of turning out champion sportsmen: I look back to Australia's finest left-handed batsman Neil Harvey, the 1940 Brownlow medallist Des Fothergill, who like Neil and his brothers also played for Victoria in Sheffield Shield cricket, my uncle Alby Pannam, Marcus Boyle and the brothers Richards.

After three years I was ready to move out into the world of industry and, thanks to some help from my grandfather, I was apprenticed as a fitter and turner at the Challenge Engineering Works in North Melbourne. I hated the place then and vowed to buy it lock, stock and barrel and have it bulldozed. The problem was that I was hopeless with tools and had the concentration span of a gnat. It was the Sinatra era and while little Louie was dreaming of the big-time and singing as he worked, the job was getting thoroughly botched. One day I was drilling brake drums with a template over the drum to guide the heavy drill. To the accompaniment of heavy metal, I was belting out a Sinatra classic *I Couldn't Sleep A Wink Last Night*. Unfortunately, the template had shifted and some 200 brake drums left the Challenge Engineering Works with the holes out of whack.

I can remember my boss now. I hated him and he had equal respect for me.

"Can't you see?" he roared.

"It's my eyes," I replied.

"Damn your eyes."

He loved to send me on errands; looking back, it was the perfect way of getting rid of me for an hour or two. He delighted in sending me to McDonald's in Richmond for compressor parts. I'd get on my bike with a haversack packed with these heavy metal parts and wobble back to North Melbourne. My shoulders would be red raw, my hatred of him the same colour. Other days he'd send me to the steel works to collect six-metre steel rods. I'd tie them to the bar on my bike and try to ride back to work. Have you ever tried riding a bicycle with a six-metre steel bar attached? I tell you, once you get the wobbles up, that's the end of things. These days I have a Mercedes. I find the ride a lot more comfortable.

Life in those days was simple but I always hankered to get into business myself, to play football for Collingwood and to make good.

III

Romance was a side issue for this very undapper 16 year old. There were moments, however. Every morning as I made the trip by bike from home in Abbotsford to North Melbourne, I rode through the Exhibition Gardens. Every morning, the eagle-eyed Richards would spy this good-looker riding in the opposite direction. Now, when you're 16 you have a fertile mind and a vivid imagination, and mine was in a wild gallop. Every morning the romance got heavier, the wedding was a Hollywood spectacular and love was in the air. There was only one problem: not once did she pay me even the scantest iota of attention; not once did she look my way.

Oh well, there were other things that made up for it. While Frank Sinatra was making the girls swoon with his crooning at Radio City in New York, I had the boss crying with my renditions in North Melbourne. Something had to give, and finally it was me. "I think we'd better end this apprenticeship," I told him one Saturday morning after I'd polished every speck of dust off his new Ford VB. I don't think I've ever seen a happier man in my life. He was that pleased to get rid of me. He reckoned that in three years I could have sent the place broke.

My football was progressing at a more luxurious pace. After school I found myself playing for Abbotsford in the now-defunct subdistrict competition. I was a 16 year old playing amongst men for the first time and boy, it was like nothing on earth. We played on a disused rubbish tip in Ramsden Street, Clifton Hill. Ex-VFL players like Nana Thomson and Piggy Harnett loved terrorising raw kids like me and in that year, 1939, I found out what football was all about—survival! It was the toughest football I ever played and it makes me wince to think about it. To make matters worse, I fancied myself as a good player and had no worries about telling anyone within ear shot. These blokes gave you a whack across the face as soon as smile at you and it was something you just had to cop. Abbotsford was a run-of-the-mill footy club that struggled through the season but as far as I was concerned it was just a detour to Victoria Park and the big-time.

Financially things were looking better, too. I'd swung a job at Diecasters in Collingwood working as a process worker. God, it was boring. Once again I proved just how hopeless I was with tools and it didn't take the boss long to spot it. I was whisked from one job to another until I found myself making toothpaste tubes, which was dull, repetitive work that made me even more determined to get out and make my own way in life. The boss there was a man called Darbyshire and we loathed each other. He didn't like the way I gave him cheek and repeatedly told him that the only way he got the position was by marrying the owner's sister. He didn't like the way I did the job. In fact, he didn't like any bit of me. One way or another the relationship dragged on through the war years. We endured four years of our own private two-man war in the backstreets of Collingwood; I blackened the blades of machetes for the blokes in the jungles and Darbyshire dreamed of sticking one in my back.

III

By 1940 Alby Pannam was convinced that I had enough talent to try out for Collingwood's seconds team. Alby was my football idol. There was never a question of his loyalty or his fitness and having played over 193 games he was Collingwood to the core. He'd played in the Magpies' great premiership sides of 1935 and 1936 and despite the fact that he was my uncle, he was the perfect bloke for a tough, cheeky little rover like myself to model his game on. In those days the seconds would play on the away grounds, usually in front of a handful of spectators who knew each other by first name. My parents went to the MCG that year to watch me play Melbourne, and Dad said afterwards that you could hear every kick echo around the empty southern stand. It was like playing in the Swiss Alps. It was a transition period for Collingwood because many of the older players had joined up and gone off to the war and it was left to kids like me to fill the gaps. To make matters worse the great Magpie machine that had so dominated football in the late-1930s had grown old and had lost the stalwarts that had made it the most feared side for close to 20 years. Money, too, had made an impression and Collingwood lost its two young champions. Ron Todd, the game's most brilliant full-forward and the reigning Brownlow medallist, and my old schoolmate, Des Fothergill, had both left. Both shocked

Collingwood by leaving at the absolute peak of their careers to join VFA club Williamstown, but more of that later.

Collingwood made it through to the seconds Grand Final that year and what a thrill it was. Melbourne and Richmond would play the main match in front of nearly 70,000 later in the afternoon but the MCG was just about packed to the rafters for our match. Collingwood beat Carlton and the media was as pleased with my roving performance as I had been myself. Later in the rooms as we celebrated our first seconds premiership since 1925, we were joined by the senior coach Jock McHale. He walked over and stood in front of me, this legendary Collingwood figure who was to coach the club for 39 years and who had already notched eight premierships.

"Young Richards," the great man said.

"Yes, Mr McHale?"

"Well played today, son. You'll be a Collingwood player."

Those few words, which were probably the most exciting I have ever heard, have stayed with me until this day. He was to be Mr McHale to me for the best part of my football career. He was a man who was adored by everyone at Collingwood, a man who did more to mould the spirit of the club than any other. As youngsters we had watched him since we were old enough to go to Victoria Park, and we'd heard the stories. One in particular sent shivers up my spine. It concerned the League's greatest full-back Jack Regan, a Collingwood champion himself. Regan had just started his illustrious career and was playing on the half-forward line. Collingwood trailed by three points as Regan marked on the bell. The skipper Syd Coventry walked over to Regan as he stood with the ball, 25 metres out from goal.

"What'll I do?" Regan asked.

"Kick the bloody goal," was Coventry's predictable answer.

Regan's kick went astray for a point and Collingwood lost the match. As the players filed into the Collingwood rooms, Jock was sitting on a chair, grinding his felt hat into a pulp in both hands. He was so upset he couldn't even look at the players. Now, Jack Regan was a good Catholic boy who had considered the priesthood; he was a gentle and kindly young man. He walked up to McHale and tapped him gently on the shoulder.

"I'm terribly sorry, Mr McHale," Regan said.

With that Jock looked up and said, "You bastard. Go and throw yourself into the Yarra."

A team-mate in that first premiership was Norm Crewther. He's been my plumber for more than 30 years. Years after that match he came to my Phoenix Hotel in Flinders Street to fix a faulty flange in the shower.

"All those tiles will have to come off, Louie," Norm told me.

"Don't be bloody ridiculous. Why don't you take off the tap and use a bit of hemp and white lead."

"I'll give it a go but it won't last."

That was 18 years ago and the thing is as good as ever. Whenever I saw Norm I was reminded of the story about the plumber who was called to the brain surgeon's home. He spent 20 minutes fixing a leaking tap and confronted the brain surgeon.

"That'll be $350, mate."

"That's preposterous," the startled surgeon replied. "I'll have you know I'm a brain surgeon and I don't charge that much."

"Yeah, I know. I used to be a brain surgeon."

III

Six games into the 1941 season I was selected to play my first match with Collingwood's senior side. I can't remember how I found out about my selection but I probably read about it in the *Sun*. That, in itself, was a big deal because the previous year you had to go to Mick Canal's fish and chip shop in Johnston Street to read the seconds team sheet stuck to the front window. The name in the paper was a very big deal indeed. That Friday night I was so revved up for the match against Carlton, I was unbearable. I rolled up my socks in a ball and ran up and down the passageway at home, baulking imaginary Carlton players and kicking goal after goal. Unfortunately one kick went astray and my only pair of black Collingwood socks sailed up through the manhole in the ceiling. Dad had to go and borrow a ladder from a neighbour to get them down.

The next day we caught the train to North Carlton station and walked across Princes Park to the ground. I'd been named in the forward pocket, second rover to Uncle Alby, and picked to play on a mini-Sherman tank named Charlie McInnes. Charlie was the most frightening-looking bloke you could imagine. He was built like John Nicholls, only 10 centimetres shorter. He had huge muscular arms and thighs that could turn you into an instant pizza if he fell on top of you. He walked up to me at the start of the match and thrust out this hand.

"Good luck today, Lou," he said with the most sincere look on his face. "Thanks," said I, hardly able to conceal my delight that this Carlton premiership player even knew who I was.

The ball went down and 'Cheerful Charlie' let fly with a backhander right across the bridge of my nose, knocking me rotten. I didn't get a kick in the entire first half; didn't even remember most of the first-quarter. Things improved after half-time, but Charlie McInnes gave me my first football lesson: when you shake hands with an opponent always stand nine or 10 metres away.

I played my first senior game in 1941, the first of 250, and from that slightly groggy debut against Carlton, I never again played in the seconds. To a youngster reared in the Magpies nest and steeped in the tradition of the most famous football club in Australia, it was bliss. To walk into the dressing rooms under the old Jack Ryder stand was a thrill in itself. I'd run to training from work at Diecasters after knock-off and arrive breathless in the rooms. It was worth the run. You'd look around and see the great Collingwood champions like Phonse Kyne, Marcus Whelan, Jack Regan, Harry Collier and Alby Pannam. Jock McHale would be there—an intimidating sight to both the young player and the veteran. The players at Collingwood were treated like superstars in those days and were paid pretty well too. I'd been earning 27/6 during my apprenticeship but a game in the seniors was worth £3 and another £1 went into the provident fund. There was coir matting on the floor, there were pictures of the great Collingwood sides staring down from the walls, and the rub-down tables were covered in clean white sheets and pillows. It was all very comfortable really.

Recently I read some comments made by Hawthorn's great young full-foward Jason Dunstall, as he approached his 100th goal for the 1988 season. Dunstall was quoted as saying how overawed he was to be playing for a champion team like Hawthorn and rubbing shoulders with the likes of Michael Tuck, Dermott Brereton and Bertie DiPierdomenico. It took me back nearly half a century because that's exactly how I felt in that first year with the Magpies.

CHAPTER 3

A STAR IS BORN

There would have been few more terrifying sights in sport than that of Jack Dyer bearing down on you at full speed, hell-bent on destruction. Now in his mid-70s and still remarkably well preserved, Jack is seen by the kids as a bloke who clowns around, assassinates names on radio and lends his famous moniker to the 'Dyer'ere' column in the *Truth*. For the best part of 20 years Jack was the biggest and most fearsome name in Australian football.

Sporting Globe writer Hec de Lacy christened him 'Captain Blood', but Jack had none of the swashbuckling good looks that swept Errol Flynn to fame and fortune. By the time I'd arrived on the scene, Jack was a godlike figure, the captain-coach of Richmond and football's meanest big man. At about 1.85 metres he was no giant by today's standards but he was amazingly fast, a superb kick and a skilled protector down at the old Punt Road oval. It was there in the mud and slush, deep in the winter of 1941, that our paths first crossed. Jack had knocked Pat Fricker to the ground. He then bowled over Phonse Kyne and had yours truly in his sights for the hat-trick. I was the next cab off the rank and wasn't going to cop it. As he bore down, I sidestepped and he slipped headlong into the mud. Quick as a flash I grabbed that famous number 17 Tiger jumper and he was penalised for holding the ball. If that wasn't bad enough, in the following Monday night's *Herald*, cartoonist Sam Wells presented his version of the David-and-Goliath act of round 13, and that stuck in Jack's craw for years.

III

The next season we were back at Punt Road again and in 1942 we were desperately short of big men. Jack was going for a boundary throw-in opposite the old wooden scoreboard in the outer, and I saw that our ruckmen had been stranded up-field. I ran in from about 10 metres, went for the knockout, missed, and punched Jack behind the ear, which was no mean feat when you look at the size of Jack's ears. (He looks like a taxi with its doors open.) In a flash Jack whipped round and gave me a short jab in the chin.

"Why don't you hit someone your own size, you big copper bastard," I whinged.

He looked down at me. "Listen, sonny, if you don't like it, take your schoolbag and go home to your mother."

I never forgot those words. Once you're out in the field, you are all men and all the same size as far as I'm concerned. Little did I realise, as I lay in the quagmire that was Punt Road, that Jack and I would form a television partnership after our playing days that would last for 30 years and become something of a folk legend in football.

In those days we struggled against Dyer's Richmond and our blokes did it hard, old Jock McHale in particular. After one galling loss at Punt Road, our players drifted off into the night, hoping to forget the afternoon's misery. I thought someone should go in for a drink with the victors so I walked into the Tigers' lair. There was 'Captain Blood' with his motley band enjoying a beer. Dyer saw me as I walked in.

"Come here, son," he said. "What'll you have?"

"I'll have a lemon squash."

Well, that was the cue for all the players to burst into hysterics.

"Shut up," the 'Captain' roared.

"He came in here by himself, so let's treat him properly. At least he's had the guts to show his face."

My estimation of Jack rose significantly that evening. But there was one man at Richmond who used to give me nightmares.

Right through my career Max Oppy used to belt the living daylights out of me. Max played in the back-pocket and was built like a pocket battleship—made of muscle and having huge forearms, the bloke was put on earth to make a rover's life hell. Dyer loved to sick him onto me, like a dog chasing an old bone, and Max, to his credit, never let him down. I once knocked Max down playing against Richmond and stupidly helped him to his feet. Afterwards I walked straight into Jock McHale in the dressing rooms. "If I ever see you pick up another player, you'll never get another game with Collingwood," the coach roared. "When there's one on the ground, they're one short."

It was a message well learned and from that day on I'd trample them where they lay. Despite our frequent clashes (and to be fair, I did a bit of damage now and then), Max was always wasted in the back-pocket. He was a skilful player with a great kick and would have been a great centreman.

Years later my brother Ronnie and I decided to fix up Mr Oppy once and for all. We had him in our sights; Ronnie was bearing down from one angle and I was doing so from the other. Max saw us at the last moment and almost got out of the way. Ronnie collected him a glancing blow. It wasn't good enough, however; if you didn't deck him he'd get his own back in a flash. Sure enough, down went Ronnie and the umpire was right on the spot. At the tribunal the following week Ronnie was asked to give his version of the incident. Now, Ronnie speaks quickly and his garbled evidence, delivered staccato style, was enough to get Max off the hook. Strangely, Max and I became the best of friends in later life, but to this day I'm still wary of those massive forearms with the hunks of fist at the ends.

III

The VFL tribunal would become like a second home to me over the 15 years I played VFL football but only once did I go there as a reported player. Seven times I was the offended party and that, in itself, should say something about the way I played football. Could this suggest, you ask, that I was the provocateur? I was called before the wise men at Harrison House in my first season on a striking charge. In those days on my tip toes I would have measured in at all of 1.68 metres, yet I was fronting the tribunal on a charge of striking Fitzroy's gentle giant of a ruckman, Bert Clay, who was 1.95 metres. During the match I'd seen Bert throw his arm back and collect Uncle Alby right across the face, knocking him out. Like a fool, I rushed in and threw a punch. In his evidence the umpire said I hit Bert in the face but to this day I can't quite figure out how I reached. My evidence was obviously second rate and I was suspended for two weeks. As I walked from the room I vowed to myself that I would never get reported and when I retired towards the end of the 1955 season, I could look back with pride and say that I had lived up to my promise.

That's not to say that I cleaned up my act. I certainly handed out plenty; but, then again, you had to in those days. My little trick was to whack the bloke and then steer well clear of the scene of the crime-hit-and-run style. There was nothing more stupid than to stand around and talk it over with the umpire and a bloke's team-mates.

III

The 1940s saw me grow up quickly. I went from a carefree teenager to a more mature adult with the added burden of VFL football on my youthful shoulders. The kids from Lithgow Street state school had grown up with me, as neighbours and mates, and in those war years helped me get in and out of the odd bit of mischief. Jack Arnott won't be remembered by even the most ardent of Collingwood supporters and I reckon his family would struggle to recollect his seven senior games with the Magpies.

Jack was a Lithgow Street boy although, the truth be known, he hailed from Richmond and could quite easily have been one of them, rather than one of us. As a teenager he was debonair, well groomed and basically a lair. His wavy blond hair was always immaculate and his signature was a camel-hair coat that he kept in absolutely pristine condition. He loved the birds and they loved him. It was that camel-hair coat that drove us all mad. Jack thought he was the ant's pants in it and woe betide anyone who messed with it. Just about anyone who could pull on their jumper and do up their own laces could get a game with Collingwood in the war years and I knew Jack had a bit of talent buried under all that camel hair. Though he was a mad keen Carlton supporter, I talked him into trying out at Victoria Park and in 1942 he cracked it for a senior game. He actually kicked four goals, at full-forward. The next week he kicked another six and he was on top of the world. He thought he was 'Nuts' Coventry and Ron Todd rolled into one woman-killing bundle. North Melbourne was next in line and the 'Shinboners' had the idea of countering this young upstart by moving a bloke named Harrison from centre half-forward to full-back. Poor old Jack didn't get a sniff and his meteoric career was on the wane.

Later his father took him aside and said, "You know why you went bad, don't you?"

"Why?" said Jack.

"It's your little mate, Richards: he won't kick the ball to you any more."

Jack confronted me with this preposterous allegation and I admit that it was pretty well spot-on.

"Listen, Jack, after you kicked 10 goals in two weeks you were starting to get a big head. It was a fluke, and I'm not going to waste my time on a no-hoper," I told him in my most matter-of-fact way. Jack's career was stuffed but, strangely enough, we have stayed friends ever since.

Jack, resplendent in his camel-hair overcoat, joined Jack Burns and me one afternoon over at Carlton where we were watching a lightning premiership. Later we went for a couple of drinks in the room under the grandstand. A few smart-arse Carlton types started having a go at Jack about his coat. Jack Burns and I sized up the situation in a moment and made for the door-better to run away and live to fight another day was our motto at the time, and a very sensible one at that. Meanwhile, Jack and some bloke were toe to toe. I can recall Jack's stance now. It was a modern version of that of John L Sullivan, the great 19th-century pugilist, one of the last of the straightbacks. As Jack was sizing up, with fists outstretched and head tilted back out of harm's way, the lights went out.

We heard a mighty thump and took off, with Jack not far behind us. It seems that Jack had biffed the bloke fair on the nose and put him down for the count. As we sprinted to North Carlton station we looked in amazement at Jack. He was in a terrible way; not hurt mind you, but ashen. When he belted the bloke, a spurt of blood had defaced Jack's coat. It took him months to get over it.

Last summer I bumped into Jack and his wife at our annual Christmas get together. We were laughing about his dress sense and he let me in on a secret. In the summer months in those far off days he would strut around in the brightest tangerine double-breasted sports coat the world had ever seen. It set him back 10 quid. Close to 20 years later, a bloke confronted him in the street and asked him if he was the fellow who used to wear the tangerine sports coat to Collingwood. Jack said he was and informed the stranger that he still had the coat at home in his cupboard.

III

I was working at Diecasters, making a bit of a name for myself with Collingwood, and three or four evenings a week I was helping out at my uncle's hotel in Fitzroy. The Marquis of Lorne was no five-star pub; if anything, it was a bloodhouse. Arthur Richards was Dad's twin brother, and pubs had run in the family. Their father Bill had run the Morning Star in Hoddle Street and the Jolly Hatter's in Russell Street, Collingwood and three or four others. Later, brother Ron and I were to go into the industry as well.

Arthur's pub was no model for any aspiring publican; just the opposite. His biggest order each week was for 30 dozen bottles of cheap port and that went straight round the corner to the sly grog shop. These were the war years when bottled beer was extremely hard to find. The clientele was as rough as the port. You'd walk in to the bar and see the biggest assortment of thugs and crooks gathered in one place in Melbourne. 'Gooseneck' Cartilege and his brother 'Dopey' would be drinking with the likes of Red Maloney, a noted street fighter of the neighbourhood, and Bull Kelly. Bull had been in so many dust-ups that he'd had a metal plate inserted in his skull.

The consorting squad were regulars. They'd call in four or five times a day to keep check on the villains. Occasionally they'd grab Bull Kelly by the scruff of the neck and drag him outside for more in-depth questioning. Often Arthur and his wife Ethel and young Louie would sit back with eyes wide open and mouths closed as the passing traffic did its business. I remember a taxi driver named Cato arguing with a mate.

"You bastard," screamed Cato. "I'll blow your bloody brains out."

"You wouldn't have the guts," came the reply.

With that Cato disappeared out the front door and the bar returned to normal, apart from the sniggers and disbelieving laughter. Half an hour later he was back, brandishing a large German Luger and inserting it in his mate's ear. Aunt Ethel was a short, heavy-set woman who evidently didn't have the same brand of courage as we Richards men. She marched around the bar and took the gun from him.

The ladies' parlour of the Marquis of Lorne was a delight, too. Two girls were having a mighty punch-up one night and it was left to me to separate them. Just as I appeared on the scene an old woman wielding a bread knife with heavy serrated edges, which she had produced from her handbag, joined in. A nice type of girl you'd meet at the Marquis in those days, but hardly marriage material. It was there I learned the cardinal rule of bar-room brawling: never leave the till unattended and never jump the bar. You leave yourself wide open to be king-hit. Always walk around the bar because 99 times out of a 100 the fight will be over by the time you get there.

I have strange memories of the pub. It was here that I decided that a hotel was all the go for a young footballer on the way up. It was here that I also managed to get my driving licence. Our friend Cato the cabbie mentioned to me that he had a friend up at the motor registration branch who might like to help me with things. Up I went and after one nervous lap of the branch I was duly licensed to drive a motor car.

The family had struggled through the depression years with Dad finding odd jobs with his electrical talents and Mum working in the boot factory for £2 a week to support Ron and me. In 1944 as I was approaching my 21st birthday, the family was hit by tragedy. Dad and a mate had been working around south-eastern Victoria in the Toora-Foster area of Gippsland, doing any electrical work they could find. One night they were playing cards on a boat in a creek near Toora. Dad had been enjoying a few drinks but said he was feeling ill and felt like some fresh air. Apparently he fell into the creek and drowned. Two days later his body was recovered and I recall the long drive down there for Mum to identify his body. It was a nightmare. I remember trying to talk to get her mind off the tragedy as we drove along. Looking back, I would say she handled it well; she was terrific, in fact.

III

The war years saw Collingwood slump down the ladder, and from 1940 to 1944 the side failed to reach the finals. In 1942 things were so bad that the Magpies failed to field a seconds side, battled to get together a competitive senior side and at one stage looked likely to lose their Victoria Park headquarters to the services. Few clubs had as many servicemen as Collingwood, who seemed to have their champions spread from the jungles of New Guinea to the deserts of north Africa. By 1945 we had peace in Europe and in the Pacific. The battle zone was closer to home; it was just round the corner from Princes Park. The MCG had been used to house troops and from 1942 to 1944 the VFL finals were played either at the Junction Oval, St Kilda, or at Princes Park, Carlton's home ground. It was the first time the club had missed more than two successive Septembers and, coupled with the fact that it was my first taste of finals football, September 1945 had very special meaning. We'd finished second to South Melbourne and met them in front of 46, 224 people for the second semi-final.

I remember little of the match. South were led by Brownlow medallist Herb Matthews. They had 'the Greatest', Laurie Nash, back at the age of 35 and Jack 'Basher' Williams, 'Gentleman Jim' Cleary and a 17 year old destined for big things in Ron Clegg. The nicknames, by the way, belied the real characters of the Swans of 1945. They were a tough, mean and dirty lot. We lost by 11 points and faced a Carlton side on a hot streak. They talked about the 1945 VFL Grand Final as the 'Bloodbath', but I can' tell you that it was the teddy bears' picnic compared with the preliminary final. We knew it was going to be tough and we went in prepared. Our full-foward Len Hustler was built like a brick outhouse and played with the same subtlety. He was about 1.88 metres and weighed in close to 105 kilograms and he knew exactly what was required of him. He was there to rough up the Carlton players, who weren't exactly backward in that area themselves. Hustler got rid of Carlton's half-back flanker Yin Brown. I can remember it now—Hustler standing over him and Brown on his back, scurrying away as quickly as he could, boots flying everywhere. There were brawls all over the ground. These were not individual fights like those which marred the Grand Final, but all-in donneybrooks. One reporter said later that it cleared the way for footballers to use knuckledusters and spikes. We'd gone into the game without our captain Alby Pannam, who had a knee injury, but by three-quarter time were pretty happy with ourselves. We led by 35 points 10 minutes into the last-quarter and had a place in the Grand Final at our mercy.

Funny things happen in a game of football and a few happened that bleak Saturday afternoon which have stuck with me for 43 years. The Blues threw a young rover, Jimmy Mooring, into the game late in the third-quarter and he seemed to spend all his time running around revving his players up. Half-forward Lance Collins kicked four goals in the last-quarter revival and for the last 15 minutes Collingwood had stopped to a walk. Our rucks had been carried by Allan Williams, easily the best player on the ground in the first half, but as the game increased in tempo and Carlton got a run on, he slowed to a crawl. He wouldn't come off the ball when it was quite obvious that someone like Hustler was the man we needed. I remember him at full-forward. "I'll kill those bastards. Just let me at them," he growled. Looking back, I think he would have been just the man, too. It was an old Collingwood ploy to start a rumpus when things looked bleak. Kick the ball over the fence into the street, belt someone—do anything to get the opposition's mind off the football, and while they fought, you got on with the game.

III

Carlton was a tough and talented team led by the toughest footballer I've ever seen. Ironically Carlton's skipper Bob Chitty was cast in the lead role in the first movie version of Ned Kelly, but unless I'm horribly mistaken, old Ned wouldn't have lived with him. Two stories illustrate the point. Collingwood were playing Carlton and our skipper Alby Pannam slipped the boot into Chitty, as he was known to do on special occasions. (Nothing flash about our Alby.) Chitty didn't even lose stride as he launched out with the most perfectly timed backhander I've ever seen. Alby did a perfect backwards somersault. I love reading about players who miss a match because of the flu or a runny nose, or because they've had their numbers taken for pulling somebody's hair. Chitty didn't worry about that garbage. He worked for K G Luke, the great Carlton stalwart and official who would later become president of the VFL and put into action the plans to build VFL Park. Chitty worked on one of Luke's presses, making badges. One day his finger got in the road and he lost a chunk of it. It didn't worry Chitty: he played the following Saturday, in the 1945 preliminary final, with a special metal guard to cover the raw stump that had been his finger. By quarter-time he'd thrown it into the mud; like a lot of other things, it seemed to upset him. I suppose you would equate him in build with Hawthorn's great champion of the 1970s and 80s, Leigh Matthews. They both had no fear whatsoever and were blessed with bodies that could dish out and take terrible punishment.

Chitty had one other saving grace: his hands looked as though they were carved from Mallee roots. His great gnarled fingers bunched up into a fist about 12 centimetres thick. I shudder to this day when I think of them making contact. It was Chitty who led Carlton into the 'Bloodbath' Grand Final in 1945 after overrunning Collingwood, and their match with South Melbourne has become part of football's folklore. I would have loved to have been out there, but there were moments during the brawling when it was wiser and much safer to enjoy the comforts of the outer.

Ten players were reported and seven received heavy suspensions; surprise, surprise, my old mate Bob Chitty was up there with the best of them. He copped eight weeks for elbowing South's Billy Williams. Ted Whitfield was spotted running down the ground with his jumper over his head so he wouldn't be recognised for this part in the proceedings. It didn't do him any good and he missed the entire 1946 season. Don Grossman of South got eight weeks for striking Jimmy Mooring, and 'Gentleman' Jim Cleary was suspended for eight weeks for punching Ken Hands of Carlton. So incensed was Freddy Fitzgibbon with the fighting that he actually jumped the fence to get to the action. He'd been out on a three-week suspension and was an onlooker. Incidentally the match was won by Carlton, with the Blues becoming the first side ever to win the premiership from fourth position.

III

On the work front things were bleak. The war was over, the job market was flooded with ex-servicemen and the powers that be at Diecasters decided to give me the boot. A very undignified farewell it turned out to be. As far as they were concerned my days of blackening machetes had come to an end; my days of making toothpaste tubes were well and truly finished. Ever the optimist, I had my beady little eyes on a job with the Melbourne and Metropolitan Board of Works, in their yard at Northcote. When things looked grim, Collingwood's greatest benefactor, John Wren, stepped in, using his not-inconsiderable influence. (It helped when you were roving for Collingwood.) The job was an intricate one, fraught with responsibility and tailor-made for a young man with my qualifications and zeal. I was sort-of an engineer. I tested the copper balls used to flush toilets, making sure they didn't leak and that they floated at the correct time. That wasn't all. I also checked pipes for leaks and taps for drips. To be honest, I was finished most days by lunchtime.

Les Almond was a bit of a rogue, a returned soldier who'd become a workmate, and when things got quiet we schemed. He came to me one day with a suggestion. "Louie, have you ever fancied pigeon pie?" he asked. We had a stock of pigeons which were used to check for gas escapes in the deep sewer pipes, and I had visions for our supply mysteriously dwindling. Les was too smart for that. "You bring in a pack of pigeon peas tomorrow and I'll do the rest." The following morning I got to Northcote with my pigeon peas and Les arrived armed with a small bottle of brandy and a bowl. We soaked the peas in the brandy all morning and scattered them under a wooden box held up at one side with a stick to which he'd attached a bit of strong. The pigeons feasted on the peas and staggered drunk under the box. Les pulled the string and presto, fresh pigeons. There were not only enough for me and Les, but in the end we were supplying the whole yard. It's a story I always bring up when I bump into Australia's former Test skipper, Bill Lawry. The 'Phantom' still races pigeons and it brings tears to his eye to think of all those potential champs ending up on the Richards' family table at dinnertime.

III

My 100th game was unforgettable. How many players get to reach such a milestone in a drawn second semi-final? Back in 1928 Collingwood had figured in the first finals tie in VFL history and beat Melbourne by four points in the replay. The time the opposition beat Essendon, rated by all the good judges as the power side of the 1946 season, the side to beat for the premiership. A record second semi-final crowd of 77,370 packed the Melbourne Cricket

Ground and were treated to sensations before the game had gone a quarter. We lost Pimm, our full-forward, before the match when it was found he hadn't recovered from influenza; and then to really throw the side into disarray, Bill Twomey, our brilliant 17-year-old centreman, was forced out with a thigh injury. Twomey had claimed before the match that he was doubtful, but coach Jock McHale, one of the best judges of a player's fitness I'd seen, decided he was ok.

Despite those setbacks Collingwood should have had the match tied up at half-time. The giant scoreboard at the MCG showed us leading by 13 points. It also showed us having 19 scoring shots to their 11. In years gone by, Collingwood has boasted a great full-forward. In the years before and after World War I the great Dick Lee was the League's best spearhead. Ten times he topped the VFL goalkicking and when he retired in 1922 he'd kicked 707 goals. Gordon Coventry did his apprenticeship under Lee and then set about breaking his record. In 306 games 'Nuts' kicked 1299 goals, became the first man to kick 100 goals in a season and in his last year, 1937, topped the goalkicking for the sixth time. Ron Todd made a sensational start at Collingwood, kicking 120 and 121 goals in his first two years at full-forward in the 1938 and 1939 seasons, but shocked everyone with his move to VFA club Williamstown. So in the years of World War II, and immediately afterwards, we were without someone up forward. Fortunately they had a couple of good rovers who loved kicking goals, and to be honest, I didn't really care if there was anyone at full-forward or not.

Getting back to the 1946 second semi-final, we went into the match without Des Fothergill but all things considered we were perfectly placed at three-quarter time when we led by 16 points. In the last term, as we'd done against Carlton in the vital match the year before, we let ourselves down. This time we had the chances but blew them. We kicked 2.7. The opposition was more accurate, kicking 5.5 and when the bell rang the scores were level—13.22 Collingwood to Essendon's 14.16. The irony of the moment was lost on me: 100 points apiece, in my 100th game. Like my team-mates, I stood dumbfounded. I recall turning to some of the Essendon blokes standing next to me and saying, "Shit, not again next week!"

One bloke who didn't mind was Essendon's captain and coach, Dick Reynolds, known to all at Windy Hill as 'King Richard'. Reynolds was not a big man but at 1.68 metres and 82 kilograms he had the size, not to mention the ability, to play just about anywhere he felt like putting himself. He'd won three Brownlow Medals in five years in the 1930s and was destined to play in a VFL-record 320 games. In many ways Dick was everything I wasn't. He was scrupulously fair, clean and adored by footy fans of other sides, and he was also a pin-up player to kids wherever the games were played. He'd no sooner kick you in the ankle or backhand you across the bridge of the nose than take a drink or bot a fag. You wonder how long he'd last today. Reynolds was at the forefront when the two teams met for the replay a week later.

Collingwood didn't have the strength or stamina to handle the Bombers in successive weeks yet at three-quarter time the scores were level again. I had visions of playing Essendon every week until Christmas or at least until one side gave in. No such luck. In the last-quarter, Essendon bolted away. I was thrilled to be named our side's best player and, looking back, I remember with some pride my performance against Essendon's champion, Billy Hutchison. In those days Collingwood just didn't have the tall players to counter the power teams like Essendon and Melbourne. It was the era of the 'Collingwood six-footer'. We didn't have the tall players so we invented them. If a player was five feet 11 inches we would pop him down as six feet in the finals line-ups in the Friday morning papers. One problem of course was that the opposition were giants compared with our blokes who were supposedly just as big.

There was one Essendon player who intrigued me. Harold Lambert was possibly one of the best half-dozen players I've ever seen. He played on the half-back flank or in the centre and had the ability to beat anyone. He would start as a tagger, get on top and then dominate the game, and it was always on our best players. Charlie Utting had been named in the centre for Victoria but when Collingwood played Essendon, Lambert cut him to ribbons. Bill Twomey and Bobby Rose found out the hard way too. Lambert stopped them all. He retired after playing 98 games, 100 would have entitled him to a hefty Provident Fund payout but he went with barely a word to anyone. He was that type of man. Years later I was giving him a rap on *World of Sport* and after the show I was given a message. "There's a call from a Mr Lambert for you." I answered the phone and it was Harold. "I just rang to say thank you for the nice words on the show," he said. And he hung up; not one for long conversations, Harold.

III

The 1946 VFL season came to a tame end for Collingwood, a week short of our target. We were again miles ahead at three-quarter time but lost the match in the most disappointing fashion. This time it was Melbourne and as we sat down for our oranges we led by 23 points. (Oh, this was so reminiscent of Carlton the year before.) This time it was the brilliant Jack Mueller who destroyed us with four goals off his own boot in the last term, to make it eight goals for the day. Again I was named our best player but again it was little consolation. Mueller was one of the greats of the game. At this time he was 30 and supposedly in the twilight of his career. He was destined to take over as playing coach of the seconds at the MCG and make a spectacular re-appearance two years later—again to blitz Collingwood in a finals match. Jack had lost a couple of fingers and wore a black glove but it didn't stop him being one of the greatest high marks football has seen and the perfect big occasion player. Melbourne's full-forward that day was Norm Smith, the red-haired and wily fox who would challenge Jock McHale's claim to being the game's greatest coach, with six premierships in 10 seasons. Smith was a great forward, possibly the most unselfish I've ever seen. He was a shrewd player and ultimately a great tactician.

At the end of the 1946 season, Collingwood enjoyed the ultimate end-of-the-season trip. We all climbed aboard the train at Spencer Street railway station for a trip to Western Australia. These days footy clubs think nothing of sending the boys to London or Mexico, Greece or the USA for a quick sojourn on a jumbo, but back in 1946 a trip to Perth was considered a very big deal indeed. On the way we stopped at Kalgoorlie—a chance to stretch the legs and loosen up with a game against the locals. Some of us had more on our minds than football, to be perfectly honest. How could you be serious about the football? The umpire bounced the ball to start the game, and on the rock-hard surface the ball seemed to go up forever. Our ruckmen would sometimes have three runs at the ball before it came down. A bloke couldn't wait to get into his good gear to get out amongst the action.

Jack Burns and I quickly latched onto a couple of local beauties. Dressed to kill we were and they weren't bad either—fur coats and all. Now, when you're 23 and on your first big trip, the sight of two heavily made-up young ladies in full-length fur coats is something you dream of, even if you are in Kalgoorlie, in the middle of the

Nullarbor, in temperatures that can touch 35°C after dark. Anyway, we young Lotharios lured the girls back to the Railway Hotel (overlooking the railway line, of course) with the promise of cool drinks. The truth be known, we had a couple of cold bottles of beer. It should be revealed that Jack and I had won the big prize in the accommodation stakes. We were sleeping on the upstairs balcony of the hotel—the ritzy part of the balcony. We had a couple of drinks and then the serious matters were discussed. "Well, let's get down to business," they said, quoting a price. That was the end of the evening.

We went on and played a match at Bunbury against a combined south-west side. We won easily and I dazzled them with five goals. The *South Western Times* of Thursday 24 October, 1946 won me with the following:

> Rover Lou Richards was the star of the day. His uncanny
> football sense and accurate disposal, whether by hand-ball
> or foot pass, was a treat to watch.

I still subscribe. Keep up the good work, fellows. It was the same story in Perth. In front of 15,000 people at Subiaco we defeated the unbeaten Western Australian premiers, East Fremantle, by 18 points. For my part I kicked three goals but collected my major football award to that date, the Simpson Medal, an honour which I still cherish.

After the match Jack Burns and I wandered back to the team hotel only to be confronted with an urgent message. "The coach wants to see you in his room immediately," we were told. Like a flash we were upstairs knocking on Jock McHale's door. "Come in boys and sit down on the bed," Jock said, pointing to the spare bed. He was sitting on the other bed next to Ted Rowell, a prominent Melbourne rails bookmaker with a big quid who had been a teammate of Jock's and a real legend around the club. Jack's eyes met mine and the same thought went through our minds together; a windfall was on the way—beauty. Mr Rowell didn't let us down either. "Well played young Richards, well played Burns," he said as his hand snaked towards his bulging coat pocket. We wondered whether it would be 10 quid each or whether we'd have to share it. The hand came out holding a paper bag. The payoff had come. "Have an acid drop," he said. As we made our way to the door with the bitter sweets in our mouths, he called us back. "Here you are fellows," he said, reaching into his pocket. "Have another one for later." I ate mine. Jack threw his the length of the corridor. "Bloody acid drops."

III

Collingwood missed the finals by half a match in 1947 but it was my most outstanding year in football. Despite my cheek and backchatting, the umpires gave me 11 Brownlow Medal votes; not enough to beat Carlton's winner Bert Deacon, but proof that I was being noticed. I was selected to play in Victoria's carnival side in Hobart, won major newspaper awards and even won a popularity contest. The Collingwood supporters were one-eyed back in those distant days. The *Sporting Globe* ran a reader's survey for the best player of 1947 and 12860 voted this Magpie champ as the player of the year. It makes me dizzy to think of all those forms I filled in with the family at the kitchen table. Second was Carlton's Jack Howell on 12 630, and way back in third was Fitzroy's great captain Freddie Hughson with 6917. The *Herald* footy writers led by my old mate Alf Brown were outstanding judges, too, and I won their £100 award by three votes from Essendon's burly ruckman Percy

Bushby, and a further vote back was South centre half-forward Ron Bywater. A hundred quid was certainly very handy, especially when you consider you could buy a weatherboard house for £1500 and a brick house for about £2500.

I had my heart set on being in the Victorian team to play in the 1947 carnival and was on the plane to Hobart that July. It is the highest honour for a footballer to reach state football, and to join the likes of Phonse Kyne, who was captain, Billy Hutchison, Fred Flanagan, Les Foote and Jack Graham was an enormous thrill. When I look back at the photos of the team lined up next to an Australian National Airlines DC one-and-a-half at Essendon airport, I see that I was strangely subdued. I was probably worried about the trip ahead. Victoria lost to Western Australia by four points but thrashed Queensland and Tasmania and tied up the Carnival on percentage by beating South Australia.

The shock of losing to Western Australia was the upset of the trip and for Fred Fanning it was a match he could never live down. At 1.93 metres and 95 kilograms he was a big bloke, and that year he won the VFL goalkicking with 97 goals—a record that stands today at Melbourne. We were a kick the difference when Fred won a set shot 36 metres out in the dying moments. You have to realise that the same bloke once kicked a torpedo from the centre of the MCG over the grandstand. He reckoned it flew 130 yards (118 metres). One way or the other it was a whopper and Fred could certainly attest to that. He was lining up and the West Australians were hurling mud at him, shaking the goalposts, screaming. Things were pretty tense. Anyway, he missed, kicked a point and we lost the match. The next morning the headlines screamed out at you from the sports pages: "Fanning loses game for Victoria." Fitzroy's Alan Ruthven gathered every copy he could find and piled them outside

Fred's door. The big Demon opened the door, saw the headlines and burst into tears. We didn't let him live it down.

It was in the game against South Australia that I first saw Bernie Smith, one of the greats. He was playing in the centre in those days and was destined to become a great player with Geelong. We just stood back and marvelled when he got the ball. Of course he went on and won the Brownlow Medal in 1951 as a back-pocket and starred in back-to-back premierships with the Cats. Rarely do you look back in sport and hang your head in shame, but I do every time I think of Bernie. We were playing against each other at Collingwood one day and Bernie was set up for an easy chest mark. I ran straight at him and punched him in the throat. When he got to his feet, he looked me in the eye and said, "Lou, I never thought you'd do that to me." It was like hitting Mother Theresa in the nose. I felt guilty and ashamed and I prayed that Victoria Park would open up and swallow me where I stood. He was the loveliest bloke in football and the game lost one of its greatest champions when he died of cancer a few years ago.

When we were there in 1947 Tasmania was in the grip of a long, wet winter, and the joint was freezing. Occasionally the players would warm up with snowball fights. North Hobart oval looked like something out of the Battle of the Somme, only muddier, and every night we were all desperate to warm up. One night we went out to a dance and bumped into a team of nurses. They suggested a friendly cuppa back at the nurses' home and offered to leave a side window open for us. Off we went—St Kilda's Harold Bray, Melbourne's full-back Shane McGrath, Fitzroy's Alan Ruthven, Fred Fanning and yours truly—in search of warmth and the tender loving care dispensed by nurses. In we piled, with the exception of Shane McGrath who offered to stand guard under a street light out the front. Meanwhile we were crashing around in the dark looking for the light cord and the nurses, but instead we found ourselves confronted with the steely eyes of the matron doing her rounds. Fred Fanning burst into tears. "Don't put us in," he pleaded. "I've just got engaged." I did all the talking and seemed to be doing alright when I looked out the window and saw Shane, our stooge, chatting to a policeman. The matron was a good sport and told us to follow her to the back door, which would have been okay but for silly Fred. He found the light switch at last, turned it on and had nurses screaming blue murder. We finally made it out the front where Shane and the copper were still chatting like best mates.

"Where have you boys been now?" the copper enquired.

"We're on our way home from a dance," I answered.

All of a sudden there was a rumpus behind us as Fred reappeared. The policeman whipped out his baton and started to look very menacing indeed. "I'll get them. I knew someone was in there. I'll beat their brains out."

He wouldn't have missed Fred—he was seven pick handles across—but fortunately we managed to quieten everyone down and head back to our own beds. I often think of Fred Fanning—just the type of bloke to have with you in the trenches.

CHAPTER 4

DANCING, PRANCING AND ROMANCING

I f this book has flipped open at this page you'll soon know why. Blame those grubby types who stand in bookshops thumbing through high-class literary blockbusters like this one, searching for smut.

The early adventures of young Lewis Thomas Charles were generally confined to the sporting fields of Melbourne and the less salubrious surrounds of factories and plant buildings within cycling distance of Abbotsford. That's not to say that the fires of passion didn't run through his veins. When you've been married to one woman for more than 40 years and in love with her for what feels like a lifetime—sometimes two—the romantic exploits of your youth tend to become a little clouded. It's been particularly difficult writing this chapter with Edna peering over my shoulder, tut-tutting here and sniggering there. Imagine Harold Robbins churning out those sexy epics on his yacht in Cannes, with his missus butting in every few pages. I constantly remind her that this is my life story, warts and all. She reminds me at every opportunity that the warts were PE (pre-Edna), and that this part of the story should be regarded as far-off fantasy, the wanderings of a grey-haired senior citizen.

As a teenager I might say that I was a suave, dark-haired sophisticate; well, dark haired, anyway. The place to go, the in-place for girls, was undoubtedly Leggett's Ballroom in Greville Street, Prahran. These days it's been turned into squash courts and a tennis complex. Often as not I'd slip into my only good suit and catch the train over to Prahran with my mates, Laurie Yates and Curly Freake. Leggett's was very, very smart. At first, Laurie, Curly and Lou were anything but. We were known as 'corks'. We got to dance in the curtained-off area reserved for beginners, making fools of ourselves as we stomped all over the dainty feet of the instructresses. With the lure of those fresh young ladies behind the screen we quickly picked up the rudiments of the foxtrot, the modern waltz and the quickstep—all the new-fangled steps of the day. When the curtain went back we generally stood there, stunned. It's amazing how the bravado disappears when you're put on the spot.

One night the boys bet me a shilling that I wouldn't ask one particular girl for a dance. In those days I would have done anything for a shilling, I can tell you. Like a flash I was over to her seat to ask her for the pleasure of the next dance. As Ern Pettifer's band struck up the music, the young lady stood up. She towered over me by at least 15 centimetres. Without exaggerating she was taller than most of the blokes I played football with. I spent the dance with my ear nestled against her navel but it taught me a valuable lesson which I never forgot: don't ask a girl for a dance if she's sitting down.

III

After six months as a learner I graduated to the Collingwood Town Hall, working up the guts to hit the big-time. I must have been all of 17, the war was on and, to be fair, there was a shortage of eligible young men around. It was only a matter of time before I was nabbed by an older woman, and before you go dreaming of Joan Collins or Kim Novak, let me put you straight. She was old— all of 24 or perhaps 25—and definitely not Miss Australia material. Obviously feeling a bit romantic since her husband was overseas, she pounced on me. We danced and chatted and, not being one to turn up an opportunity, I offered to walk her home to Johnston Street. The moment she walked me through her front door and into the bedroom I knew which direction the evening was headed. I might have been only 17 but I wasn't stupid. The light was turned off and as the moonlight flooded the room I was ordered to undress and hop into the big double bed. There was nothing romantic about it at all. As I lay back on the verge of an historic event in my young life, she was taking off layer after layer—corsets and girdles and all the other paraphernalia. Crikey, it took forever. The act itself, I can report some 50 years on, didn't. The old saying, "faster than a speeding bullet", might have been Superman's catchcry in the 1950s, but it was mine in the early-1940s. I was out of bed in a flash, dressing on the run and bolting for home. Strangely enough I've never seen her to this day, not that I've been searching all that hard.

The Collingwood Town Hall dance, run by the Freemans, was a marvellous social event in those days. It was one of three dances run by the company. The other two were held at the St Kilda Town Hall and the Masonic Centre in the city. One ticket got you into all three dances, and that was a pretty slick marketing ploy in those war years. Hardly anyone had a car so once you started off at a dance you stayed the night. If you were lucky enough to have a mate with a car you guarded him jealously. You made sure he had a girl, too, because that motor car was the passport to a whole range of extra curricular activities when the band stopped playing.

My Collingwood team-mate Jack Burns had a friend with a car and a shocking stutter. By the time he'd finished asking a girl out, the dance would be over and she'd be halfway home. One night Jack and I both got lucky early. We had our girls organised but spent hours lining up a third girl for Jack's mate with the mumbles. Luck went our way and the three of us were heading off for a romantic interlude in our friend's Chev. It wasn't the most comfortable of rides but those were the sacrifices. While our driver shared the front seat with his three female companions, Jack and I were squeezed into the dickie seat in the back. Everything was going well as we headed along the boulevard on the banks of the Yarra when the car spluttered and came to a bumpy stop. "I think we're out of petrol," our driver stuttered. "There's a spare tin in the back." We pulled out the can and took off the top. With that, our driver lit a match and peered into the can, the match disappearing into the spout. "Plenty there," he said, but it was too late for Jack and me. We were already in the bushes looking for cover and waiting for the explosion. It never came but this did put a dampener on the evening.

III

Although I've been married for years and have two lovely daughters, and despite the fact that my first three grandchildren were girls, I've never really been a ladies' man. Edna reckons she met me during a blackout. I can't quite work that one out. If she met me during a blackout, how on earth would she have fallen for my dark, swarthy looks?

Football and, in particular, Collingwood have figured largely in my life but it was a chance meeting with a young lady in 1943 that made them pale into insignificance. Edna Bowie was about my age—20, give or take a month—and a real looker. I was introduced to her at Victoria Park one day by her cousin, and I suggested we might have a dance at the Town Hall that night. When you're a rising megastar in the VFL you have to fight your way through the backslappers after the match and this particular night things were pretty hectic. By the time I left the social club it was getting close to 10 o'clock. I hadn't forgotten my promise, so I walked around to the Town Hall, preparing to trip the light fantastic with the delectable and shapely Miss Bowie. I saw her right away and went over.

"Righto, Edna, my dance."

"Sorry," said Edna. "I'm booked out."

Just like that; given the old 'lemonade and sars'. The next week it was the same story but I was a cheeky little rover, blessed with perseverance and patience. This time I asked whether I could escort her home. Little did I imagine that she wasn't going to her home just down the road, but to her cousin's home in Westgarth, miles away. I was taken in for a cup of tea and then shown the door. She knew how to treat 'em mean and keep 'em keen, even then. It took me three weeks to get my name on her dance card but once I was there, I was in for keeps. While I thought she was a stunner, the feeling wasn't mutual. Years later it wounded me to read in a magazine that she had thought I was arrogant, and it shocked me to the core to discover that she had also thought I was a member of the feared Don gang. This was the gang of hooligans, thugs and toughs who stood outside the chemist on the corner of Johnston and Hoddle Streets in Collingwood, picking on the unwary. This was the same unsavoury mob who jeered and whistled as I rode by on

Edna's lady's bicycle some nights (a bicycle equipped with a skirt guard to stop a young lady's attire from being wrapped up in her spokes). It was lucky I played for Collingwood. I can tell you that.

For five years we went together and from the outset I was positive that she was the woman for me. Over the years Edna has kept those great looks and maintained her dignity, and no one has had a greater influence on my life. I remember asking her to marry me after we'd been going together for three or four years.

"How much have you got in the bank?" she asked me.

"£62," I told her.

"Not enough," was her matter-of-fact reply, but it was enough to get both of us saving like mad.

Apart from being the drummer in her father's dance band, Edna was making a very healthy living as a tailoress, doing piecework for Howards on the corner of Hotham and Hoddle Streets in Collingwood. While she was earning between £20 and £25 a week, I was still at the Board of Works making my £9. With the glut of ex-servicemen around Melbourne in those days, it was hard to get a job, let alone gain rapid promotion. The plum jobs went to the blokes who'd been overseas, so when I saw a job advertised for a trainee sewage designer I held out little hope. Once again the legendary John Wren came to the rescue. At a time when I was playing my best football for Collingwood and Victoria, I won the job—on the condition that I went back to night school and earned my leaving certificate.

At the age of 25 I returned to school, which was an august establishment by the name of the Austral Coaching College in Little Collins Street, Melbourne. It was murder. Here I was, a VFL superstar, sitting amongst all these pimply faced 16 year olds, battling with George Bernard Shaw and having my brain tied in knots as

I wrestled with my logarithms. How could you concentrate? Every kid and most of the teachers were more interested in the fortunes of Collingwood than the work at hand and if it hadn't been for Edna's cousin, who was a teacher, I don't think I'd have ever made it. You might be wondering what George Bernard Shaw had to do with my elevated position as a trainee sewage designer; 40 years on, I'm still wondering myself.

My job was to inspect sites and approve alterations to existing sewers. It was painstaking work, I kid you not. One day a week the boss would say to me, "Young Richards, take the car today." That, in itself, was an invitation to disaster. I hadn't driven a car since I visited the motor registration branch years earlier to collect my driving licence with my friend Cato. The garage of this establishment was like a maze and on the first day at the controls it took me 90 minutes to get the car out of the parking spot and pointed in the vague direction of the road. I scraped the bumper bar and slightly dented the mudguard. On another occasion I had my foot in plaster and managed to smash into another parked car. To this day I've improved only marginally and must be one of the only people in Australia to write off a BMW doing 25 kilometres an hour in a No Through Road. Digressing slightly: I was ordered to go and pick up some plants one morning at Portsea, from my old mate Jack Cannon's place. After the job I picked up a can of Coke for the return trip and was merrily minding my own business, with the can resting on the dashboard, when I turned into my street. McGregor Avenue in Portsea is a lovely ti-tree-lined avenue, an unmade road that winds through the properties of the rich and famous. I was wandering along, thinking of nothing in particular as I am known to do, when crash: the place exploded around me. I came over a hill and ran head-on into a Toyota Celica, wrecking the Richards family saloon. Feeling moist, I touched my shirt and almost fainted as I noticed a wet, sticky substance—blood! Then I spied the Coke can and I've never felt so relieved in my life. Edna could supply a million more examples of how my driving hasn't improved over the years, but I won't let her.

III

In our courting days we had quickly established that our future in business lay in the pub game and we worked like crazy with that end in sight. Money was the key and she was the ideal manager. We lived on my money and banked hers. On 30 October, 1948 we were married at the Wesley Church in Lonsdale Street, Melbourne, and then adjourned to the Melbourne Town Hall for the reception. Arthur and Molly Bowie put on a magnificent wedding, entertaining 300 guests. Molly always had a special effect on me. When I first spotted her I thought she was a better sort than Edna but our personalities led to some crackerjack arguments.

We fought like cat and dog for years while Arthur, the laid-back and placid bloke he was, would look on bemused. "Why create an enemy when you can make a friend?" he'd tell me as the verbal war raged around him. "Why use vinegar when you can use honey?"

They were terrific to us and in later years would help us get our life into very respectable order. Molly always had her reservations about me. Like her daughter at first, she thought I belonged to the notorious Don mob and was just another uppity footballer.

In fact, I don't think she believed Edna and I were playing mothers and fathers until our daughter Nicole was well on the way.

By 1950 we had saved some money and, with the help of my uncle and aunt, managed to acquire the lease to the Town Hall Hotel in Errol Street, North Melbourne. Arthur and Ethel had been lessees of the Marquis of Lorne in Fitzroy and knew the pub trade inside out. Edna and I were rookies. Edna, in fact, had never been in a pub, nor had she ever had a drink in her life. From the outset it was the worst kind of partnership imaginable. Edna was young and attractive, the sort of young lady that the blokes would want to stop and talk to. Ethel was older and a little on the plump side. I was a VFL footballer at the height of my career with the most popular team in the land and a regular state representative, while Arthur was just another publican. The inevitable blue wasn't long in coming, which isn't to say we weren't always at each other's throats.

One particular night Ethel had been dipping into the brandy, the favoured way at the time for women in the pub game, and was well and truly under the weather. We were cleaning up and had all the glasses stacked on the bar to dry. All the jealousy and nastiness of the previous months erupted. There was name-calling and finally Ethel did her block. With one swing of her arm she cleared the bar of glasses, smashing them everywhere. Two days later my uncle and aunt came to me and suggested that we break the partnership: they wanted out of the Town Hall and it was ours if we could raise the money. We had saved about £900 and needed another £600 for the lease. For the first of a number of times in the early years of our marriage, my old sparring partner Molly Bowie and husband Arthur came to the rescue.

Our pub was owned by the Richmond Brewery, which in those days ran in direct competition with the mighty Carlton and United Breweries. This should have been a disadvantage but in the early days of our venture it was an unexpected blessing. No sooner did we take over than CUB went on strike. There was no beer available in North or West Melbourne except at our pub in Errol Street.

Mum had decided to get married again and my young brother Ron, then about 21, asked if he could move into the pub with us. He couldn't have come at a better time. The Town Hall did a reasonable trade in normal circumstances. We used about 12 or 13 18-gallon kegs of Richmond beer a week. In the first week of the strike we pulled 60 kegs and in one day Ronnie pulled 11 on his own. People came from everywhere to sample the hospitality. They drank on the footpath, up the side lane, anywhere they could find. The first week was costly for us when we found that 12 dozen glasses had gone missing. By the end of the strike we had 20 dozen more than when we started; drinkers wouldn't bother waiting for a fresh glass but brought their own from pubs near and far. It took Carlton and United years to get back into their rhythm but for Edna and me it was a glorious and lucky start in the industry.

We quickly discovered the pub game was to our liking. It was bloody hard work but there was money to be made if you were prepared to hack it. Just getting the beer in those days could be a handful. I used to borrow a converted Chevvy tourer from a mate, Lou Livingstone, and drive over to the Richmond Brewery to collect my allocation. The car was a sight. It had been cut in half and a tray had been fixed on the back. When we stacked the beer on board the front wheels would lift off the road. You'd drive along and have to stop now and then to get the wobbles out of the wheels. It was our first taste of the pub trade and we were hooked. It would become our life for nearly 25 years.

III

In those days of six o'clock closing, bottled beer was a rare treasure and many pubs still had trouble getting a fair supply of barrels. With the licensing police breathing down your necks, it was a futile exercise to break the law and sell beer after hours, yet most of us did so. There was always a mate who'd call, looking for a couple of bottles after hours, and when they were good customers it was hard to knock them back. One night at about 11 o'clock I got out of bed to answer the telephone. Some of the locals played for the Happy Valley football club, a Sunday League team who played down near the Royal Children's Hospital. The blokes were having a bit of a turn and the beer was running low. They wanted an extra nine-gallon keg. I reminded them that it was going to cost 10 quid-roughly the equivalent of 220 glasses—and they would have to come and get it. "Park the car at the end of the lane, open the boot, keep the motor running and give a quick toot on the horn," was my instruction. I went into the next bedroom and woke brother Ron. "Come on, you're stronger than me. You can give me a hand," I told him. We went downstairs and rolled a keg out of the cellar. They were big wooden kegs with steel rings, and I can tell you they were bloody heavy. We heard the bloke pull up and a few seconds later toot his horn. Ron went out the back door into the lane and proceeded to carry this keg nearly 60 metres to the car. I was at the car and was about to take the money when I saw a car turn the corner into Errol Street. It was the licensing police. Quick as a flash I ran down the lane, almost colliding with Ron. If there was an Olympic event for barrel carrying, Ronnie would have taken the gold. I flipped him round in mid-stride and pointed him towards the back door. He kept on going. We deposited the errant keg in the cellar and hightailed it to our bedrooms. The expected knock at the door came moments later. I opened up and there stood the coppers, two of them.

"Why did that car have its boot open out the front?" one of the policemen said. "No idea, constable," I replied. They couldn't prove any wrong had taken place and promptly left. Many of our customers used to bring their own gallon jars and I'd fill them with draught beer for them to enjoy during the evenings in the comfort of their own homes. One of my boarders, named Ronnie, used to keep his gallon jar in our fridge. One night he asked me refill it after hours, but considering the state he was already in, I decided to pour him half a gallon instead. Edna and I were about to go to bed when we heard a ruckus outside. Ronnie had taken his beer and joined some of his mates in the laneway. They'd been there only a few minutes when the police arrived. There was the customary knock on the door and we scattered. My brother Ron jumped into his bed with his clothes on; in fact, he still had his boots on. Edna was more of a quick thinker (come to think of it, she still is). She grabbed our infant daughter Nicole and lay back on the bed breastfeeding her. I opened the door. The licensing policeman wanted to know whether I had served the blokes in the lane and I pointed out that Ronnie was, in fact, our boarder who had kept the beer in the fridge to keep cold.

"Who's inside?" the policeman asked. "My wife is in bed upstairs." He demanded to see for himself so he marched upstairs and knocked on the door. "Come in," Edna said and as the bloke peered around the corner he saw Edna breastfeeding Nicole. "Terribly sorry, mother," he said and hastily made his exit, apologising profusely as he went. Thank goodness he didn't go into the next room where Ronie was cowering under his blanket.

Despite my experience with my uncle in Fitzroy, Edna and I were relative rookies in the hotel game when we began working at the Town Hall Hotel. We'd settled into North Melbourne but we looked back in horror at our initiation. I guess we'd been in the hotel game six hours when I heard a shocking thud outside the window. Arthur and I met outside in the hallway.

"What on earth was that?" I asked him.

"We'd better go and look," he said.

We opened the side door onto the laneway and as we did a figure clad in singlet and underpants darted past us and up the stairs. It was Bill, our boarder. Bill was a shunter for the Victorian railways at the North Melbourne yard and quite partial to a glass or two at night. This night he'd had more than enough, leaned out the window of his first-floor bedroom and fallen about three metres onto the serrated galvanised iron fence. When we went up to have a look at him we found that he'd taken a huge triangular chunk of flesh out of his side. The booze probably saved him because if he had been sober, I reckon he would have died of shock.

Edna couldn't believe what she had let herself in for. In the years ahead she found out. As an expectant mother she thought nothing of carting the beer every Thursday night or doing other menial tasks which were hard work for a League footballer, let alone a mother-to-be. Even in the early-1950s we had trouble getting bottled beer. The strikes had played havoc with production and we got an allotment of bottles in ratio to the amount of bulk beer we sold. I remember getting 100 dozen bottles of Richmond beer every week and then doling them out in varying amounts to my customers. If they were a run-of-the-mill customer I might give them two bottles; if they were my very best they might get a dozen. In those days that might have cost about a quid. On a good night I could get rid of the whole 100 dozen in 20 minutes. Jimmy Sexton, a mate of mine who had the Racecourse Hotel opposite Flemington racetrack, had a far brisker draught beer sale and was allocated about 500 dozen bottles a week. He had a great idea. He'd keep the semitrailer laden with beer out the front of the pub and just take out the cash registers.

He'd sell his load off the truck inside an hour. Richmond Beer was regarded as second best to Carlton and United's product but in those days it would sell like dynamite. Regular CUB drinkers always complained that the Richmond stuff tasted like "panther's piss" and was only palatable if taken chilled. Come to think of it, can you imagine drinking a glass of warm Foster's?

CHAPTER 5

STRIFE AND SUCCESS

Impartiality should be the byword for football commentators, writers and broadcasters but, personally, its absence has never worried me one bit. I'm a Collingwood man and I'm proud of it. The Magpies gave me my finest sporting memories and, unfortunately, some of my darkest. It is a club with a grand heritage and you only have to walk into the rooms and see the old photos of past greats to understand the history of the place. In my day Collingwood was the number-one football club in the nation; a team to be loved with fervour or hated with passion. And that's the way we liked it. While the other 11 clubs battled for column space in the newspapers, any football story was big news at Collingwood; it still is.

The club always portrayed itself as bigger than the individual, and that's why the defection of top players bordered on heresy. Collingwood put you on the field in that black-and-white jumper and controlled your destiny. The club decided when it wanted you to leave, not the other way around. Back in 1940 Ron Todd went to the VFA, joining Williamstown for £500 and double the match payments he was getting at Collingwood. Todd was a youngster, a local and the outstanding goalkicker in the VFL. In 1938 he kicked 120 goals to top the VFL goalkicking. The next season he kicked 121. If that wasn't bad enough, triple Copeland trophy winner and the 1940 Brownlow medallist Des Fothergill followed suit and went to Williamstown with Todd. No side could afford to lose one of these players, let alone the two most gifted players in the team. They were huge stories but the behind-the-scenes battles weren't revealed for years. Once you left the fold you were virtually an outcast and despite repeated requests from Todd to return, the club held fast. Fothergill did return in 1945 and played for three seasons, topping the goalkicking for the club twice and underlining his great talents. In 1950 the same attitude prevailed as Len Fitzgerald left for Adelaide where he would win three Magarey Medals, and in later years we would lose Bobby Rose and Murray Weidemann at the peak of their careers.

In the 1960s, 70s and 80s we would see the club split down the middle in a series of torrid election campaigns. In 1963 Tommy Sherrin and Frank Galbally did battle resulting in success for the football manufacturer and failure for the eminent legal eagle. Eleven years later a slick and brash businessman named Ern Clarke swept to power, defeating former ruck great, Neil Mann, for the presidency. The photos at the club were taken down, history was shoved into the cupboards and a modern era was ushered in. In fact, the club hit rock bottom under his leadership. Personal bickering hit a new high, players squabbled over match payments and eyed jealously the huge sums being paid to Len Thompson, Phil Carmon and Des Tuddenham, and the relationship between president and coach Murray Weidemann verged on all-out war. Something had to give as the club plummeted to the wooden spoon for the first time, in 1976. Clark resigned because of business pressure, Weidemann left at the end of the season to be replaced by Tommy Hafey. Airline captain, John Hickey, took the helm but in 1982 another reform movement, aptly labelled 'the new Magpies' and spearheaded by Ranald Macdonald, the publisher of *The Age*, would take charge and plunge the club to the verge of bankruptcy.

Recent Collingwood history has been a sorry tale of administrative bungling and bureaucracy gone berserk, but I mention the potted history to highlight the big news stories that have kept Collingwood on the front page over recent decades. And that has been off the field. Add to that little mess the fact that the club has not won a premiership since 1958, and has appeared unsuccessfully in nine Grand Finals (losing eight and drawing one, in 1977) and you get a better view of the situation that has befallen us. Hard as it is to believe, all the stories I have illustrated fall way behind the biggest to ever break at Collingwood: the 1950 coaching fiasco, which I remember like it was yesterday.

III

In the late-1940s we had a good, talented side, and we'd been finals regulars but hadn't got past the preliminary final. By 1949 Jock McHale had decided to stand down as coach after 39 years, 752 games and eight premierships. He was indeed the prince of coaches and only the fourth man to have coached the club in its VFL history. His replacement would be of critical interest, not only to us, the players, but to everyone associated with the club. There were five contenders for the post but it boiled down to a head-on battle between the seconds coach Bervyn Woods, who had played under McHale in five successive Grand Finals from 1935, and our skipper and great ruck star Phonse Kyne. Kyne desperately wanted the job; Woods, unbeknown to most of us, had already been promised the job three years earlier on that end-of-season trip to Western Australia. To understand the political climate of the day you must realise that Collingwood was run by three men: president Harry Curtis, who had held the job for 26 years; secretary Frank Wraith, who had been there for 20 years; and treasurer Bob Rush, who had been in office for 42 years. Add to that the awesome power wielded by the VFL's longest serving and most godlike coach Jock McHale, and you see how a feeling of complacency could have snuck into the place. That is exactly what happened.

The Curtis-Wraith-Rush power base had become bombastic and almighty. These men figured that their word was supreme. When they offered the coaching job to Bervyn Woods they expected it to be upheld without a whimper. I recall the predicament the players were in. We all felt tremendous loyalty to the club and therefore to Woods, the duly appointed coach; but on the other hand, how could you look past Phonse Kyne? He had been a mighty ruckman for the club since he joined in 1934 and although he had played his best football before the war, he reminded us of his extraordinary talents by winning a hat-trick of Copeland trophies from 1946. To say he was a living legend would not be overstating matters.

Collingwood had made it known that they would not be interested in appointing a playing coach, and Messrs Curtis, Wraith and Rush were known to be furious that Kyne had put them in a pickle by applying, and worse still, by making the application public. To add insult Kyne promptly announced his resignation as a player, to make his application fit their bill. I believe that the committee meeting at which the coach was decided was probably the fiercest brawl ever witnessed in a room which had seen plenty of action.

Accusations of double dealing raged for years, but in the end Woods won by a solitary vote. Local boot manufacturer, Bill Nimmo, was incensed by the committee's decision and began calling for a special general meeting to protest the appointment. Kyne meanwhile kept true to his word and continued in retirement. At the final practice match in April 1950 the supporters went mad, hurling abuse at new coach Woods, our president, secretary and treasurer. When Kyne popped into the ground to watch the game he was carried shoulder-high around the arena. It came as little surprise to any of us when Woods stepped down the next day in favour of Kyne. He had lasted five days and never coached Collingwood in a senior game. His predecessor had lasted 39 years. The furore was front-page news and I doubt if there has been a longer or more intense press campaign in the history of VFL football, but to Collingwood's fury, it was far from over. As Richard Stremski wrote in his excellent history of the club, Kill for Collingwood, "other clubs had reform movements; Collingwood had a revolution."

The rebels, headed by John Wren junior and Jack 'Jiggy' Harris, still wanted their meeting and on 17 May called for the resignation of the old guard. I remember sitting with the other players in the Collingwood Town Hall listening to an impassioned plea for peace from Percy Page, the secretary of the Australian National Football Council, and to the words of Jock McHale. Both men were booed by the huge crowd which was out for the blood of Wraith, Curtis and Rush. A division was called for and those in favour of the 'revolution' were asked to move to one side of the hall. The players had agreed to back the rebels and stood as one and moved to the appointed side. Only a small number of people remained against.

Legend has it that Bob Rush, who was hard of hearing, turned to Harry Curtis and said, "Are they for us?"

"For us be stuffed. They're agin us," Curtis told him.

This bitterly fought campaign ended the football careers of men who had known long and truly loyal service to the club. They were more than household names; they had guided the destiny of the club for more than two decades, had been tougher than any other administrators in their day and had put Collingwood on a pinnacle. Unfortunately for them they didn't know that they had run their race. Their bombast and complacency had been recognised in the nick of time. I recall that John Wren junior had been summoned to see his father, the legendary power broker at the club and one of Melbourne's wealthiest men. John Wren senior was aghast that his son could back the rebels against three trusted and proven allies in Curtis, Wraith and Rush. After Wren junior outlined his argument, he went ahead with his father's blessing.

III

At no stage in my football career was I ever politically active, nor did I want to be, but there was one fleeting moment when I was regarded as a pocket-sized Castro, a mini Mussolini. In the late-1940s we had a bad run, losing four or five games in a row, and I was concerned that the slump would worsen. I mentioned my concern to fellow players Jack Burns and Mac Holten, a future Liberal politician, and they agreed. It was suggested that instead of talking to Jock McHale about our predicament, we would ask the players to get together after training for a private meeting. This would be a chance to thrash out our problems. The club secretary Frank Wraith got to hear of our plans and was furious. The three of us were summoned to his office. "Jock McHale wants to see you three," Wraith said. It was like being called before the headmaster, only Jock in those days wielded more power. In we went. All standing before him in a line we looked very contrite. "Burns, you're a good Catholic boy. Holten, you're a Liberal voter, and Richards, your family has been involved with this club for 50 years. Now the three of you are acting like commos, trying to hatch a conspiracy. While I'm coach there'll be no meetings. Now get out and get ready for training," Jock roared. Suitably chastened, we left quickly and, needless to say, there was no meeting.

III

Under Phonse Kyne, Collingwood would not make the finals in 1950, but great things lay ahead. The players could sense a change; they could feel that Collingwood was about to embark on a new and successful era despite the setbacks of 1950.

Phonse was a fine on-field leader who, having replaced Alby, took us into the finals in 1946, 1948 and 1949; but in those three campaigns we won only one of six matches. There were more than 70,000 at the MCG for the first semi-final in 1948 and they saw Collingwood get off to a patchy start against Footscray. Our kicking let us down and at one stage Bobby Rose had 1.4 on the board. To make matters worse Bill Twomey injured his ankle, and it was touch and go whether he'd see out the game. At half-time Phonse and Jock McHale were in a quandary. Should they take the brilliant Twomey off the ground or should they see if he could prop up an end in the forward pocket? Luck was with us this time. Twomey went to the forward line, kicked five goals in the third-quarter and three more in the last to finish with eight goals from nine shots, and we won by 35 points. I always felt that Bill could have been even better than he was at Collingwood. He was the sort of bloke who, when he was good, was very good and when he was bad he was horrid.

The 1948 finals series was one of the most remarkable in League history. First there was Twomey's match, as it was affectionately dubbed. Then, after a lacklustre second semi-final in which premiership favourite Essendon trounced Melbourne, the Demons sprung one of the shocks of the year. They recalled veteran Jack Mueller, 32, to play alongside Norm Smith, 33, on the forward line for our preliminary final encounter. Mueller is close to being the best footballer I have ever seen. A magnificently versatile player, a great mark and a fine kick, Jack could take a side apart. As a teenager he lost the tops of his two middle fingers on his right hand above the knuckle, and he wore a protective leather glove. The accident, which had happened in the machine room of a box company in Carlton, did little to hinder his great career. Many thought he was over the hill when he was recalled from the seconds, where he had decided to see out his career as a playing coach: if only! We kicked three quick goals but then Mueller and Smith mauled us. Jack kicked eight and Norm added six and we were out of action, losing by 65 points. Melbourne drew with Essendon in the Grand Final the following week and won the replay the week after. Mueller kicked six in both matches to tally twenty in three finals—not bad for a bloke who played only two games out of the first 18 for the season.

While Mueller, the old bloke, stole the limelight in September 1948, it was a young rookie from the Mornington Peninsula town of Hastings who claimed the title as the first superstar of the postwar years. John Coleman's arrival in League football was breathtaking. He'd been reared in Moonee Ponds and had played a few games in the Essendon and District League before his parents moved down to Western Port Bay. Playing for Hastings, he kicked 11 goals in the 1947 Grand Final to take his season's tally to 136. In 1948 he kicked 160. In both seasons he'd tried out in practice matches with Essendon but had been unimpressed with the way he was treated and went back home. By 1949 he'd been approached by 10 VFL clubs (goodness knows what was wrong with the recruiting officers from the other two clubs). In the opening match of the 1949 season he made his debut for Essendon wearing the number-10 guernsey. He kicked twelve goals against Hawthorn and overnight he was a football sensation. Previously his Essendon team-mates had ignored his leads, but once he joined the club proper everyone was on the lookout for him. He led to the likes of Billy Hutchison, Ron McEwin, Greg Tate and Keith Rawle and repaid them with bags of goals every week.

Despite having Coleman, Essendon lost six of their first 10 matches but later won eight straight to nudge Melbourne out of the finals race and take fourth spot. Collingwood finished third and we met in the first semi-final. It was a wet, muddy afternoon and the Bombers were anything but happy with the hard-hitting, or should I say, rough-house manner in which we greeted them.

To be honest, Collingwood was never in the game, and we got slaughtered by 85 points. Essendon kicked 20-16-136 which was a record score in any final, and their winning margin went into the book as well. Coleman was superb. He kicked six goals to take his tally for the year to 91. On Grand Final day he would kick another six to move from 94 to 100, becoming the first rookie to 'kick the ton' in his first year. His career started explosively and would end dramatically in his 98th game, against North Melbourne in the eighth round of 1954. A knee injury would end the dream.

Having been around football for so long, I have had the joy of watching the great full-forwards, from Gordon Coventry, through Bob Pratt, Ron Todd, Bill Mohr to the greats of recent times like

Doug Wade, Peter Hudson, Peter McKenna and Bernie Quinlan, yet I have never known a player to have won the public's heart quite like Coleman. The kid had everything: the enormous leap, great hands; he was a lightning fast lead and could top it off with the accuracy that sets the great full-forwards from the rest. In those 98 games he kicked 537 goals at an average of 5.48 per game, and of the greats, only Peter Hudson with 5.59 has done better. Essendon, with Coleman, won the flag in 1949 and again the following year when he kicked 120 goals in another *tour de force*.

III

To be captain of Collingwood was to me the single greatest football honour that could befall any youngster. The club had a tradition that was unparalleled in that area and knowing that my grandfather and my uncle had both reached that pinnacle, it was always my burning desire to follow them. The Magpies had a number of great captains between the wars, including Syd Coventry, Harry Collier and Jack Regan, and afterwards Phonse Kyne. When Phonse retired to take over as coach there was little argument that Gordon Hocking should replace him in 1950. His vice-captain was ruckman Neil Mann and that appointment had me red with rage: as a more experienced player I figured that I was next in line, but evidently I wasn't that popular with my team-mates. Those who knew me then, and to some extent now, would know that I expect perfection. I like things being done properly and don't mind delivering a blast when I feel it is justified. In the 1940s I was playing well, I was roving for Victoria and I was one of the key players at Collingwood. I wasn't scared of telling my team-mates that they were playing badly and delivering the withering blast within earshot of all and sundry. In fact, I'd often roar the tripes out of them in front of their team-mates and/or opposition. When Neil was made vice-captain it made me reappraise the situation.

By 1951 Collingwood had regrouped. We had got over the departure of Jock McHale, adapted to the coaching style of Phonse Kyne and had put the 'revolution' out of our minds. Essendon were again a force to be reckoned with, but the suspension of John Coleman from the finals series, after being found guilty of striking Carlton's Harry Casper, took the wind out of their sails. A new force had emerged—the Cats from Sleepy Hollow—and they weren't bad either. In 1951 Geelong would win the Brownlow Medal through Bernie Smith, the goalkicking courtesy of George Goninon, and the premiership. (Collingwood had done the hat-trick twice back in 1927 and 1929.)

Early in 1951 the players met for their pre-season dinner—a ritual which went back donkey's years at Collingwood. We'd all troop in and listen to our president Syd Coventry, and then get the annual warning from Jock McHale, even though he'd stood down as coach.

"Don't forget, you young fellows: take it easy with your wives; you know it's Thursday night," Jock would tell us. "And you young fellows with girlfriends, see them home by all means, but keep the picket fence between you when you say goodnight."

To this day I'm not quite sure what it meant, but Jock obviously thought it was of vital importance because I heard the same line every year for a decade. Later in the evening there would be the vote for the captaincy. In 1951 I'd put Ronnie up to nominating me. No one seconded the nomination. I almost sank through the floor with embarrassment. Gordon Hocking got the job and Neil was again his deputy. While I was moping around later, contemplating this bitter blow to my ego, Ron fronted me. "I've never felt so embarrassed in my life," he said in his usual machine gun delivery. "Don't you ever do that to me again, you bastard."

III

That season it was a new me. When our players looked down I would encourage them rather than yell at them and the results were an improvement. When Gordon Hocking injured his knee, Neil Mann took over as captain and I was elevated to vice-captain. Later in the year I took over as skipper when Neil went down with injury. It was a position I revelled in and at the pre-season dinner in 1952, with Gordon Hocking's retirement leaving the position open, I was elected captain unopposed.

We met Geelong in the second semi-final and George Goninon had one of those days you dream about. He kicked 11 goals on Jack Hamilton—the future boss of the VFL—including six in the last-quarter, and the Cats won by 82 points. Ron and I put together good games and were Collingwood's best, I recall rather humbly. We went into the preliminary final with confidence, and with 20 minutes remaining, we led Essendon by five goals. I can't remember what happened next but I was reliably informed that I was knocked out. Collingwood obviously missed me because they blew the lead and lost by two points.

In the 1970s the Magpies would be hit with the derogatory tag, 'Colliwobbles'; this was a term that summed up their inept and fumbling performances under pressure in finals matches. Crikey, I reckon we had a bad case of it in the 1940s and early-1950s. We got through to the finals easily enough but blew the big ones. The 1951 preliminary final was the fourth time in seven years that we faltered one game short of the Grand Final. Not surprisingly we made it through to the finals in 1952, my first year as captain, and proved little opposition to Geelong in the second semi-final. Once again we were the drawcard on preliminary final day. This time our opponents were Fitzroy; a pretty tough mob captained and coached by the debonair Alan Ruthven. He was one of the great rovers of his time, the winner of seven club best and fairest awards and the 1950 Brownlow Medal. While his was a tough side, he played the game fair. He was known universally as 'the Baron'. Friends at Fitzroy tell me that he dressed so loudly as a youngster at the club that they called him this after Baron Rothschild, and the moniker stuck. This day I flattened him in front of the Members' Pavilion at the MCG and 'the Baron' lay prostrate on the turf.

"Get up, you bludger," I yelled at him.

"Not till they stop hooting you, you little bastard," came the deadpan reply in 'the Baron's' famous gravelly drawl.

III

Over the years we became firm friends. We were both in the pub game and later panellists on *World of Sport*. 'The Baron' loved a wager and loved a game of golf, so Ron Casey and I would indulge him in both passions each week. We'd play at Kew and 'the Baron' and I had a standing bet. He'd wager a dozen bottles of French champagne that I couldn't break a hundred. I'd put up four dozen cans of beer. One particular day at Kew I played the best golf of my life. Everything fell into place, the putts rolled uphill and into the cup, the drives went long and straight. After nine holes I tallied up my score and found I'd shot 38. By the 14th I was in magnificent shape, just a few strokes over par. 'The Baron' was getting nervous. He started doing all those things that upset a player's concentration. He'd fart when I went to drive the ball. He'd rattle his clubs as I putted. He'd drop a branch as I played an approach shot.

The Richards resolve was like steel. On the 15th I found a bunker, or should I say it found me, and it was determined to keep me. I took 17 shots to get out and my game went to pieces. In the end I shot 104 and 'the Baron' kept his champagne and my beer. To this day I'm shocked at his behaviour—from a Brownlow medallist, too!

III

Getting back to the football, I did exact some revenge and we won the preliminary final quite easily. Bob Rose was brilliant. The win set us up for another crack at Geelong in the Grand Final, my first with the club. The day remains vivid in my memory; the details of the match elude me. Ron and I made it a practice to get to the ground about half an hour before we were needed. It gave us a chance to relax and unwind. Grand Final day in 1952 was no different. We jumped into my Holden station wagon and drove from the pub in North Melbourne and somehow found ourselves in the MCG car park, near the Richmond ground. The attendant took one look at us and directed us towards Punt Road, in quite the opposite direction of the ground and leaving us with a three-day hike.

"Listen you bastard, don't you realise we are performing here today?" I growled at him. "I'll be exhausted if I have to walk from Punt Road. If it wasn't for us, youse bastards wouldn't have a job here."

Ronnie was trying to calm me down and that was making me worse. I was getting so fired up I couldn't contain my rage. "What did you call me?" the attendant finally said.

"I said, youse ... ewes, like in sheep," backpedalling furiously.

It didn't do any good as we were directed to the parking spot he had originally picked out. I parked the car and Ronnie grabbed his gear off the back seat. I went to the back to get mine and, blimey, it wasn't there. I'd left it back at the pub. Into the car I got, out the gate and I was off at breakneck speed through the city, back to North Melbourne. Flying down Flinders Street, I heard a police siren, and a bloke on a police motor bike waved me over.

"You're speeding, driver," the copper said.

"Look, I'm Lou Richards, captain of Collingwood. I'm performing in the Grand Final this afternoon and I've left my gear at home."

"So it is, Lou. Follow me."

With that he took off, with me in pursuit. He didn't have the lights flashing but he guided me through the traffic, home to Edna where I grabbed my bag, and he was there to guide me back to the MCG. You wouldn't want to know it, but I ended up at the same gate and the same bludger was there giving instructions. This time I tried to be polite. It didn't work and I didn't bother arguing. He had the same spot put aside, the farthest spot from the MCG imaginable. By the time I walked into the rooms I was a wreck; and it pains me to say, but I played atrociously and Collingwood lost. I could barely raise a gallop all day.

III

Geelong was a side built on class. The Cats were fast, balanced and supremely cocky. Looking back at some of the champions who played in those back-to-back premierships under coach Reg Hickey, it isn't hard to see why this combination was rated as one of the best ever. Skipper Fred Flanagan epitomised the Western District look with the moleskin trousers, the Harris tweed jacket and the elastic-sided riding boots, off the field that is. He might have looked like a cow cocky but he could play football. In his first eight seasons with Geelong he represented Victoria. George Goninon lived in the shadow of John Coleman, like every other full-forward of the time, but he kicked plenty of goals and was the VFL's top sharpshooter in 1951. The side was packed with talent. Leo Turner wore the number-nine guernsey 130 times with pride; his son Michael would inherit it and play 245 games until his retirement at the end of 1988. They had great rovers in Peter Pianto and Neil Trezise and, of course, there was Bob Davis.

Bob is one of my best mates and I wouldn't say this to his face, but the bloke could play football. He was about 1.78 metres and weighed in at 92 kilograms and could run like the wind. They still talk about him running 100 metres bouncing the ball at the MCG against Collingwood in the 1952 Grand Final. He is known everywhere as 'Whoofer' but he likes to be remembered as 'the Geelong Flyer'. Sometimes I think that nickname stuck because of his way of driving along the Geelong Road: the bloke thinks he is Nelson Piquet, but drives faster. Personally, you wouldn't catch me dead in his car. Bob was one of the great stars of that Geelong era, a half-forward flank with explosive pace and a player we found nigh-on impossible to stop. Then there was Bernie Smith, one of the great gentlemen of football and, incidentally, the best back-pocket player of all time. Some back-pocket players treated me with respect; others treated me like the front door mat and wiped their boots on me, if they could catch me. Max Oppy of Richmond, the man with the most fearsome forearms in the business, would ride roughshod. Charlie Sutton, the human tank and captain-coach of Footscray, liked nothing better than seeing me squirming on the ground. Bernie Smith just tried to outplay you, and frequently did.

By mid-1953 Geelong looked invincible yet again and were steaming towards a hat-trick of VFL premierships. They had started football's greatest winning streak with a draw against Essendon at Windy Hill in round 11 in 1952. When we made the trip to

Kardinia Park in August 1953, they had won 23 on end. They hadn't lost a game at home in 16 appearances. At three-quarter time we trailed by two points and I remember sitting sucking on my orange as the Cats moved back to their positions for the last-quarter. "Come on suckers," they seemed to be saying. "It's only a matter of time." The boys put on the sort of last-quarter burst that makes your heart swell with pride. We kicked 4.4 to a goal and ended our opposition's winning streak. Geelong was stunned. After the match it was normal for the sides to mingle and enjoy a drink. In fact, the hospitality at Geelong then and now is unrivalled. That day there was nothing. I don't think it was done on purpose; it must have just slipped their minds. On the eve of the finals it was the perfect boost, knowing that the hot premiership favourites were only human after all.

Collingwood had put together a pretty good team and we felt that we could beat Geelong in the finals. The Magpies hadn't won a flag since 1936 and after our harrowing loss in 1952 had plenty to prove. Looking at the side, there were some fairly ordinary players scattered through the line-up but we had plenty of champions in there as well. Neil Mann had finished third in the Brownlow count, Bob Rose second and for the second year in a row our teenage winger, Thorold Merrett, had finished in the top ten. Merrett was a marvellous player whose career was tragically cut short with a broken leg. He was only 26 when he retired in 1960 and the dual Copeland trophy winner had already played 179 games. He came to the club with a huge wrap at the start of the 1950 season. My former team-mate Jack Murphy had seen Thorold playing for Cobden in western Victoria and raved about his skills. "This kid can stab-kick a pellet of wheat up a chook's arse from 30 paces and not ruffle a feather," was Jack's no-frills report. Looking at Merrett you'd think he was in primary school. He played his first game against Footscray mid-way through the season and kicked six goals from a forward flank. He was 16 years old, stood about 1.75 metres and must have weighed 50.8 kilograms. He was a freak.

Geelong created a new record in 1953 by finishing on top of the ladder after every round, but we beat them in the second semifinal and knew we could do it again on the day that mattered most. There were 89,000 at the MCG for the Grand Final and the atmosphere was electric. As usual I walked over with Geelong's skipper Fred Flanagan to toss the coin, to decide ends.

Fred, always the gentleman, extended his right hand. "Good luck today, Lou."

"Don't wish me the best of luck. You see that flag pole on top of the stand? Put your head down and I'll kick your flaming head right over it," I replied.

Fred was flabbergasted; he still is to this day. As for me, I don't quite know what made me say it. We were that keyed up. It was like no match I'd ever played in. Before the game Phonse Kyne and I had told the players that no one was to go down. "If you are down and out, get up. Run past your mates and tell them to get on with the game," Phonse reminded them. It was a warning that I'll remember. Late in the match I cramped. The ground was rock hard and I'd run out of steam. Down I went. A familiar voice yelled in my ear, "Get up, you weak bastard," screamed brother Ronnie. I recall getting to my feet and running on, having no feeling whatsoever in my legs. Things went our way in that match. Our pre-match plans worked to perfection. Terry Waites was to play only a dozen games for the club yet he put Geelong's John Hyde out of business. We knew Hyde had a crook thigh so we told Waites to run him all day and the kicks would come. Bill Rose tagged the Cats ruck star,

Bill McMaster, out of the game. Neil Mann was great in the ruck, Bob Rose brilliant as usual, Des Healy a match-winner on his wing, and little brother Ronnie was my choice as best on the ground.

In the last-quarter Geelong made a spirited revival and I thought they might just knock us off. Healy went down with a cramp and I ran over to him and told him to rest in the forward pocket. I decided to look after his man, Bert Worner. By this stage Bob Davis was going crazy. He'd kicked two goals and set up a couple of chances. He was running riot and this bloke Worner was running like a gazelle. He kept getting the ball and taking off like the 'road runner'. "If this bastard will stop long enough, I'll knock him rotten," I remember saying to myself. Fortunately Des recovered from his cramp and relieved the situation. In the dying moments of the game, which, incidentally, felt like an eternity, Ronnie somehow got the ball over to Bob Rose who kicked the clincher. The bell rang and the ground was invaded by thousands of Collingwood supporters. In those days there was no cup or medal presentation; the players were swamped and the captain was carried shoulder high from the ground. I don't think I've felt anything like that elation as I was hoisted up and carried from the MCG. Back in the rooms the beer flowed like water. As captain it was my responsibility to join Phonse Kyne at the post-match radio show at 3AW. I quickly showered and was walking out with Edna when a well-known Collingwood barracker and prominent wharfie, Len Stewart, picked me up and carried me on his shoulders through the milling crowds. It felt terrific until he trod on a beer bottle and dropped me on my back. I was in agony as I finally made it to the car park, to our secretary Gordon Carlyon's old Buick. I threw my gear in the back seat and as I got into the car, Gordon slammed the door shut, neatly jamming my fingers. It was a night I'll never forget.

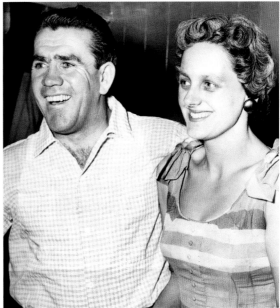

WEDDING DAY A youthful Mr and Mrs 'Kiss of Death' tie the knot. Edna was a real looker and I was introduced to her at Victoria Park by her cousin. I was a lucky man with Edna, who kept me in line and was my best mate.

YOUNG FATHER Taking time out from football with my children Kim (left) and Nicole.

COLLINGWOOD FOOTBALL CLUB
2nd EIGHTEEN   PREMIERS 1940

Allan Studios, Collingwood

P. Blokkeerus   D. Morehouse   J. O'Connor (Timekeeper)   W. Arthur (Head Trainer)   F. Story

P. L. Scott   Cr. R. L. Friend   H. W. Edmonds   Cr. J. Eastman   F. Westlake   J. Dicker
Com.   Com.   Coach   Chairman   Manager   Asst. Timekeeper

H. Coventry   W. Johnstone   A. Aldridge   K. Sullivan   D. Knott   J. R. Carnie   R. Howell

K. Barrett   C. Newman   L. Tyrrell   W. Unwin   W. Noonan   J. Pimm   L. Hustler   J. Jones

N. Crewther   A. L. Hill   C. Shields   C. MacRae (Capt.)   J. McHale (Vice Capt.)   P. Busbridge   R. Smith   C. Rose

L. Richards   R. Carruthers   H. Mears

EARLY DAYS Sitting proudly (front row, left) in my black-and-white guernsey at 17 years old.
I shared my first Collingwood premiership with vice-captain 'Jock' McHale (we beat Carlton junior by 22
points in the reserves), son of the legendary coach. The next season we'd both make our senior debuts.

100th GAME The young superstar, standing in front of the most famous grandstand in football and on the hallowed Victoria Park. A publicity shot to celebrate my 100th game, before the 1946 record semi-final against Essendon. We had drawn the previous week— I kicked four goals—but lost the replay, and the preliminary final to Melbourne.

TALKING THE TALK Seven's commentary team at Waverley in 1980. Bobby Skilton, the 'Kiss of Death' and Peter Landy. Sometimes it was so cold at Waverley I'd wear a pair of Edna's tights under my slacks!

A FORMIDABLE TRIO Three of the very best. Yours truly, Ron 'Mr Football' Barassi and the world champion boxer Lionel Rose. During *World of Sport*, I liked nothing more than to enjoy a drink afterwards with the likes of Barassi.

UP FOR A BET I take my punishment after a dopey dare gone wrong, sweeping Collins Street with a feather duster after declaring Melbourne a certainty to beat Footscray in 1959.

HOT PIES The three wise monkeys—Bob Davis, Jack Dyer and I—tucking into a few Four'N Twenty pies before presenting *World of Sport*. They were the three that Doug Elliot had obviously overlooked.

MONKEYING AROUND 'See no evil, speak no evil, hear no evil.' *League Teams* on Seven was the popular forerunner to a multitude of late-night footy shows.

© CHANNEL 9 ARCHIVES

↑ ORGANISED CHAOS
Executive producer Gordon
Bennett explaining the
running order on *World of Sport*.
It didn't matter because after
10 minutes we were always
running 20 minutes behind.

← CAPTAIN BLOOD
The best partner a man could
ever have. A dumb ruckman!
In his 312 games with Richmond,
Jack Dyer put the fear of God
into every opponent he met.

LOOKING GOOD
After 30 years at Seven,
I found a new home
co-hosting *Wide World
of Sports* at Channel Nine,
where the make-up and
hairdressing 'department'
made this publicity
shot sparkle.

We finally celebrated at the Magpies' Nest, a secret rendezvous which remains just that to this day. John Wren had thrown in about a thousand quid to split up and we were feeling pretty happy with our lot—all except me. My finger throbbed, my back ached and I was stuffed. If this was winning, I'd hate to know how losing felt. Collingwood's first success in a Grand Final since 1936 had its effects off the field as well. The drama of the moment claimed two victims: Jock McHale suffered a heart attack the day after the Grand Final and died a week later, and John Wren suffered a similar fate. He was struck down with a heart attack the Monday after the match and died a month later. I reckon they died happy men because Collingwood was a big part of their lives and the wait for success had been a long and bitter one.

CHAPTER 6

THE END AND
THE BEGINNING

It makes you bleed when you hear about young players today getting paid hundreds of thousands of dollars to play football. Thank goodness the VFL has come to its senses and introduced a salary cap on each of the 14 clubs and a draft system. Both these highly controversial changes to the game have had teething problems but together they might just be the salvation football has been searching for.

Money was never a high priority over my 250-game span with Collingwood. You might believe that it has taken higher profile in my life since the day I hung up my boots; too right it has, and I reckon I've worked very hard for it. When I started with Collingwood I was paid 30 bob a match. We all were: from my captain Jack Regan, the prince of full-backs, through to the youngest player in the side, who in 1941 was yours truly. Even our coach Jock McHale copped his 30 bob. Jock had been the game's most successful coach and had been at the helm at Victoria Park since 1911. In the 1930s he had been offered as much as £40 a week to coach rival sides but his love of club and guernsey held him steadfast to Collingwood. Right to the end, in 1950, he took the same payment as his players, and I ask you how many of our current crop of coaches would do that?

The game in those days was regulated financially by the Coulter Law. Framed in 1930, it set down strict guidelines as to how much a player could receive. For example, in the 1930s it was £3 a match, in the war years we did our bit and the fee was cut in half, but in 1946 it rose again to £3. In 1951 it rose to £5 and in 1955, my last year, we all took home £6. Inflation wasn't a word many of us had heard about and football wasn't our major source, or should I say only source, of income, as it is with many young players today. Bonuses were frowned upon during the season but were allowed to an extent at finals time, when all the payments were increased. At Collingwood we were fortunate to have one of Victoria's wealthiest men as our patron. After nearly every game we would troop into the dressing rooms and be greeted by Jock McHale and a little bloke in a black overcoat with a felt collar. John Wren wasn't a tall man but around Collingwood he was a giant, by name and reputation. Many a player in financial difficulties would hit John Wren for a hundred or even two hundred quid to get them over bad times. The money was never repaid; it was rarely expected. The man who operated the famous tote in Johnston Street and sued for criminal libel after the publication of Power Without Glory (the story of a fictitious bloke from Carringbush named Jack West, who also operated an illegal tote) played a not insignificant part in my life. I never had need to seek financial help from him but he did help me get work on two occasions when work was hard to come by.

III

John Wren was a bandy-legged bloke who loved players at Collingwood who could kick straight—the goalkickers who took the limelight. One memorable day, in a match against North Melbourne, I was in marvellous form and kicked seven goals, which was the best sharpshooting performance of my career. Afterwards I marched into the room and spotted Mr Wren chatting with the coach at the door. The players loved John Wren because, among other things, they knew he richly rewarded good performances and the rewards came in the form of the folding stuff. This day I was on line for a healthy payout but for some reason Mr Wren hadn't noticed me. I made my way across to the lockers. (At North Melbourne in those days the lockers consisted of a row of nails on the wall and the veterans took the precaution of bringing their own nails and borrowing the bootstudder's hammer. I was one of those thinkers.) By the time I'd stripped and sauntered slowly to the showers there was still no contact from our wealthy patron and to be honest I was getting a little concerned. I showered, dried off and walked back to my nail. Jock and Mr Wren were still deep in conversation. Back I went for yet another shower and another until finally I reckon I'd been in the bathroom 17 times. I'd never been so clean in my life. Just as I was about to give up all hope, Jock caught my eye.

"You know Mr Wren, Lou?" he said.

"Yes, Mr McHale. How are you, sir?" I replied in my most polite manner.

"Well played this afternoon, young man," he said, pressing something into the palm of my hand as we shook.

"Thank you, sir. Thanks very much," I managed as I made my way back to the nail, anticipating the sight of a £10 note when I unclenched my fist.

You can imagine my shock when I peered down and there was a £1 note, all squashed and clammy with my sweat. When I got outside, Edna was waiting and she saw straight-off that I was crestfallen.

"How much did he give you?" was her opening line.

"A quid," I said trying to hide some of my disappointment.

"He might be going through a hard time. He's probably down to his last 10 million pounds," she added in a way that just rubbed salt into the wound.

His generosity was legendary; and a pound, although at that time a third of my weekly pay, was still well below par for a seven-goal haul. The next week we played St Kilda at the Junction Oval. Afterwards I saw Jock and Mr Wren again chatting about our win. I walked past him and he called out to me.

"Young Richards, how much did I give you last week?"

"A pound, sir."

"I thought so; I've been worrying about that all week."

With that he put his hand in his pocket and pulled out a £10 note.

"Here, this is a little better," he said.

I was delighted but as I walked away a thought struck me.

"Do you want that pound note back Mr Wren?" I said.

"No, you keep it."

III

Twice in the course of my career I was tempted with big money to leave Collingwood: once to join the Victorian Football Association and later to play with another club. The thought of financial security was the key factor. In 1946 the VFA was going through a rebuilding process. The association had snared the biggest names in football. Among them were men like Laurie Nash from South Melbourne, the great Bob Pratt, who held the VFL goalkicking record, Harry

'Soapy' Vallence from Carlton and the Collingwood pair of Ron Todd and Des Fothergill. For a decade from the mid-1930s, the VFA offered a very credible alternative to the power of the VFL. The offer was a simple one for me, as I was then on the basic £3 a match. I was promised £300 a season, or £15 a match plus financial help buying a house. In those days I wasn't married, was still living at home and, to tell the truth, was flattered to be singled out. One night there was a knock on the front door and when I opened it I was confronted with one of John Wren's emissaries. It was a straightforward discussion. He pointed out that I was a Collingwood boy through and through, with a proud family heritage. He also suggested that after only five years at Collingwood, I would be leaving the club before I had shown the Magpies my best football. I knocked back the offer and never regretted it.

In 1950 I was approached again, this time to play with North Melbourne, a side that had developed into a tough, mean and quite successful club under the guidance of coach Wally Carter. At the time I was the angry young man. I was annoyed that I had been overlooked as vice-captain in favour of Neil Mann and I was bitter that the club had dropped my little brother Ronnie to the reserves. It would be fair to say I was ripe for the plucking. The Town Hall Hotel in North Melbourne was a popular watering hole for some of the local players, and some days you might bump into the likes of Ted Jarrard, Alan Marchesi or Pat Kelly enjoying the Richards' hospitality. They obviously passed on the message that I was disgruntled because out of the blue came an invitation to Edna and me to join North's president Frank Trainor for lunch at his House of Commons hotel in the city. I informed him that it would be impossible to go as we were both needed to run the pub, but he was persuasive. Finally Ronnie took over for the lunch break and we headed into town. Frank Trainor was quite open. He offered me £12 a week to play with North. He pointed out that the money would be handy and with a hotel smack in the heart of North Melbourne territory, the rub-off would be enormous since fans would clamour to drink there. He just about had me convinced. Word must have spread like wildfire because the next day I was working in the public bar and in walked Collingwood president Syd Coventry and committeeman Jack 'Jiggy' Harris. They'd heard about the offer and wanted me to reconsider. Running the pub and playing League football was taking its toll and I poured out my worries. I told them I had to go to market each Monday morning at five o'clock and didn't have the money to put any staff on to help out. The next Monday morning I was setting off to buy the fruit and vegetables and who should be outside the pub but Syd and 'Jiggy'. "We're here to give you a hand," the club president and former premiership captain said. So for the next hour I was treated to the amazing sight of one of football's most decorated heroes and alongside him a prominent Melbourne businessman pushing my long barrow around the stalls as I packed the fruit and vegetables on board. That swayed me and I decided to play out my career with the Magpies.

III

Over the years I copped my fair share of injuries, including three depressed fractures of the cheekbone, a broken nose, a broken forearm, a broken collarbone and a broken foot, but I think the wear and tear of running a pub did more to shorten my career than anything else... The constant pressure of being on your feet and on the move all day took a lot of sting out of me over the seven years in the pub.

It's funny how you tend to forget the pain of being injured but the aftermath stays with you. In 1950 I broke my arm playing against Essendon at Victoria Park. The arm was set in plaster and I met Edna outside the club rooms after the game, feeling low and with my arm in a sling. We walked over to my car, a Vanguard utility, and then realised that I had no way of driving and Edna didn't know how to. "You'll just have to drive," I told her. Well, she got into the car and somehow managed to jump the car all over the road from Collingwood to the pub in North Melbourne. It was one of my most frightening memories. Another time I copped a backhander right across my face, smashing my nose and fracturing the cheekbone, in a match against Hawthorn. Evidently I was carried off on the stretcher. I do recall lying there in great pain when Jock McHale appeared. He jabbed his finger into the cheekbone, sending shockwaves through my body.

"You'll be right," he said, and promptly marched on out. That night I had no intention of sitting at home moping so I suggested to Edna that we should pop down to the local picture theatre and take in a film. The Austral Theatre in Johnston Street, Collingwood, was the neighbourhood flea house. You took your own flea powder to dust down the seats and some of the better looking sorts would wear flea collars; Edna's would be jewel encrusted. All through the film I kept blowing my nose, trying to clear the congealed blood. It must have been quite a night for the people sitting around us. Apparently it's the worst thing you can do when you have your nose broken. When the lights went on I saw Edna recoil in horror.

My eyes had blown up like large red plums and I was peering at her through narrow slits. I always liked to go past my mother's home each Saturday night just to reassure her that I was alright. That night we took a detour. It would have put her in an early grave.

My 15th year with Collingwood was 1955 and it was a milestone that I had been looking to, something that my grandfather had hoped I would attain. I was playing quite well in the pre-season matches and felt that the year would be a formality. Just to be on the safe side I approached coach Kyne and asked for a chat. I'd been reappointed captain for a fourth term but at 33, I was slowing down. Bob Rose was the champion rover in the side and I was planning to play out the year in the forwardpocket with the occasional burst on the ball.

"Listen, Phonse," said. "I want to keep playing but if my form goes I'll quit. I won't embarrass you or the club."

"Righto, Lou," he said, and that was that.

III

One of the major benefits of being captain is that you get to sit in on the selection committee and you get to put up your name first. At mid-season, however, one of the other selectors, 'Jiggy' Harris, who was a member of Collingwood's great premiership sides in the late-1920s, dropped a bombshell.

"Lou should stand down; he's playing shithouse," he told the assembly. Syd Coventry was enraged.

"Don't be ridiculous, you can't drop Lou. He's the captain," Coventry said. With that he picked up a pencil and threw it at 'Jiggy' hitting him square on his bald head. "Don't be a fool," he added.

'Jiggy' was pretty well spot-on. The old skipper had run out of gas. I kicked six against St Kilda in round 14 and by the time we played Essendon three weeks later, the end was closing fast. Trips to Essendon's headquarters at Windy Hill were a sheer nightmare for Collingwood sides throughout my career. During that period from 1941 to 1955 we played 13 times at Essendon and won only twice, once by a solitary behind. We did even things up when they played at Collingwood. In that period we won eight of 11. I realised as I drove out to Windy Hill that this was the last major obstacle between retirement and another round of finals football. Collingwood and Melbourne had dominated the season and looked destined to playoff for the premiership the following month. The game lives in my memory as a disaster from start to finish. When we came in at half-time I hadn't touched the football. That was bad but worse was to follow. Collingwood was being badly mauled and only Des Healy was saving us from annihilation. He had the ball in the centre and I led like a rocket—a pretty slow rocket mind you. His stab pass was a beauty, hitting me right on the chest. It knocked all the wind out of me and ricocheted about 35 metres. The crowd went mad. I was given the raspberry by the Essendon fans and to make it worse by my own supporters as well. It was a moment when I wished the ground would swallow me up.

Poor old Billy Hutchison, Essendon's captain, would remember the game for years. He had the dubious distinction of being the last player I whacked in League football. He was going for the ball and I went to punch it away. I missed and hit him right in the Adam's apple. He couldn't speak for three weeks. If I was unpopular before, this was completely new territory. Billy was a saint at Essendon. He was the winner of seven best and fairest awards, a Brownlow medallist and also one of the cleanest and most skilful players ever to pull on a boot. Just as I was getting over that indiscretion, Healy raced out of the centre again looking for me and I led perfectly. Unfortunately I took my eye off the ball and it hit me on the head. The crowd was going wild. We lost by 73 points and that night I made my decision. I walked into the pub and confronted Edna.

"How did you go?"

"Terrible. I've decided to give it away," I told her.

"If you feel that way it's no use playing," she said.

The next Tuesday night I rolled up to training at Collingwood, got changed and walked out into the middle of the ground that had been my stage for 15 years. Phonse Kyne was directing circle work. "I think I'll give it away, Phonse," I told him in a way that left room for negotiation.

"OK, Lou," he said in a matter-of-fact sort of way that also left no room for negotiation. "Kick it there, Bobby. Over here, Des." And training went on as usual.

The next day the story was all over the papers. Alf Brown, the chief football writer at the *Herald* and one of the great sports writers Melbourne had produced, was in touch early in the morning. I gave him the exclusive and it was plastered all over the front and back pages of the *Herald* that day. It was quite a story—the captain of Collingwood quitting one week short of the finals. In my heart I knew I made the right decision, even four weeks later when I watched Collingwood play off in the Grand Final against Melbourne; more so when I saw them lose by five goals. Strangely, Phonse Kyne thought the opposite. When I bumped into him after the game and was consoling him, he told me that I'd been sorely missed. "If you'd played I reckon we might have had a chance," Phonse confided. "I reckon you might have kicked a couple of goals and given us a bit of leadership up forward." It would also have meant that Melbourne would have had the added pressure of covering a very experienced player. His words were nice but did nothing to alter my feelings or make me regret my decision.

III

Mine had been a good innings. I'd played exactly 250 games and led the club to a VFL premiership. I'd played interstate football for Victoria, won the club goalkicking and booted 425 goals which at that stage made me the 17th highest goalkicker in VFL history. Perhaps my finest achievement was that I'd come from the backstreets of Collingwood and made a name for myself. Little did I realise what it would lead to as I bowed out. The response from the media was immediate. The Argus, a morning paper which is now defunct, asked me to be its celebrity football writer over the finals series and I was entrusted to a young sports writer named Peter Banfield. He would later become my sporting editor at the *Sun* and his boy, also named Peter, would go on and play League football with Essendon and the Brisbane Bears. I was outlandish, as loud in the columns of the *Argus* as I'd been on the field for Collingwood.

In my authoritative preview of the first semi-final that year I suggested that Essendon would have no trouble at all beating Geelong. In my inimitable way I was right off the mark. This was a promise of things to come in my journalistic career and indeed the first 'Kiss of Death'. Geelong won the match because they used their rover Neil 'Nipper' Trezise to tag Essendon's captain and champion little man Bill Hutchison. ('Nipper', by the way, would become the minister for sport among other portfolios in successive Victorian parliaments under Premier John Cain.) That day he was undoubtedly the match winner. On Monday morning our readers were confronted with a blazing headline: "Oh, for a king hit." Beneath was my article laying out the correct procedure for removing pesky taggers. I suggested that Billy Hutchison would have been quite within his rights to whack Trezise right across the bridge of his nose with a backhander. It created a sensation and a media career was off and running.

In those far-off days before the birth of television, the wireless coverage of football was huge. Panel shows were all the rage as the experts previewed and reviewed the round of matches. At 3KZ Phil Gibbs hosted the Pelaco Inquest on Saturday nights from seven until eight and I was quite stunned when he called at the pub one day and asked me to join him on air. I told him that I wasn't interested but deep down I wondered if I could handle the assignment. "I haven't even got a pencil and notebook," I told Phil, trying to wriggle out. Phil disappeared and an hour later was back at the pub with pen and paper in his hand. I thought about it overnight, discussed it with Edna and finally agreed. On Saturdays I would sit alongside Phil in the commentary box at the MCG, adding my pearls of wisdom to his kick-by-kick description. That evening we'd go back to 3KZ and dissect the game. These days you can't shut me up when I'm on air and some producers have told me that they'd have to amputate to get the microphone out of my hand, but in those days I was a complete novice. Thank goodness I got over it quickly. I would arrive at 3KZ with reams of notes that I'd scribble down during the match, trying to sort them out on air. Phil was intrigued, being the pro he was. "I've got more notes here than Margaret Mitchell made when she wrote *Gone With the Wind*," I quipped to him one night. The listeners lapped it up and my nerves disappeared.

At least I wasn't as bad as Jack Dyer. Phil told me recently that after each match he'd dispatch a stenographer to Jack's pub, the Post Office Hotel in Prahran, and listen to Jack's version of the game, complete with the full array of Dyerisms (or Dyer'ere as it became known in the *Truth* years later). She'd rush back to the studios and type up a five-minute script, condensing the unique Dyer version of the match, and Jack would arrive later and read it on air.

I enjoyed my month at the *Argus* and loved working with Phil Gibbs at 3KZ. I realised quickly that there was a big opening in the football media for a smart young boy like me with the right credentials. There was one problem-the Collingwood Football Club. The Magpies wanted me back in the nest to pass on the Richards magic to the youngsters. They wanted me to become Phonse Kyne's understudy and coach the reserve grade side in 1956. Edna was at the pub one night with our dear friend and bookkeeper Ivy Sheehan when I told her of Collingwood's offer. It was to be £7 a week and I thought that was pretty handy pocket money. They were horrified and tore into me. They pointed out that I'd bury myself if I took a job coaching the seconds and that I'd be a forgotten man inside a season. I knocked back the job and to this day I reckon their advice was the best I've ever had.

CHAPTER 7

RADIO DAYS

I n 1956, after 25 years of football carnage, Jack Dyer decided to don his topper and tails and head to England for a year's sabbatical. He took in the French "Riverina" and dined on "spaghetti marijuana" with the toffs. With his close mate Ted Rippon and under the watchful eye of Test fast bowler Keith Miller, the pair were seen at Epsom for the Derby and Lord's for the Test match between Ian Johnson's Aussies and Peter May's Pommies. Since Jack had been replaced by my uncle Alby as coach of Richmond—a sore point that still festers—he'd made a marvellous name as a radio commentator and newspaper columnist with the *Sun*. Jack's departure opened a whole new world for me and I can't say that I was all that sorry to see him bid Australia farewell.

III

Clyde Palmer, father of well-known sports journalist and multimedia punchliner Scotty Palmer, had been in touch and asked me to write for the *Truth* in 1956. Unfortunately Clyde fell ill and while he was away from the controls, the football column was offered to Footscray's captain-coach Charlie Sutton. The *Sun's* sporting editor Harry Gordon approached me and said that his editor Frank Daly would be interested in having a chat with me. They needed a replacement for 'Captain Blood', who was no doubt enjoying the good life in the 'Old Dart', and thought I might be just the man. When I visited Mr Daly I told him bluntly that I knew Jack was being paid £6 a week and that I would do the job if they paid me £10.

"What happens when Jack gets back from England? Will I get the flick?" I enquired.

"If we're happy with your work you'll stay," he told me.

The radio stations weren't exactly beating down the doors of the Town Hall Hotel in North Melbourne to recruit this former Collingwood captain so I was thrilled to hear from Frank Mogg, the boss of 3XY.

"Would you be interested in calling the football for us this year, Lou?" he asked.

"I've never called a game in my life," I warned him.

I had listened to Jack Dyer and thought he did a great job and there was a hankering to do it as well. He told me I'd be working with Doug Elliott, one of the biggest names in radio, and as an afterthought he suggested a weekly payment of £20. It's amazing how those afterthoughts win you over. It was the start of a 30-year working relationship with Doug; a man also known as 'leather lungs', 'Uncle', 'Unca', or any other tag you cared to throw his way. Doug was a legend in Melbourne radio. He had a booming voice and the ability to get both the caller and the listener enthused; and as a young untried talent, I was lucky to get one of the finest teachers around.

In the early-1950s Doug compered the fabulously successful Kia Ora sports parade, a show that might well have been the forerunner to *World of Sport* on HSV 7. Max Reddy and Stella Lamond provided the entertainment, VFL stars would take part in quizzes and do their own bit of song and dance and then there were the variety acts. It never ceased to amaze me how Doug could work with Captain Miller and his cockatoos. The birds could count and were amazingly trained but had a bad habit of flying around the venue dropping large loads of fertiliser on the audience. Then of course there were Freddie Brown and his monkeys who had similar problems with their toilet habits, and to top it off there was Billy Bargo, the country's foremost whipcracker. If Doug could handle a line-up like that, a 1.68-metre former Collingwood rover should have been a mere formality.

III

In 1956 we called the football together, beginning with the practice matches at Essendon. Doug had decided that I needed practice so he decided to borrow a tape recorder and we set ourselves up on the roof at Essendon's Windy Hill scoreboard. Week after week we called the games until I was starting to get the hang of it. I loved it and I will always be indebted to Doug for his painstaking training. He taught me to talk from the diaphragm, insisted that I learn my numbers each Friday night and dinned into me the need to continually update the score. These were the three basics for football commentators which hold fast in any era and in any electronic medium. When Jack returned from England he found things had changed. I was looking after his old column in the *Sun* and had no wish to depart, and I was comfortably ensconced at 3XY. Jack Dyer and Doug Elliott were always great mates and I felt that with Jack's return from abroad I would no longer be needed. I went to Mr Mogg with my worries.

"Jack's back, so there's no need to keep me next year," I told him.

"Lou," he said, "We want you back next season."

There was a pause and another of those afterthoughts.

"Oh, and we'll up your pay to £30 a week."

In those days that was great money.

In 1957 football fans were treated to the amazing sight of the 3XY football commentary team: the portly frame of Doug Elliott separated the ankle tapper from Collingwood and the collarbone cruncher from Richmond. Thinking about it, you couldn't have done better; the big bloke and the little bloke, the ruckman and the rover, the traditional enemies of Collingwood and Richmond, the slow drawl of 'Captain Blood', the incessant chatter of 'Louie the Lip'. It was the perfect team. Uncle Doug was the barb of every joke. He'd appear hurt and mortally offended but he'd play it along like the perfect ham that he was. His calling should have been saved for posterity because there has been no equal. A typical example of his skill when a bloke kicked a goal was "Oh, he's put it through the big sticks. The ball is perfectly silhouetted against a dark August sky…"

Commentating wasn't the plush job it is in the 1980s. At Footscray we were working from the rickety old scoreboard at the Geelong Road end. We'd sit on a plank and peer out through a gap in the scoreboard. There was no toilet and no time to find one but Doug always carried the empty beer bottle in case of emergency. He was always a thinker. Jack was a great target with those big flapping ears of his. One day a spectator at Fitzroy got so irate he pitched an apple at Jack and hit him on the nose—an amazing shot that prompted Jack to suggest on air that the bloke would be ideal material for the Australian cricket team. We all played to the crowd and loved it and both Jack and I were taught a very valuable lesson by a master showman. Doug always told us to be ourselves: in show business it's a must. Over the years those words rang true. Jack massacred the English language like the linguistic lunatic that he was and I just kept talking.

III

The advent of the transistor radio made football commentary a whole new game. In the past the commentators had that bit of licence. They could say what they liked and no one was any the wiser but as pocket radios became more popular accuracy became essential. I remember watching Essendon's skipper Jack Clarke being flattened in a most crude way; steamrolled, in fact. Doug was going on and on.

"This is a black day in football. That was one of the most disgraceful incidents I have witnessed, a blot on the game. The League must intervene," he preached, and then he turned to Jack.

"With me is Jack Dyer, 'Captain Blood'. Jack, how did you see the incident?"

"Quite a fair bump," said Jack, completely flooring Doug, who, incidentally, barracked for Essendon since the day he ate his first pie and sauce.

Doug could flog a dead horse if he had to and when it came to getting publicity for our radio coverage he was magnificent. Leading up the 1957 finals he came up with the idea of arriving at the Melbourne Cricket Ground in a horse-drawn carriage with his motley team of commentators, Richards and Dyer, suitably attired in top hat and tails. We drove through the city, waving to our adoring public and even the stern faces of the MCC members softened as 'Captain Blood' and I made our way to the commentary position. The photograph duly appeared in the *Sun* the following Monday. That year we blitzed the opposition and at the beginning of 1958 Doug rang me with some exciting news.

"Louie, we're leaving 3XY. We're off to 3UZ. I've already signed up," Doug told me.

Once again I was on the phone to Mr Mogg, outlining Doug's planned departure.

"He's gone but you and Jack are staying with us. Oh, and by the way, it will be £40 a week this season," he said.

Jack felt the same as I did and it was with some sadness that we told Doug that he was going by himself. He was shattered. "You can't do this to me, boys," was the plaintiff cry. "You're letting me down."

"Pig's bum," said Jack in that long drawl. "You've signed on for more money."

III

So in 1958 Jack and I handled the job as a team. It was an enjoyable year and a long-lasting friendship was forged. Sure, we got stuck into each other at every opportunity but the moment the microphone was turned off we were again the very best of mates. Unfortunately it was a radio partnership that was quickly shattered. The *Herald* and *Weekly Times*, who employed me as the football expert on the *Sun*, also owned the radio station 3DB and were annoyed that I was working in direct opposition and beating them hands down. The editor Frank Daly, who was paying me £10 a week for my incisive and articulate prose, told me that I had no choice but to work for 3DB. "You either work for 3DB and the *Sun* or neither," was his blunt ultimatum. I rang Mr Mogg with the sad news.

"Lou, we'll give you £60 a week to stay with us," he said. It was a tough decision to make: the *Sun* paid me £10 a week, 3DB would pay only £29 and then there was another major concern. We'd bought the Phoenix Hotel opposite the *Herald* building in Flinders Street and relied heavily on the newspaper clientele. We agonised over it before I decided to throw my lot in with the *Herald* and *Weekly Times*. The money from 3XY was tempting but we felt that in the long term my future lay with the burgeoning interests of the *Herald* and my profile would be better served by staying on with the Sun; and then there was the prospect of television, as the *Herald* and *Weekly Times* owned HSV 7. Once again it was a vital decision and 30 years later I have no reason to believe I made an error. It isn't a matter of how much you are paid; it's the rub-off that really counts. When you work with the biggest media organisation and the largest daily newspaper in the country you can't go wrong.

My on-air partner and boss would be 3DB's sporting director Ron Casey, a youthful radio commentator with an encyclopaedia tucked under a very smooth short-back-and-sides haircut. Crikey, we looked young—overweight and young. Since I retired from football Edna had put me out to graze in a pretty good paddock and somehow my weight had ballooned to a respectable 90 kilograms.

Casey, or Case as he was known to all and sundry, had been put in the same paddock years earlier by his wife Pauline. It was little wonder that we became known as 'the Bookends'. In 30 years of radio and television I've never been lucky enough to work with a commentator like Ron. He was a very tough, demanding boss, but the moment you went on air things happened the way they should have. He knew his sport inside out, always kept well informed and preferred to commentate and let the expert make the outrageous statements. Ron had been an amateur wrestler in his younger days and I dread to think what it would have been like to be pinned to the canvas under that barrel-like frame.

He opened my eyes to sports other than football and cricket. He got me interested in his first love, boxing, and we enjoyed many a night at the stadium in West Melbourne. He took me to the bike races at the old Olympic velodrome and it was here that I'd cross tracks with one of our greatest cyclists ever, the former world champ Sid Patterson. I was at the Phoenix one night when the phone rang. It was Sid. He was riding in a six-day race at the velodrome against the might of Italy and when I spoke to him he was taking a breather.

"Can you bring over a couple of cans?" Sid asked. "I'm bone dry."

"How'll I get in?" I asked.

"Just tell the gatekeeper you've got some urgent supplies for me," he said. I was about to hang up when I had a brainwave. "How many do you want?" "Four cases should just about see me out tonight," Sid said, and he was gone.

Four cases of beer in those days meant 96 small cans or roughly the equivalent of a nine-gallon keg, but it didn't worry Sid. It was a sip in the ocean. When I got there with my precious load the gatekeeper was waiting and he helped me out into the middle of the track. A grateful man was our Sid and it did nothing to stop him winning the race.

Horseracing was a bit of a mystery to me but Casey was a great teacher. Along with our wives we became regulars at city meetings after the football season and finally became members of the metropolitan clubs. It got to the stage where we decided to become active participants and started racing our own horses, the first of which was a lovely two-year-old filly named Grable. She had nice legs like her namesake but she wasn't a huge box-office winner. She did win at Sandown and that was a thrill I'll never forget.

III

In the mid-1970s we went looking for another horse and entrusted the search to Jack Dyer's old travelling compatriot and former Essendon player Ted Rippon. Ted was a good mate of Colin Hayes and made the trip to Adelaide to inspect his latest crop. There were two promising youngsters and Ted couldn't decide between the two.

"Take the two of them," Colin Hayes suggested.

"No, we'll take her," Ted said, pointing to a filly that would race under the name Rondelay and in the years ahead would start 20 times, twice winning, once at the Geelong Oaks Trial, and bring in about $14,000. The one Ted left behind raced under the name How Now and apart from winning the 1976 Caulfield Cup, the Caulfield Stakes, the AJC Oaks, the Wakeful Stakes, the Craiglee Stakes and Kewney Stakes it also amassed $210,660 in loot. Every time How Now saluted the judge, and that was often, we'd all turn on poor old Ted Rippon and give him hell. "That could have been ours," I told him until his ears rang. Jack Dyer was even harsher. "I wouldn't send Ted to a used-car yard to buy a secondhand camel," Jack said on *World of Sport* one Sunday. I'll give 'Captain Blood' his dues, he kept his hands in his pockets and kept out of some of our hare-brained money-making schemes. He stood back and laughed to himself when our syndicate purchased a nag by the name of Pavement Art, out of Streetfighter, which was a beautifully named horse if I don't mind saying so myself. The problem was that it couldn't win a race. We'd be forever bunking it up on *World of Sport* and it was forever letting us down. One week we'd obviously gone overboard. It started at Bendigo at 101 on the books with Harry White on board but the publicity from *World of Sport* had seen it shorten to 7-4 on the tote. You don't want to know where it finished. Finally at the urging of Case and the boys we relinquished our hold on Pavement Art, chuckling to ourselves at our good luck to be rid of it. It won its next six races on end in the bush!

Still, we had some fun along the way. There were others that brought no joy at all but until you've had a horse and won you couldn't know the joys the sport can bring. Along the way we somehow got mixed up with the dishlickers, too, and a wonderful greyhound named Chief Dingaan. Ron and I raced it with Bill Collins and Doug Elliott under the *World of Sport* syndicate. The Chief won 16 races, from memory, from sprints through to distance races but saved his best for a stud career that seemed to go on forever.

The horses and dogs were fun but at times were a costly pastime.

That's where Case and Uncle Doug were brilliant. They could sniff out a business opportunity at 20 paces. We bought a radio station—3CV in central Victoria—and we built country clubs at Wimbi and Rich River and we diversified. Looking back on my partnership with Ron at 3DB, it was a rich apprenticeship for calling the football on Channel Seven years ahead.

Ron and I were at the microphone every Saturday for 14 years and in those days the conditions were anything but plush. A home game at St Kilda's Junction Oval headquarters could be a nightmare. The game was called from a booth out in the open in the St Kilda cricket club stand and anyone who has been to see the Saints play will know that there are few more parochial spots in sport. They always got a good go from me. Each year we'd travel away for the annual interstate matches. Perth is a lovely place to visit but hell to call football from. As the visiting commentators you get the worst position, generally out in the crowd and definitely out in the cold. I have vivid memories of calling a match that saw Victoria fight back ferociously to grab the lead in the last-quarter. As a former Victorian star, and remembering that our broadcast was being heard only in my home state, I felt it was my duty to be just a touch one-eyed. It infuriated the locals who were within earshot. Suddenly a bloke turned around and belted me right across the head with his umbrella. It knocked my headphones askew and almost took my breath away. That's where it was great to work with Case. He just kept going, completely unfazed by the whole episode.

We had considered moving our two-man show across to television but had enjoyed such a long and rewarding partnership that there seemed little need.

CHAPTER 8

THE TRAVELLING CIRCUS

For more than 10 years the Ron Casey/Lou Richards travelling circus bumped around the country roads, crisscrossing Victoria and spreading the sporting gospel to untold numbers of towns and hamlets. We might not have been the first to do the sports night circuit but we can unashamedly take credit for building it into a massive industry.

Radio station 3DB broadcast into rural areas through its regional station 3LK and it was felt that the country folk should get to see and hear their favourite personalities and sporting heroes up close. Virtually every week through the footy season Case would have a night organised. It might be Rupanyup one week, Avoca the next. Ron would organise a couple of big names and we'd climb into his Vanguard station wagon and take off during the afternoon. After the show we'd drag our weary legs, climb back into the car and drive home, often getting back to the city towards day-break. Today it's a big business with big bucks for the best speakers as well as the worst. The likes of Max Walker, my good mate from *Wide World of Sports* Leon Wiegard, Sam Newman and 'Crackers' Keenan have been hot gospellers on the sports night circuit for years and have done very well out of it, too. When Case and I were on the trail we did it for nothing. If we'd charged, I'd now own five pubs and half of Toorak.

III

Ron had a fine panel to select from in those days. There might be Doug Ring, Colin Long, Merv Williams, Bill Collins and Jack Dyer, plus the assortment of football champions who were only too willing to help out. The drive was always good fun. It was a time to tell stories, to tell the odd sporting lie; and I was always in good company. Doug Ring was a member of Don Bradman's Australian team which went through the 1948 tour of England undefeated. A fine spin bowler and a great raconteur, Doug would later become the cricket expert on *World of Sport*. Colin Long loved his golf but his main string was tennis and he had played in Davis Cup finals for Australia in the 1940s. Merv Williams was a legend and in the years to come his cliches would endear him to a generation of fight fans through *TV Ringside*. "He's hit him everywhere but the roof of the mouth and the soles of his feet," was always my favourite. He could talk boxing for hours on end and Case, being a fight fan himself, wouldn't slow him down. For racing fans there was 'the Accurate One', Bill Collins, who could also liven up any trip anywhere with the suggestion of a small wager on just about anything.

In the early-1960s we'd been asked to appear in Warracknabeal, about 350 kilometres north-west of Melbourne, in the wheat-growing area known as the Wimmera. This particular night there were five of us. Ron compered the show as usual, Jack Dyer and I argued as usual and we had on hand the former VFL Grand Final umpire Allan Nash to adjudicate and Brownlow medallist Bobby Skilton to talk some sense. The hall at Warracknabeal was packed to the rafters. We did the show and enjoyed some country hospitality before starting the long trip home that night. I was tucking into some excellent cream sponge cakes when I happened to remark to one of the ladies' auxiliary that Edna adored sponge cake. Next thing we knew, the ladies were packing Case's Vanguard station wagon with cream cakes. There were enough cream cakes in the back to feed a football tea. The car looked like a Herbert Adams delivery van. Although we all enjoyed a beer we rarely had a drink on these trips because of the long drive home, so after we'd had our cuppa we hit the road. It was a very long trip and as we neared Deer Park on the outskirts of Melbourne Ron leaned across and tapped me on the knee. I was sound asleep.

"Louie, we're nearly home," Case said, his voice sounding a little muffled. "I'm feeling a bit weary myself."

"You'll be right," I assured him, and promptly fell back to sleep.

The next thing I was woken by Allan Nash screaming from the back seat. I looked out and we were heading straight for a power pole. Case woke up, swung the wheel and managed to avoid a head on collision but did collect the pole anyway. The car rolled and the cream cakes flew everywhere, coating us all in thick country-style cream and chunks of soft sponge with an assortment of strawberries and passionfruit for good luck. 'Captain Blood' had been asleep in the back and had woken. What a sight! He looked more like 'Captain Creampuff'. Bobby Skilton had been out like a light, curled up in the corner, and he was looking very groggy. Dyer was panic-stricken. "How's Bobby?" he kept asking. "Is he OK? Gawd, don't tell me we've injured him." It's worth pointing out that Bobby Skilton had won two Brownlow Medals and half a dozen club best and fairest awards at this stage of his career and was miles and away the most valuable footballer in the VFL. Fortunately the South Melbourne star was a lot better than he looked under his coating of cream cake and this reassured Jack enormously. "I was only worried about the insurance," Jack wailed. "It would have cost us a fortune." The following week the *Truth* came out with the story—the crash, the cream cakes and Jack's worry about Bobby Skilton's fate. They also claimed that we had been drinking something stronger than buttermilk. They were wrong on that count but there was nothing we could do about it.

III

Some years later Jack and I found ourselves on a double bill at Port Fairy, down on the Victorian south-west coast. We'd entertained the locals at the football club and they were so pleased with the night that we were offered a hotel room each plus a huge bag of prawns to take back to Melbourne. The next morning I knocked on Jack's door.

"Jack, can you lend me a comb so I can do my hair?" I asked the big log. "I haven't got a comb," he told me. "You don't need one. When you're in the bush you have to learn to improvise. Use a fork."

Now I ask you, have you ever tried combing your hair first thing in the morning with a fork? The next matter to be settled was the question of the prawns.

"How will we get the prawns home?" I enquired.

"Easy. We'll divide them down the middle and you can take the bag containing your share," Jack said matter-of-factly.

"But how will you get yours home?"

He looked at me with that look he always reserves for rovers, that look of disdain. He walked over to his bed, grabbed his pyjama pants and proceeded to tie a knot in both legs. With that he poured in his half of the prawns, pulled the drawstring tight at the waist and tied a knot.

"That's what I mean by improvising," he said. To this day I reckon he still wears those pyjamas—I just wish he'd wash them.

This might well be my story and you may wonder why Jack's name keeps bobbing up. The truth is that we have had such a marvellous partnership over the years that if you mention Jack's name, mine will inevitably creep into the conversation, and vice versa. Jack was the star of the show on those long road trips, make no mistake about that. The crowds loved him, and they still do. He has always been larger than life and loves nothing more than the chance to settle back with knockabout people and talk about the things he loves, mainly himself. We'd frequently finish our part of the show at about 10.30pm and be looking for a polite way out; Case to get back to Melbourne and back to the office for work the next day, and me to get home to Edna and the Phoenix Hotel. Jack on the other hand liked to loiter. Occasionally he might enjoy a friendly glass or two as he told stories we'd heard a million times. However, the great thing about Jack is that no matter how many times you've heard the story you still chuckle when it comes round again.

III

In my book *The Footballer who Laughed*, Tom Prior and I recounted a number of the great Jack Dyer stories and to this day they bring the house down. One of my favourites concerned a match between Melbourne and Richmond in the early-1940s. Just before half-time Jack shirt-fronted the Melbourne ruckman so hard it seemed to make the grandstands shake. The Demon went down as though he'd been hit by an axe and didn't move as the trainers examined him and called for a stretcher. Don Cordner, a doctor who played for Melbourne (and went on to win the 1946 Brownlow Medal), pulled a blanket over his team-mate's face as he was carried from the ground.

Jack went white when he saw this. "My God," he said. "He's dead. I've killed him." Terribly upset, he went into the Richmond dressing room. The first person he saw there was the then-vice-president of Richmond Ray Dunn, a famous and successful criminal lawyer. "I can't play in the second-half," Jack told Dunn, "I've murdered that poor bastard."

The legal eagle didn't blink an eyelid or turn a hair. "Go out there and play the game of your life in the second half," he told Jack. "Win it for us and I'll get you off on a manslaughter charge."

Happily the Melbourne player was okay and no charges were laid. I love the big ox but I love to see him squirm. Nothing gives me greater pleasure than to see a little bloke put the knife in and twist it slowly.

One year I flew to Swan Hill for a night with Jack, Bill Lawry, former Australian captain and my *Wide World of Sports* colleague, and an ex-jockey named Peter Bakos. We arrived at Moorabbin and were amazed to see Jack swallowing airsickness pills. Evidently he could fly for a mark but had trouble if he was more than 15 centimetres off the ground. Jack's worries were compounded when he spotted our mode of transport, which was a light plane— a twin prop job—with propellers at the back of the wing. Jack was staggered. "Are we flying up there backwards?" he wanted to know. I sat up front with Bill Lawry while Jack sat in the back with Peter Bakos. As a jockey Peter Bakos was a lot of fun. He was a pint-sized hoop who could ride the lightweights with ease. He could make the weight in a Shetland pony race. Of Hungarian descent, Peter has made more out of his public speaking, I venture, than in his entire riding career and is now a very successful businessman, making whips and Lycra colours for his former workmates.

Jack was intrigued with him, intrigued with his cheeky grin, his high-pitched voice and, most of all, his size. "How come you're so little?" he demanded. Bakos explained that he came from Hungary and over the generations, each third or fourth, out popped a little'n like him. "Pig's arse," said Jack in that famous Tiger drawl. "I reckon you're a dee-warf." It was a funny trip with the intellectually superior Bakos making up for his small stature with a succession of one liners at Jack's expense. Up front Bill Lawry wasn't travelling too well either. He'd heard that Swan Hill had been the centre of an outbreak of encephalitis and the mosquitoes along the Murray River had been to blame. The fearless Australian opening batsman who'd weathered the likes of 'Fiery' Freddie Trueman, John Snow, Wesley Hall and Charlie Griffiths was a little uneasy about confronting the local mozzies.

We duly arrived at Swan Hill and were assembled at the top table for dinner. Midway through my meal I dropped my fork and when I bent down to pick it up I noticed that Bill had tucked his trouser legs into his socks.

"What have you done that for?" I said, pointing to his ankles.

"Do you know where mosquitoes breed?" he said.

"Yeah, of course I do," I said, not wanting to be outsmarted by this pigeon-racing ex-cricketer. "They breed in swamps, along stagnant creeks and on dams."

"And they breed in the dark," Bill said. "Look under the table; it's dark, isn't it?"

You can see how Bill Lawry, with logic like that, developed into one of the finest and wittiest after-dinner speakers in Australia. We got through the night and settled back in the plane for the trip home. Jack was violently ill, as was Bill. I was content to sit back and watch as Peter Bakos ran riot. He walked over the top of the very white-faced 'Captain Blood', he prodded him, he taunted him and he watched gleefully as the former scourge of League football turned numerous shades of green. To make matters worse, Bakos had a bottle of gin and after a few was three parts. This had Jack incensed. "When we get on the ground I'm going to murder you, you little bastard," Jack growled, on one of the rare occasions when he lifted his head from the paper bag.

On another night I ended up in the same country pub as Peter Bakos and I was astounded when I walked into his room and saw him shaving. He was standing up in the handbasin, so he could see his face in the mirror. I love short guys: they make me feel so tall.

III

These days it's not unusual to be flown somewhere to speak at an engagement but in the late-1950s and early-1960s the car was the only mode of transport. Invariably it was Ron Casey's car and Ron always got to drive. One year we were returning from Stawell, home of the famous Easter Gift in western Victoria. It was mid-winter and bitterly cold. None of us saw the stone that shattered the windscreen. We helped clear the broken glass and I promptly gave up my front seat and huddled in the back with Doug Ring and Bill Collins. I've never felt so cold in my life as the wind whistled through, but Ron was blue and shivering. We arrived at Ararat and had to wait some hours for the windscreen to be replaced. Standing at the service station, Bill Collins saw a billiard parlour and suggested a frame or two of snooker to while away the time. Bill grabbed Case as his partner, figuring Doug Ring and I would be the patsies, and calmly informed us that we'd be playing for two quid a corner. He wasn't far off the mark either. Ron and I used to play at the City and Overseas Club once a week and it could take anything up to four hours to complete one game. I could play a frame without potting a colour. Doug was the mystery man. Bill broke and Doug just about cleared the table. In the car later we quizzed him about his prowess with the cue. "I wasn't a slow bowler in an all-fast attack in England for nothing," Doug told us with that wicked grin lighting up his face. While Miller and Lindwall were ripping the Poms apart, Doug was sharpening his skills on the green baize and he wasn't bad either. I loved it. Over the years I found it hard to catch Bill Collins out and on this occasion he was outwitted by an expert.

Ron Casey's cars took a real hammering over the years. He must have logged tens of thousands of kilometres and spent hundreds at the panel beaters. Before the VFL organised its junior development program the *Sun* put together football clinics and took the superstars to the kids in the country. Ron, Doug Elliott and I would act as the comperes and on each trip we'd take away three big names like Ted Whitten, Bob Skilton and Polly Farmer who'd demonstrate their skills. Coming home one night from Benalla we were chatting to the great Geelong ruckman Polly Farmer.

"What are your plans when you finish football, Polly?" I asked him.

"I'd like a job like you and Ron have got," Polly said, "a job where you don't have to do anything."

I thought Case would drive off the road. He was a workaholic and I was trying to combine running a pub with my multimedia engagements.

The crowds varied and the receptions we received varied but two nights stick in my mind. Jack Dunn, the long-time sportswriter on the *Sun*, had organised our panel to appear at Terang, which was a three-hour drive down through the Western District. Case, Colin Long, Doug Ring and I arrived in the town and it was abuzz. We had a quick bite at the local pub and headed across to the hall.

The place was all but deserted. At the advertised starting time there were 10 customers out the front and there was no queue fighting to get in. There were red faces everywhere. It seemed that this was the night of the local hospital ball and the whole town was there enjoying a bit of old-style country hospitality. To make matters worse the show had to go on and we had to sit and endure 90 minutes of whipcracking from some country bumpkin. We were bored rigid and the show we staged that night was the fastest I've ever been part of.

Rarely and only rarely do I put my life in Jack Dyer's gnarled old hands and when I do I usually come unstuck. Jack and I were topping the bill one night at Poowong in south-east Gippsland. (Poo-where? You might ask.) Jack suggested a brief interlude along the way in a tiny country town at a pub owned by a mate of his who was a mad keen Richmond supporter. It sounded like a pretty good idea at the time. We enjoyed dinner and were looked after like kings. At seven o'clock we decided to head off into the night and make for Poowong. Three times I asked Jack if he knew where we were heading and each time he assured me that his navigational skills were second to none. Three hours later, after being hopelessly lost in a tangle of unmade country roads, Jack declared that we had arrived. The hall in Poowong was packed to the rafters and they were all roaring drunk. They'd been waiting for us for hours and had settled into the odd keg or 10. "They'll kill us," I whispered into Jack's monstrous, flapping ear as we walked in. Quite the opposite was the case, in fact. The reception was magnificent and the night went without a hitch. It taught me a valuable lesson though: never trust a ruckman, no matter how small the job may be.

While there wouldn't be a town in Victoria we haven't appeared in over the years, we occasionally got calls from interstate as well.

In the early-1970s I went to Whyalla in South Australia with Bill Lawry, who was fresh from captaining Australia in India. The place was packed with some 1500 people who'd paid their hard-earned money to listen to the 'Corpse with Pads On' and the 'Kiss of Death'. Bill by this stage had started to develop into a fine speaker and was waxing eloquent about the horrors of touring India—the rotten food, the bloody Indians and the stomach upsets that greeted them all just about every day. So bad did it get, Bill told his wide-eyed audience, that the batsmen were tucking their trouser legs into their socks in case they had an accident while running between wickets. Bill spoke beautifully about the subcontinent and as he finished he asked for questions from the assembled multitude. You wouldn't want to know, but a bloke right down the back stood up like a shot. "I'm Doctor So-and-so and I'm an Indian and proud of it," he said. "I think you are a racist, Mr Lawry." Bill copped it sweet but when he got the chance he leaned over and whispered in my ear, "You have to be stiff. We've travelled 800 miles, there are 1500 people here and I have to strike the only Indian in town."

One of the greatest shows we ever put on was witnessed by only a handful of people in a tiny Wimmera town, so tiny that the name escapes me. I recounted it in *The Footballer Who Laughed Again*.

III

Years ago when former top VFL umpire Jeff Crouch took over running the Royal Children's Hospital appeal for the *Herald* and *Weekly Times*, he invited Jack Dyer, Alan 'Butch' Gale and me to do a sports night for the appeal. I may have been in smaller towns but I can't remember any. Apparently the main local entertainment was watching the streetlights go on, so you can imagine what a hit Jack was with his lies, self-praise and exaggeration. After the show, which was a great success even if I say so myself, everyone went back to the little weatherboard pub where we were staying. 'Butch' Gale, a big and tough champion ruckman for both Fitzroy and Victoria a few years earlier, grew tired of Jack's glowing stories about himself and went to bed. I stuck around (for once Jack was buying) and it was just as well that I did. In Jack's audience there was a cocky; a local footballer so tall and craggy that he made 'Captain Blood' look positively anaemic. Eventually the cocky grew tired of being told by Jack that he "couldn't fire" and decided he could. After one look at his fists, which were huge, I went looking for reinforcements. I knocked on 'Butch's' door and shouted, "You'd better come quickly, 'Butch', or we'll be taking Jack home in a box. There's a big bloke out here getting ready for murder." 'Butch' said he was coming, as I knew he would, so I ran to try and save Jack from execution. The big cocky was facing me as he and Jack shaped up and I saw his face drop. Then everyone, including the cocky, burst into laughter. Turning around I saw why. There standing at the door was hairy old 'Butch' Gale wearing a lady's nightie, a pink one with lace around the neck and arms. It was such a horrible sight that all thoughts of fisticuffs were instantly forgotten. 'Butch' explained later that he had neglected to pack his pyjamas and had asked the female publican if she could lend him a pair. She told him she was a widow and couldn't oblige with pyjamas but offered her best nightie. 'Butch' said he could hardly refuse after the lady had been so obliging. I believed him and I am sure the locals did, too; but Jack Dyer still shakes his head at the memory. "I don't know what the modern man is coming to," he says sorrowfully. "Who would have ever thought that a good ruckman like 'Butch' Gale would have turned into a transistor?"

CHAPTER 9

A BIRD OF
ANOTHER FEATHER

With eight good-sized steps you'd walk straight past the Phoenix Hotel, nestled at the 'Paris end' of Flinders Street in Melbourne. With a 22-foot frontage and a view over the railway yards, the pub was one of the smallest, cosiest and most unusual in the country. It was always a newspaper-person's pub and with the massive grey headquarters of the *Herald* and *Weekly Times* a few paces away across Exhibition Street, there was a steady river of drinkers. Downstairs in the public bar the compositors and printers would mix with a few of the knockabout reporters and sub-editors while upstairs in the press bar the intellectuals from the reporters' room across the road aired their views. Melbourne didn't have a journalists' club as such, but the Phoenix was the next best thing.

After seven and a half years at the Town Hall Hotel in North Melbourne, Edna and I decided that we should get out and find a pub of our own; one where we could take over the freehold and build up our own goodwill. It was the perfect opportunity for us to take our first holiday and we arranged to spend some time at the Chalet at Mt Buffalo. Skiing in those days was quite a novelty and for us a new adventure. Our ski instructor was an Italian named Tony and he put us through the whole routine from snow plough to herringbone. I must admit, I was a very willing pupil. One afternoon we were on a fairly steep slope and Tony was called away from the group by another instructor. "Louie, you look after the class," he said and whizzed off down the mountain. Somehow I slipped, fell sideways and in a matter of seconds wiped out the whole class, sending them flying everywhere—it was the domino principle on a human scale. By the end of the week I had earned my white star and despite this massive honour I didn't return to the slopes until 1987 when *Wide World of Sports* sent me on a mission to Mt Buller. Funny thing that; if I recall, I spent most of those few days on my backside, too.

III

By 1957 I was already working as the football expert on the *Sun* and I had noticed the Phoenix was up for grabs. We had been out of North Melbourne and living with Edna's mother and were desperate to get back into business. There was only one small problem: cash. The going price was £60,000. We had £12,000 tucked away and the bank wouldn't accept anything less than £15,000 as a deposit. My mother-in-law came to the rescue as she had years before and lent us the difference.

I've been told the Phoenix was built last century and started its life as The Fail Me Never Inn. Over the years it was owned by the likes of former Hawthorn player Tom Fitzmaurice, Elty Reeves and the McIntosh family. When I took over it had a grain store, Burston Brothers and Barrett, on one side and the Victorian Cricket Association building on the other. Like a slab of salami it was wedged between the two. I never minded the VCA people; they were fine. It was the constant influx of visitors from the maltsters next door that got in my hair. The place was full of rats and mice and when they had had their fill in the grain store they'd come in to us for a change of diet. I'd be in the cellar changing a keg and it would be nothing to feel a large rat run right across my skull. It would frighten the daylights out of me. Edna on the other hand was a true ratter. One afternoon Nicole was celebrating her 14th birthday party at the pub with all her toffy schoolmates from Merton Hall. I looked around and said to Edna, "Look over there. A rat!" It was like something out of *Fawlty Towers*. The rat was sitting in the middle of the hallway lapping up the excitement of the birthday party. Cool as a cucumber, Edna emerged from nowhere and dispatched the beady-eyed little brute with one swipe of her golf club. It staggered me to see Edna use the five iron with such skill. Take her out onto the golf course and she sprays them everywhere.

Another night I was going into the bathroom for a shower and there sitting in the middle of the bath was another large rodent, eyeing me intently. I did what comes naturally to a former Collingwood captain and champion—I leaped into the air and screamed. Edna ran in and I raced out, accidentally locking the door behind me and leaving my beloved alone with that furry monster. Moments later she emerged victorious. The rat had met its match. Eventually they ripped down the old grain store and the rats invaded us in force. It was so bad that one rat had made its home in the straw-thatched roof of the press bar and would occasionally peep down at startled drinkers. Old hands wouldn't rate him a second glance. "Oh, that's Fred," they'd say, and keep on drinking. The answer to the problem came in through the front door one day—a stray cat with a ravenous appetite for rodents of all shapes and sizes. We named her Susie, kicked her down into the cellar and the last time anyone looked she was nearly one and a half metres long.

The Phoenix might not have looked much from the outside but it was a happy pub with a great clientele. More than 70 per cent of the customers crossed the road from the *Herald* office, about 20 per cent worked further along Flinders Street at Dunlop Australia's headquarters and the remainder seemed to work in the rag trade that flourished in Flinders Lane. The pub has had many facelifts over the years. In the 1930s it had a plain brick exterior decorated with ugly great gargoyles. When I left we had completely remodelled it, adding a mezzanine bar. Back in 1957 it was a pretty uncomplicated three-storey structure, with the public bar at street level, the press bar up a flight of stairs and then the living accommodation for the family. The Phoenix was the second hotel in Melbourne to be granted a tavern licence, which meant in effect that we didn't have to offer rooms, and with the space at our disposal that was a godsend. There were seven bedrooms and a living room but with a 22-foot frontage you can imagine how cramped we were. Over the years I dined out on jokes about the size of the Phoenix: it was that small, the furniture had to be painted on the walls; the honeymoon suite is on the 13th floor—not bad for a pub with three floors, but then again we didn't cater for too many weddings; if you put the key in the door you could break a window on the other side; the rooms were so small that we couldn't fit in a bed... All the oldest gags in the world fitted the Phoenix to a tee. Former St Kilda captain and Brownlow medallist Neil Roberts was a regular client and loved ribbing my staff and me about our cramped confines. He was drinking up big one afternoon and the barmaid was getting sick and tired of him.

Finally, she leaned over. "Where's the tip?" she said.

"You're standing in it," Roberts told her.

III

I'm sure that if Damon Runyan had visited Melbourne he would have made straight for the Phoenix because it was his sort of pub, filled with larger-than-life characters. In the days of six o'clock closing the pub would be packed from five o'clock onwards. It would be filled with blokes trying to get through the six o'clock swill. It was nothing for me to fill 36 glasses and place them on the bar in front of six drinkers at five to six. They knew the rules; they had until quarter past six to drink the lot or they went down the drain. One afternoon the finance editor of the *Herald*, John Eddy, strode into the bar. The place was packed, the bar chock-a-block with full glasses, the clock ticking towards six. "Give me half a dozen bottles, thanks Louie," he said. It was one minute to six and I was flat out. I packed them in a paper bag, took the money and as I was putting it in the till I saw Eddy pick up his parcel and, somehow, part of the bar towel. As he stepped away from the bar about 60 glasses of beer went flying. Right in the firing line was the *Herald*'s racing editor, Jack Elliott. Jack prides himself on being immaculately dressed and on this afternoon he was at his sartorial best. The light-grey suit looked magnificent—until the best part of 30 full glasses of Carlton Draught turned him into a sodden mass. John Eddy meantime was oblivious to everything. He was casually sauntering downstairs and out onto Flinders Street, the bar towel hanging limply in the breeze behind him.

"John, John!" I cried out. "You've got the bar towel there." With that he hurled it at me. "I'm not trying to pinch the bloody thing," he said, and kept walking.

John was a true eccentric. He had a standing order. To prepare it I'd pour a small beer and warm up a seven-ounce glass under the hot water tap. Then I'd tip in the beer and serve it. He called the concoction a "little hotty". On a trip to the United States John found himself in a cocktail bar in New York with one of those smart-arse barmen who said he could mix any drink ever invented. "A little hotty, my good man," John said. The bloke was stunned. "Pour me a small beer, serve it in a long hot glass and call it a little hotty," John demanded. "What sort of a place is this? Everyone where I come from knows what a little hotty is. They even serve it at the Phoenix."

John had been married three times and was forever complaining about the financial ruin. He told me in all seriousness, "If they leave you, offer to go with them. It's cheaper to stay unhappy." John's bad luck extended from marriage to constant run-ins with the local parking officers. These run-ins were the curse of everyone who worked at the *Herald*. One afternoon I was walking down Exhibition Street hill towards the hotel and I saw John's head appear from under a parked Volkswagon.

"What on earth are you doing?" I asked him as he brushed dirt and dust from his navy-blue suit. He looked like he'd been working in a flour mill.

"The bloody parking attendants are getting sneaky. They're marking your tyres on the inside now," he said. It was logic that escaped me.

As a reporter John was brilliant. He was the *Herald* economist and had a knack of writing about complex financial matters in a way that the layperson could grasp. One afternoon Professor Sir Douglas Copeland from Melbourne University walked into the bar.

"Is John Eddy in?" he asked me.

"No, but he won't be far away," I answered. Seconds later John walked in, greeted his academic friend and ordered his usual. Later, I walked past them as they were engrossed in deep and meaningful dialogue and I heard the professor ask John whether he intended taking any notes. With that John brushed some of the cigarette ash away from his lapel, which looked like a snowstorm, reached into his pocket and pulled out a cigarette packet. Casually he opened the lid and tore off a very small portion of cardboard. He made a couple of microscopic jottings and announced he had enough information. John Eddy was different, but also typical of my clientele. The best thing about him was his love of Collingwood and it was here that he really was quite different. He'd go to the footy every week and stand behind the goals with the Collingwood cheer squad, his navy twill suit standing out in a sea of black duffle coats.

III

The Phoenix was once described as the busiest pub in Australia (per square foot) and it wasn't all that hard to run. Our customers were generally regulars and we had virtually no trade on Saturdays. During the week we had the morning trade from the *Herald* blokes after they knocked off, a good counter lunch trade, and afternoon trade from the *Sun* staff. Business became even better when 10 o'clock closing came in; not that 10 o'clock meant anything to our best customers. Once the door was locked there might be card games in progress, two-up or other forms of adult pastimes with gambling overtones. Wednesday night was pay night and frequently two-up night. Tom Prior, Rex Pullen, David Aldridge, Alan Auldridge and a few others were regulars. They'd be at me to get together a school and there wasn't any problem there. I'd just ring up the *Sun* racing department, then the finance department and they'd flock over; Keith Hillier, Tony Meany, Bernie O'Brien, Ray Huxley and all that mob would be up the stairs before I'd hung up. They'd buy their beers at the bar and the action would be on for young and old. Rex Pullen had worked as a sports writer on the *Sun* for years and loved a bet. He'd often get away to a great start and be a couple of hundred bucks up by midnight.

"Well, china, that'll just about see me out," he'd say to all and sundry and then make towards the stairs.

"Pig's arse," would be the reply. "You've got to give us a chance to win our money back."

It would be the same old story. By 4am Rex would have clipped me for a couple of hundred and he'd go home broke. Des Keegan, the finance editor of the Sun, was a particularly popular guest. Des made a big bundle in the nickel boom in the early-1970s but he was never quite in that league as a two-up punter. He'd lose his couple of hundred each Wednesday night. I miss him a lot. The great thing about Des was that he would come looking for you the next day with a cheque book to settle his debts. The others tended to try and ignore you for a week or so.

One evening Peter Kaye, a reporter on the *Sun*, was spinning, and going very nicely. We had our money on the floor and were waiting anxiously. Behind us there was a huge crash. No one paid any notice at all. Edna ran into the bar.

"Lou, come quickly. Trevor Sykes has fallen down the stairs. He's lying down there and not moving," Edna said breathlessly. Peter Kaye barely moved a muscle. "Break it down, Ed. I'm going for my fourth head," he said.

Trevor must have recovered because I noticed recently that he's the editor-in-chief of *Australian Business*. As for the fate of Peter's fourth head, it's disappeared in the sands of time.

III

Stragglers had a bad habit of turning up at any time after the first edition of the *Sun* went to bed and the standard mode of entry was to throw a small pebble at the side window. Someone would then open the door and admit the fresh money. One night somebody got too exuberant and threw half a house brick, shattering the window and halting the game, but only temporarily. Keith Hillier, now the *Sun*'s racing editor, always chips me about those two-up games, claiming that the game could never finish until I was square. He was fairly close to the mark. If I was in front I had a standard remark: "Half an hour more and we'll finish up. I'm a bit tired." It worked every time. Wednesday was two-up night but most nights you could get a game of poker if you so desired. On these nights the old Collingwood upbringing would occasionally rear its ugly head. I was playing cards with Tom Prior late in the evening and by 3am we were still at it. Finally I suggested we cut the cards for a hundred dollars. He cut a three.

"I've got you, you bastard," I gloated, and promptly drew a two. "Double or nothing," I challenged. He cut a four. You wouldn't want to know it, I drew a three and lost $200. With that I launched myself at him and wrestled him to the floor. Tom's no slouch. He's a former boxing champion from his University of Western Australia days and he was in fairly good shape. We were rolling around on the floor when Edna appeared. She was mad. "Tom, you get home to Allison; and *you* get up to bed," she said. We crawled out like two mangy dogs.

Another night I was playing cards with Geoff Bell, a freelance TV cameraman. We were playing blind poker and I'd bet $356. I was sitting on three kings and feeling pretty cocky. I looked.

He put down three aces. "You bastard, you've been sitting on me all night," I said as I moved towards him. I leaned over and grabbed him by the tie. As I grabbed it, I fell backwards and the tie came with me. I thought I'd broken his neck. It was one of those elasticised ties, and this was enough to break the seriousness of the moment.

Occasionally I did win but it could come at a price. We were sitting there one night. There were four of us—Tom Prior, Rex Pullen, a big bloke named Lou Hoffman and me. Lou was a mad punter who had a penchant for large diamond-encrusted rings, and not just your simple rings but huge rings that would look at home on the Queen Mother. I had a terrific hand with three queens and stood to win $356; only Lou stood between me and the pot. He had three jacks. Solemnly he rose, walked around and kissed me flush on the lips. Tom went purple. He was spluttering. I looked across at him and said, "For $356 I don't care where he kisses me. He can kiss me on the bum for all it matters."

III

One of the highlights of the sporting year was the annual Phoenix Olympics staged upstairs, generally after one of the big sporting extravaganzas like the VFL dinner. There would be 10 or 12 well-oiled sportsmen and reporters looking for further diversions. Among the regular competitors were Tom Prior, *Herald* artist Oscar Skalberg, *Sporting Globe* reporter John Rice, Neil Roberts, the *Sun*'s Scot Palmer and, of course, Ian McDonald, who is now the media manager of the Australian Cricket Board but was then a highly respected football and cricket reporter. Neil Roberts, with his football and physical-education background, was sporting coordinator of the night and a hard taskmaster. One of his favourite exhibition sports was to back up to an open door, grab the top with his clasped hands, pull himself up and sit on top of the door.

It sounds complicated, and I can tell you it's bloody near impossible sober—totally impossible for all but the strongest when you have enjoyed the VFL's hospitality for the best part of six hours.

Neil might have been physically perfect but the biggest winner of gold medals was invariably my old mate Tom Prior. He was a standout in the head-bashing competition. The idea was to limp fall and hit your head on the door. You kept moving back and falling forward, banging your scone. Tom could stand one metre from the door and fall forward, perfectly rigid, and slam his head into the door. He always rubbished Neil's Adonis looks and claimed to have the perfect formula for success. "I've got a concrete head," Tom would boast. I don't know, but I reckon Tom used to wake up the next morning with a thumping headache. I get one thinking about it.

My forte was the standing jump onto the bar stools. I could jump onto one bar stool, balance, jump onto the ground, onto the next stool and so on. It won me the gold medal year in and year out. I had some imitators but more often than not they'd go flying, knocking themselves rotten. Oscar Skalberg had played football with North Melbourne and managed to keep his remarkable physique despite an unnerving habit of eating a vase of flowers at every party he went to. In the end he had me eating them too. I loved the gladdies but the carnations gave me heartburn. Oscar's speciality was chest-crushing. The idea was that you had to stand there perfectly still with your chest puffed out. Oscar would run full tilt with his massive barrel chest thrust out and try and bump you over. He knocked people down like skittles. One night he was about to knock over his latest stooge and the bloke stood aside at the very last second. Oscar went hurtling down the stairs. Oscar has always had a special greeting for the unsuspecting: he's got the world's meanest handshake. When he grasps your hand it stays crushed for weeks. We all had our favourite party trick and got envious whenever we were upstaged. John Rice covered the football and the golf for the *Globe*, and his trick was a beauty. He could do a handstand with his legs bent and managed to pick up a half-opened matchbox with his nose. One night John had been trying unsuccessfully for two hours and the refreshments of the night were having a marked effect on his performance. For two hours he tried and failed and in the end went home a shattered man. The next day he wandered into the pub and I almost fell over. He had a blister the size of a passionfruit on the end of his nose. He looked terrible. His schnoz was red and inflamed and for a while he could have passed himself off as WC Fields.

"What happened to you?" I asked.

"It's carpet burn from that bloody matchbox trick."

One of the most publicised sporting events ever to occur at the Phoenix took place on a non-Olympic night. It was billed the most brutal punch-up ever to take place but now the truth must be told. Three of us—Tom Prior, Neil Roberts and I—had been out and came back at about midnight for a couple of large cans of beer. We were alone in the upstairs bar and conversation turned to a friendly debate as to the merits of boxing against those of karate. Roberts was the proponent of boxing. Prior was the advocate of karate. To prove his point that the karate man would be superior, Tom arranged an impromptu demonstration. He placed a large empty can on the bar and set himself to chop it in half. He breathed deeply, yelled and chopped down with his right hand perfectly taut. Just as he was about to make contact the can rolled onto the floor and Tom slammed his hand into the bar. The mock oohs and aahs turned to screams of pain. We packed it in ice. Tom recovered quickly and took up the topic again. He came at Neil with a series of cutting blows saying, "If I came at you like this, you'd stand no chance."

One of the blows accidentally flicked Neil on the lip and being the super-alert and well-trained sportsman he was, he reacted instinctively. Neil delivered three of the fastest jabs I've ever seen. The first one caught Tom on the nose, the second in the eye and the third took off half of his ear lobe. You've never seen so much blood in your life and it was all an accident. We cleaned Tom up and the last I saw of them they were walking back towards the *Sun* office. Tom took Neil in to see the editor, Lyle Turnbull, and was leaning over the desk explaining what happened.

"It was an accident," Tom said, with his eye puffed up and ear lobe and nose still bleeding. "We're still good friends." Lyle wasn't amused. "I don't care if it was an accident or not, but you're dripping blood all over the copy here."

Word went round the office like wild fire that it was the Battle at the OK Corral all over again. It was anything but. I loved having a go at Tom about it and for years called him Kid Candle; one blow and he was out. In his case though, it was three.

III

Another famous club at the Phoenix was the Morning Tea Club, which consisted of half a dozen middle-aged men who'd meet for their heart starters every day at 9.30am. They'd stand together in the public bar and discuss the events of the world. There was Roy Hodgkinson, the *Herald* artist; the aforementioned John Eddy; Murray Walsh, a *Sporting Globe* racing writer; Tommy Spence, who was the Brisbane *Telegraph* Melbourne representative; a local businessman, Hubert Goldsmith; and Roy, a taxi driver. They were an unlikely-looking team but always in earnest conversation over their drinks. One morning the topic turned to women. A drunk had been eavesdropping and walked unsteadily towards them.

"What would you silly old bastards know about women?" he slurred. John Eddy took instant offence.

"My good man, I'll give you $10,000 if you can walk into any bar in the world at 10 o'clock in the morning and find six blokes drinking who've had 11 wives between them," Eddy said, and went back to his drink.

They were a very strange mob, but beaut customers.

One of the great pranks in Melbourne journalistic history had its origins in the press bar of the Phoenix. In typical flamboyant fashion Bob Clarke, the florid western rounds man of the *Herald*, and Murray Walsh, the racing writer on the *Sporting Globe*, were offered a bet they just couldn't refuse. Someone bet they couldn't stop the trams in Bourke Street. Clarke and Walsh took up the bet with gusto and made their way up Exhibition Street to Bourke Street and walked onto the tram tracks opposite the Society Restaurant. Bob Clarke had been a radio repairman up Mildura way before becoming a well-known industrial reporter and investigative journalist. What he didn't know about electronics wasn't worth knowing. Bob got down on one knee and started tapping the tram tracks. Murray stood next to him, notebook open, pen in hand. "Three thousand eight hundred electrodes, five hundred and nine ohms." Clarke recited and Walsh duly wrote it down. Minutes later along rattled a tram. It pulled up in front of Clarke and the driver jumped out and confronted the men.

"What's going on here?" the driver said quite indignantly. "Get back into your tram at once," replied Clarke. "Tramways electronics division. We're testing for electrodes."

With that the driver jumped back inside his cabin. Clarke and Walsh continued the charade; Clarke reciting figures, Walsh jotting them down. Both blokes were obviously hard at work.

After 15 minutes there were 17 trams backed up, bumper to bumper around the corner from Bourke Street into Spring Street. Finally a policeman walked over to investigate.

"What's going on here?" the copper asked.

"Tramways electronics division, officer. We're testing for electrodes," said Clarke, still reeling off these mythical figures and tapping away at the steel tracks with his pen.

The policeman held up the traffic; the trams continued to pile up in the distance. At last Clarke and Walsh figured that they'd caused enough disruption and turned to the policeman.

"All finished now, officer. Thank you for your help," Clarke said, wandering back towards the pub.

"Very good, sir," said the policeman and the trams started rolling again. The bet was a beauty but you can take it from me, the money would never have been handed over.

III

No matter how kind I was, the word spread amongst the troops that I was a tight-fisted publican, that I'd never shout a drink, that I watered down the beer—all rubbish, I might add. Jack Elliott reckons to this day that the Phoenix was the only pub in the world where you could have 64 double scotches at a sitting and walk out stone-cold sober. His racing writer mate Tom Moon used to say that my mother-in-law Molly could pour him a scotch on the rocks without staining the ice. For the record I did, in fact, shout—generally on Tuesday. This Tuesday was known as Black Tuesday, the day before the journos were paid.

Occasionally we'd entertain boarders and one of our favourites was the well-known Australian author Hal Porter. Hal lived at Garvoc and every six months or so he'd drag himself away from his writing and come to the big smoke. We'd put him up at the Phoenix and he'd sit around and drink himself into a stupor for three weeks and then head back to the bush. If you didn't know Hal, he could rub you up the wrong way. He was another of our eccentrics; he was a haughty and educated man who had his own air about him. Many took him to be totally sarcastic. This day he was having a quiet drink in front of the famous celebrity wall. His signature, of course, was there with the other big names. He was chatting to Bob Johnston, the chief of staff of the *Sun*. The talk turned into an argument.

"Don't talk like that to me, boy!" Hal said in that manner that was certain to offend.

"Who the bloody hell are you anyway?" Bob replied.

"Up there, boy," said Hal, thrusting his thumb backwards towards his signature on the wall. Johnston leaned forward, peering at the wall through his thick glasses.

"I don't give a stuff if you are Herb Elliott."

One of our long-term boarders was a young bloke from Perth named Peter Simunovich. He arrived from Western Australia in the early-1970s. He was a huge lump of a kid with massive hands and an appetite to match. He was working as a sporting sub-editor on the *Sun* and came to me and asked about boarding with us. I couldn't say no. He was like one of those refugees, wandering aimlessly around a big city. I talked it over with Edna and decided that he could have full board with us for $15 a week. This healthy 21 year old was a massive eater and made my old pie-chomping friend at *World of Sport*, the one and only 'Uncle' Doug Elliott, look like an anorexic. It got to the stage that he was eating us out of house and home.

"Peter," I said one afternoon, "we're putting up your board."

"How much?" he asked with a crestfallen look on his face.

"It's $16 a week."

He stayed for years and became part of the family. He rose to become chief football writer on the *Sun* and held that job until 1989, when he took off on a sabbatical to New York and Yugoslavia. Edna and I have a strange suspicion that he's gone on an eating holiday, in search of the world's biggest steak.

There were a million stories about the blokes at the Phoenix, the regulars and the strangers; just too many to put down on paper. I remember the doctors from Prince Henry's were always calling in after work and one particular night had booked the front room for a buck's night. The bridegroom-to-be had his brother-in-law-to-be along as his minder. It didn't do him much good. Midway through the evening all these young interns were well on the way and I noticed the guest of honour had lost his pants. Someone had thrown them out the window and they were fluttering from the tram wires outside. They couldn't be retrieved so the bloke went home naked from the waist down. Home was where he was heading but along the way he got sidetracked, or ambushed would be a better term, and he ended up back at the hospital. When he woke up the next morning he was covered from head to toe in a plaster cast, with his brother-in-law-to-be in a similar state alongside him. If you've woken up with a hangover, just imagine what it would be like to wake up like an Egyptian mummy.

III

The secret of running a pub, in my opinion, is to have a wife who knows and understands the business. With Edna I was the luckiest bloke alive. She has always been a great businesswoman with a head for running the show. She kept me in line, she also kept some of the unruly element in line and she was great support when I was trying to combine my multimedia interests. There was a time in the early-1970s when she did, however, expect to see me behind bars. We'd finished work for the night and were planning to turn in relatively early. The last drinkers had straggled out of the hotel at about 10.15pm and we were cleaning up. I walked into the small parlour at the front of the press bar and noticed a bloke sitting alone in the dark. "Come on mate, it's time to get out," I said impatiently. I recognised him as a fellow who I'd chucked out earlier in the night. He was about 1.78 metres and to my knowledge he didn't speak English. I went over to move him and the next thing he lunged at me. We fell over tables. He threw punches at me. He was kicking and struggling. I yelled out to Edna and she appeared with a former Collingwood team-mate of mine, Brian Dorman, who was staying with us at the time. They must have distracted my attacker for a moment because he let down his guard and as he did I let him have it, right in the gob. He went down like a sack of spuds. He was out cold. I said to Brian Dorman, "Quick, pick him up and we'll drop him out in the lane." We propped him out in the doorway by the VCA building. About 15 minutes later we'd finished our cups of tea and I suggested to Brian that we pop outside and check the condition of our punchy customer. We walked down, out the back door and peeped around the corner. The bloke was still lying there, not moving a hair. "I might have killed this poor bastard," I said to Brian, and visions of Pentridge and thoughts of Edna and the kids alone at home with me locked inside flooded through my mind. As we stood there a man strolled up, took one look at the body and stepped into the phone booth on the corner. When he emerged I confronted him.

"What have you been doing?" I asked.

"I rang the police. I think that bloke there is dead."

My legs went to rubber. Brian was useless. He kept saying, "Imagine going to Pentridge. Jail will be hell. I know you didn't mean it but who'll believe you?"

The next thing the police dog van pulled up. "I'm going to confess. I couldn't live with this for the rest of my life," I said to Brian. I walked over to the policeman.

"Excuse me, sergeant. That bloke there was playing up in my pub and I whacked him. I put him out there," I said.

"No worries, Lou," was his reply.

With that he walked straight over to the body and gave it the best kick up the arse you've ever seen. The bloke jumped about four metres in the air and as he came down the sergeant grabbed him by the scruff of the neck and threw him in the back of the van. As they closed the door the drunk turned to me and went, "Ha, ha, ha." I could have kissed that sergeant.

By 1974 my newspaper and television commitments were taking up so much of my time and putting so much added pressure on Edna that we decided to get out of the pub. We decided to keep the freehold and leased the business out of Lou Molina and Jim Smythe, two well-known Melbourne publicans. Edna and I moved into an apartment in Toorak, our first real home since we'd been married. Later we'd buy a holiday house in Portsea where we could dabble in the garden, grow a few vegetables and enjoy family life. It's funny you know, it was terribly hard to alter our lifestyles. We'd grown so used to having our customers and friends around us virtually 24 hours a day, and living in the hustle and bustle of the central business district; leaving the pub was like beginning a whole new life.

CHAPTER 10

ORGANISED CHAOS

Victoria went into mourning at 11am on Sunday 22 March, 1987. An era had come to an end, an institution in Australian television was about to take its final bow. As Frank Sinatra sang about the good times, viewers across south-eastern Victoria had one last look at the men who had become part of their lives for what seemed like a lifetime. It was one of the saddest days of my life.

Episode number 1355 of the world's longest continually run sporting show, *World of Sport*, would be its last. The greats of sport, the blokes we at *WoS* had known since they were battling kids, gathered to witness the show's passing. There was anger, there was resentment and there were tears. There was nostalgia by the bucketful and there was laughter and the usual array of whoppers. The show that had been given 13 weeks to prove itself back in 1959 had grown into the most loved, watched and talked about sporting institution in the land. It was described by American turf legend Eddie Arcaro as "organised chaos" but week in and week out for 28 years it had been a regular and invited guest at Sunday luncheons across Victoria, southern NSW and Tasmania. Looking around the packed studio you could see the long-time contenders for the crown of Mr Football, Ted Whitten and Ron Barassi, chatting with former world boxing champion Lionel Rose, and VFL chiefs Allen Aylett and Jack Hamilton reminiscing with former Australian Test opener Keith Stackpole, racing great Roy Higgins and basketball coach Lindsay Gaze. All had played their parts in the amazing history of a show that sadly became an early victim of television networking.

III

It was fitting that Ron Casey, Doug Elliott and I should make our final on-camera appearance together for HSV 7 on that final *World of Sport*. Back on 16 May, 1959 the three of us had joined forces for the Saturday morning debut of *Westinghouse World of Sport*. We'd all gone through the auditions. Ron had tried out successfully as anchor man, Doug had sold himself as the on-camera live ad plugger and I was to be the football expert. Jack Ayling was 'Long Shot Louie' the racing expert, and we even had a fishing expert, but in true *World of Sport* fashion that didn't quite go according to plan. Restaurateur Geoff Brookes had been invited to tryout; and, to be truthful, not many people know as much about drowning a worm as our boy Geoff. This day he decided to bring along his mate Tom Davidson who, apart from other distinctions, was conductor for the Victorian State Orchestra. While Geoff was being auditioned, Tom was sitting back in his checked suit with a battered felt hat on his head, puffing on his pipe and generally keeping out of the way. The floor manager saw him, said "You're next" and, can you believe it, he got the job. The word was that they didn't talk to each other for years.

Golf was enjoying a boom period with Peter Thomson, arguably the world's number-one golfer, and naturally we had to have a golf segment. It was decided that Colin Campbell would give a weekly clinic but poor old Colin could never get the club out of his bag. His was always the last segment and even then the show was always running late. I remember one day when Colin slid the seven iron out of his bag, or half out anyway, and looked as pleased as punch. It was as close as he ever got. Case wound him up and got him off.

Our 13-week run on Saturday mornings came to an end and, despite our pleas that the show was viable, HSV 7 decided otherwise. Enter Doug Elliott. 'Uncle' Doug went to the Seven management and suggested that he buy the time on Sunday morning and package the show for the station. Over the years I've heard people talk about *World of Sport* being owned by Doug, Ron and me but that was utter rubbish. Doug employed us all for that first year on Sundays but when the executives of HSV saw how well he was doing they didn't let him continue. Instead they kept the show going; they used the same cast and format and pocketed the profits themselves.

III

The secret of the show was its informality. It was a show where the unexpected happened, where the unlikely occurred and where the biggest names in sport, both local and international, bobbed up. It was the type of show where an argument could rage on camera and be resolved over a friendly ale in the privacy of the dressing room half an hour later. For close to 30 years the walls of the men's dressing room were privy to the great secrets of VFL football; it was a sanctuary for League coaches on Sunday mornings, a place where they could chat off-the-record to the greats of yesteryear. I always told them to spill their guts, safe in the knowledge that no one would speak about it, and frequently they took my advice. One of the great innovations was Club Corner. Every Sunday through football season the previous day's matches were analysed, with our probing interrogators firing questions at the opposing coaches. It was one of our most popular and enduring segments and despite the changes to the show over the years and the upgrading and modernisation, it was one part of the show that remained unaltered. To me there was nothing more enjoyable than washing off the make-up and enjoying a friendly can with the likes of Allan Jeans, Ron Barassi, Percy Jones and Teddy Whitten. In later years when Ron Casey was the boss of the station the beer was supplied by HSV 7, thanks to our close contacts with Carlton and United Breweries.

III

In the old days, however, it was a different story. There were the fledgling days of the *World of Sport* footy panel, which was an elite band whose job it was to preach and pontificate over all manner of football topics. Back at the very start Jack Dyer and I sat on opposite ends separated by former Collingwood premiership star Bruce Andrew, ex-Carlton coach Jim Francis, Fitzroy's Brownlow medallist Alan 'the Baron' Ruthven and my former team-mate Kevin Coghlan. We were a talented band, finely tuned by our ringmaster Ron Casey. Kevin Coghlan liked to analyse and his school teacher background made him perfect for the post. Bruce Andrew, with his long background in the game stretching into the ancient past, was ideal to explain the laws and the theory of the game while Jack was great with the bullshit. After all he is a ruckman: big and dumb. One day we were talking about high marking.

"You know I flew for a mark one day," Jack chipped in. "I went up so high that I grabbed a seagull."

"What did you do then?" I asked.

"I handballed it, of course. I was always a team player."

That was typical of Jack from the late-1950s until his retirement in the mid-1980s. He could never tolerate smart-arse types and when St Kilda's Neil Roberts, a club captain and Brownlow medallist, joined the panel in years to come, Jack was always on the alert. He figured the impeccably dressed, well-mannered and superbly athletic Roberts to be one of those intellectual types because he was a school teacher.

"Is it still hot in the Exhibition Buildings in December?" Jack asked Roberts one Sunday.

"Yes, I guess it is," replied our new boy. "I remember sitting for my matriculation," reminisced Jack. "It was so hot my plasticine melted."

It was pretty hot under those lights in at Seven then and we used to develop quite a thirst. Fortunately Alan Ruthven solved our problems. 'The Baron' was a publican and each Sunday morning he'd fill the boot of his car with cold beer from his pub, the Provincial, in Fitzroy. The beer would be stocked in the dressing room and we'd help ourselves, leaving a few bob on the table as we went. All went well until one day in the early-1960s when 'the Baron' found himself to be a few quid short week after week. One day we spotted St Kilda's former champ and our new panellist Neil Roberts chatting to his two youngsters Michael and Tim. They had handfuls of lollies, ice creams and drinks.

"Where did you get the money?" Neil asked them. "No worries, Dad," they replied. "There's heaps on the table over there in the corner."

That paved the way for the exercise to become more commercial and in stepped a real entrepreneur in Billy Webb. Billy worked on the show behind the scenes and his promotion to the refreshment booth was the beginning of the good times for all concerned, especially Billy. He converted the cellar into a bar, installed three large refrigerators, put on entertainment and at the height of his career was flogging upwards of 80 dozen cans each Sunday. You could play darts in Billy's emporium or take part in a little gambling. He'd installed a mouse track and it was nothing to see the top footballers of the day, their coaches and mates having a bet as the mice did their laps. It's a wonder Ron Casey didn't put it live to air. Nearly every other hare-brained scheme made it over the years. All went well for Billy until one day a couple of strangers made an appearance. The place was virtually deserted at this stage, as the show was in progress and thirsts were being built for Billy to look after later on. A young fellow, a police cadet whose brother 'Hank the Goose' was one of our cameramen, was playing darts with a couple of kids. There was not a drink in sight.

"Any chance of a beer," asked one stranger.

"Sure," said our unsuspecting dart enthusiast. "Grab a can out of the fridge and throw your money in the tin."

"Gotcha," said the stranger, and our boy suddenly found himself arrested for sly grogging.

There was no sign of Billy as he'd shot through, but our dart-playing mate lost his cadetship with the Victoria Police and business was temporarily closed down.

III

Over the years only the great names in Australian football were invited to join their peers on the *World of Sport* panel. Jack Dyer and I lasted the whole 28 years providing, in Jack's case, a link with our prehistoric past. The panel grew and was revamped from time to time. Amongst the Brownlow winners who graced the desk were triple champion Bobby Skilton, Neil Roberts and Alan Ruthven. We had the VFL's great goalkickers-hundred-plus men in Doug Wade and Peter McKenna, 403-game veteran Kevin Bartlett, and his team-mates Neil Balme and Kevin Sheedy who both went on to coach with distinction. Peter Patrick Pius Paul Keenan was known to us all as 'Crackers', and he was. Sam Newman hung up his white boots after his 300-game career with Geelong and joined his former coach Bob Davis to defend the inhabitants of football's Sleepy Hollow down on Corio Bay, and we were joined by 'Gentleman Jim' Cleary, the South Melbourne veteran who never had a nasty word to say about anybody. It was hard to imagine but Jim had been a culprit in the 1945 'Bloodbath' Grand Final.

Football ruled the show and now when you look back on the gaping hole it left on television you can see how much the game misses the show. It made characters out of players, gave them an extra dimension and enabled them to display some warmth and humour. Right from the start Ron Casey was open to suggestion for ideas that might liven up the show. Every Wednesday at one o'clock I'd finish up the counter lunches at the pub and meet him for lunch at the Society Restaurant in Bourke Street. We'd scheme and plot over a couple of glasses of wine, dreaming up ideas for the show. One particular day I was chatting about the long-kick competitions that had been so popular in the 1940s. I could remember Fitzroy's premiership captain-coach Fred Hughson being very hard to beat. Ron liked the idea but suggested we make it a more all-round test of kicking skills, so the *World of Sport* champion kick was born. We'd spend a complete day at the Junction Oval, filming players competing against each other for length, style and accuracy. They had to kick a drop, a stab and a punt, and Jim Cleary, Thorold Merrett and Bruce Andrew stood as judges. Who could forget Bruce? The immaculately brilliantined hair with the part down the middle was unforgettable. We often joked that he used a theodolite. He was the stickler for the taut instep and was a master of style.

There was big prize money at stake so we had no trouble getting the big names along. I would wait behind the goals and peg the distance of the kick. Bob Davis would run the ball back to the players and Ron was compere.

All went well until Neil Roberts was called in to deputise for Bob Davis one morning. Carlton's great ruckman John Nicholls was kicking this day and he was in fine touch. 'Old Crystal Eyes' let one big torpedo fly. It was going forever, through the goals and towards the 60-yard line, when out of the corner of my eye I saw Roberts shaping to take the mark of his life. Case saw him, too. "Let it go you dopey bastard," yelled the boss but to no avail, and 'Big Nick' was forced to kick again. I was so glad it wasn't me. I couldn't have faced Nicholls with those eyes cutting through your skull. Another day Bobby Skilton arrived and informed Case that he had hurt his left knee and, being a natural left footer, he could be in trouble for his heat. "I'll give it a go with my right," Skilton informed Casey. It didn't matter. Bobby put up a great performance and won his heat easily. He was "amphibious", as Jack Dyer used to say; he could kick with either hand.

III

The championship kick was a showcase of the kicking talents of a generation of footballers. From Paul Vinar, Geelong's most prodigious kicker, through to the 'Superboot', Bernie Quinlan, we always enjoyed the best. I remember Paul Vinar winning £500 one year. He was a carpenter by trade and he was elated with his win. "What are you going to do with the money?" we asked him afterwards. "I'm going in to McEwan's in town to buy a new hammer," he told us excitedly.

The handball competition had its start over a lunch one Wednesday. We decided to invite the best exponents of the handball art to compete for prize money, live-to-camera each Sunday. A target was devised with a hole in the middle for the bullseye and that would be worth 10 points. Rings were then drawn, with scores of seven, five, three and one points awarded. The players stood about 15 metres from the board and had five handpasses at the target with each hand. In those days the great handballers were Geelong's ruck star Polly Farmer and Carlton's captain and coach Ron Barassi. Polly was the classic handballer whereas Ron was a lobber, but both were deadly accurate. Polly revolutionised ruck play in the VFL and his handpassing really changed the whole face of football. It was a skill that was acquired, polished and honed daily by the big Cat. He told me once that he carried a footy with him everywhere and during his lunch break (and they could be reasonably long because Polly wasn't a great one for work) he'd wind down the car window and fire handpasses through from 10 to 20 metres. Looking back over the years I remember how his accuracy amazed us but really it was only the forerunner of things to come. His fellow sandgroper and Western Australian team-mate Barry Cable took over his mantle as the master and ruled supreme through the mid-1970s. He was a delight to watch.

When Polly's Geelong understudy Sam Newman wasn't eating wedding cake (he got married virtually every season) he wasn't bad at the art himself and enjoyed great tussles with Hawthorn's Allan Goad and Melbourne's skipper Robbie Flower. Flower was a genius with either hand but, looking at him in the studio, you'd think he'd be more at home at a knitting circle. Frighteningly skinny and baby-faced, Flower would quietly slip through half a dozen bullseyes but to this day I'm damned if I can work out how. He wore glasses that looked like the bottom of Coke bottles and squinted like Mr Magoo, but he had them fooled and was champion on a number of occasions.

I'm often asked who'd rule as the handball champ these days. I have no hesitation in saying Sydney's Greg Williams. He's in the same league as Farmer and Cable, a master of his craft and a real thinker who might lack pace but makes up for it with the shrewdest football brain around. It's also worth noting that the handball targets, which were a novelty designed for the show, have become standard issue for football clubs the length and breadth of Australia. There was never any trouble instilling atmosphere into *World of Sport* any Sunday I care to think of over my long years with the show. It was a meeting place where the very best sportsmen and women gathered. They'd swap yarns, they'd tell outrageous lies about their own ability and they'd back their judgement, often as not with a $5 note, during the woodchop, the handball or the tug of war. Every Monday morning I'd hear the tales of woe in my pub: the fellows who'd backed Farmer to beat Barassi in the handball, who'd laid Jack O'Toole in the woodchop or who'd fancied the market gardeners from Werribee in the tug of war would be there. It seemed that right across Victoria, in footy club rooms, behind locked doors in country pubs, or wherever people gathered to watch the show, there was a dollar riding on every outcome. Ron certainly gave them their money's worth. We had the roller derby with two cyclists on rollers battling the clock, and the cream of Australia's cycling fraternity joined in. From world champion Sid Patterson right through to the greats of today, they covered about 1.5 kilometres on those rollers, sometimes handicapped, sometimes from scratch. The woodchop lasted until the end and was so popular that the voice of Australia's greatest axeman Jack O'Toole was used to start the boys, even though he'd died some years before. Ron Casey or Sandy Roberts would merely say, "The voice of Jack O'Toole." Someone would press the button and Jack's voice could be heard, "Axemen ready, one, two, three." His sons Lawrence and Martin have followed the old bloke and become multiple world champions and worthy successors to his crown, but in the back of my mind I can't help but think that big Jack would have been more than their match.

III

Jack Dyer and Jack O'Toole had been great mates over the years. They were both big and burly ex-coppers who had known just how tough life could be during the depression years. Some 18 months after the champion woodchopper had passed on to the big forest in the sky, and when his recorded message was sending today's crop of axe men into a frenzy, Jack is reported to have turned to Sam Newman and said, "Good to have Jack O'Toole back. Where is he?"

"Oh, he's up in the voice-over booth," said Sam, slightly nonplussed. "Gosh, I hope he comes down for a drink before he heads home," said Jack as he wandered off.

One Sunday Ron had the boys standing on their logs. We'd gone through the introductions and they were away, slamming their razorsharp axes into the mountain ash. All the axemen kept a spare axe leaning against their logs in case of emergency and this day this almost spelt disaster. Somehow an axeman lost balance and hit his spare axe, which flew across the floor of the studio like a boomerang. Now if you know Ron Casey, he's not the lightest man on the twinkling toes. Somehow he jumped a couple of centimetres (darned to this day if I know how) and the axe chopped a thick cable neat in two. It came within a whisker of taking him off at the ankles.

The tug of war was another Casey innovation to bolster the show with live sport. We used to sit back and watch these sweating great hulks, who trained in a public bar down Werribee way, grunting and groaning as they tugged on the rope. The anchor men all weighed 125 kilograms plus and their faces would go the colour of beetroot. I used to rib Ron and tell him that we'd get plenty of publicity if one of them had a heart attack on air. He was a funny bloke to work with, Ron. The next thing, he's telling the cameramen to point their cameras the other way if anyone dies during the Tug. No one did, but the floors were often an ocean of sweat which was replenished outside just as quickly.

They might have seemed to be contrived little contests, tailormade for television and designed to fit in a TV studio. In fact they were, but by golly they were great fun and became part of the show's unique character. Some of these activities went astray, like on the day Ron introduced a quoits champion. He started throwing his quoits at the start of the show and three hours later was still going. He just went on with it oblivious to everything that was happening around him. We never had him back. Publicity was always a problem, so one day we tackled the situation head on. Ashtons' circus was in town and we came up with the idea of Jack Dyer walking through Richmond's training session with a tiger on a leash. He would be the most famous Tiger of all with a genuine man-eater on a chain.

"Do you reckon Jack'd do it?" I asked dumbfounded.

"Course he would," answered Case.

So off we went down to Swan Street, Richmond, in search of the Big Top. The bloke from Ashtons' was most obliging. "You want a tiger do you?" he asked.

"Yes," said Ron, "a big one that Jack Dyer can take for a walk on a leash."

"Over there you'll find the major; he's in charge of our big cats."

Off we strolled, positive of success, already seeing the picture on the front page of the *Sun*. The major was dressed in breeches, with leggings and boots, and was slapping his riding crop against his leg. "Certainly," said he, pulling back the flap in front of the cage. "Sure he'll be big enough." Inside the cage was the biggest Bengal tiger you've ever seen. He must have been four-metres long and weighed half a tonne with teeth 15 centimetres long. "Have you got something smaller?" I asked. In the end we had Jack walk through Richmond's training at Punt Road leading an elephant. It wasn't quite what we had in mind but it was a hell of a lot safer.

III

Jack and I established a fabulous rapport on *World of Sport* over the whole run of the show and remain best of friends to this day. Jack was the big dumb ruckman, the man who epitomised Richmond and its working-class roots. He was the bloke who could slaughter the English language and who had the biggest ears in football history. I was all Collingwood, a smart alec little rover who chipped in with annoying questions, a dapper dresser; in fact the total opposite to Jack. While we argued for years, it's not unfair to say that I have had nothing but respect for his ability as a footballer. He's one of the legends, and off the field I love him like a brother. A month before *World of Sport* came to its premature end, Jack announced his retirement. Seven had lost the rights to VFL football, the station had been taken over by ATN 7 in Sydney and at 73, Jack had decided that he'd had enough. It moved me to write a farewell piece in the *Sun* with my long-time ghost writer Tom Prior. Let me quote some of the story:

Jack Dyer has been after me for years, to let him read this story: his obituary. It started when my old mate Tom Sherrin, the former Magpie president, was killed in a car smash after a game at Geelong. I was so shocked by Tommy's untimely death that I wrote a pretty emotional tribute to him in the *Sun*. Jack, an old softie at heart, was most impressed. "I want you to write something like that about me when I go, Louie," he said. "You know, about how I was clean-living, modest and kind; how I always did the right thing, even when I was cruelly provoked!" This week Jack, 73, announced his retirement from *World of Sport*. As his TV sparring partner for more than 20 years, I'm shattered. I can't imagine life without his ugly mug at the other end of the footy panel. Jack Dyer, 'Captain Blood', has been a 'legion' in his own lifetime. There was his historic hatred of Collingwood, evidenced when Kevin Sheedy, then a Tiger star, wore a black-and-white tie on *World of Sport*. Jack was so disgusted he immediately ripped into Sheeds. "A black-and-white tie," he said with his famous sneer, flapping his nose, lips and big ears. "I wouldn't even watch a black-and-white movie." This was the Jack Dyer who invented such immortal football terms as a 'good ordinary player', the 'ackers' (academics) and the 'ammos' (amateurs) who were ruining football, players who kept 'going where the ball ain't', the gangling ruckman who looked like a 'tarantulope', the coaches who gave 'motification' speeches before the Libs had ever dreamed of 'incentivation'. In his own time as coach he instructed his players to 'pair off in threes' at training. I'll never forget the time he complained that too many modern recruits seemed to spend their time sitting around smoking 'marinara'. In a more benevolent mood Jack recalled the 'unbelievable mark' he'd held just before three-quarter time in an interstate match. "I went up so high that I was kind-of hovering there when the bell went," Jack said. "They had to throw my orange up to me." That is what has come to be known as a 'Dyerism'. Footy fans treasure them like premiership posters, and heaven help the rival raconteur who tries to compete.

And so it went on. The main reason he wanted it written was so he could show his mates over a beer.

III

I have magnificent memories of *World of Sport*, of the blokes who worked on the show, of the crew who helped put it together week after week and of the amazing and seemingly endless list of celebrities who made their way through the portals of that cramped studio. These included men like Billy Pyers, the famous Australian jockey who was headquartered in France. He arrived by cab, straight from the airport, and was on air before he realised that he was supposed to be on the rival show over at GTV 9 in Richmond. There was the great Rocky Marciano who stopped by for one of our most memorable interviews with Ron Casey; some say it was the best boxing interview ever on Australian television. Arnold Palmer was a guest as was Lee Trevino and countless tennis greats, from Rosewall and Hoad, Laver and Fraser through to Newcombe and Cash. The Harlem Globetrotters bounced me around the studio every year and after 20 years I reckoned I was no slouch with the round ball. Racing was one of our specialities and the list of jockeys, owners and trainers would read like a who's who of the international turf scene; these included men like George Moore, Willie Schoemaker, Lester Piggott, Scobie Breasley,

Roy Higgins, Geoff Lane, Bart Cummings, T J Smith, Geoff Murphy and Colin Hayes.

We rubbed shoulders over a beer in the back room with horse owners of the ilk of British pools millionaire Robert Sangster. We didn't actually have the horses in but one Sunday Carlton's star centre half-back John 'Ragsy' Gould did bring two of his polo ponies into ·the studio. The cleaners had a job and a half that afternoon, I can tell you. Ron Casey's great contacts in sport ensured a never-ending supply of big-name guests and I remember watching him interview a quartet of our greatest—Ron Clarke, Herb Elliott, Merv Lincoln and John Landy—surely the four great distance runners of the 1950s and 60s, together at the one desk to discuss the state of athletics in Australia. It was engrossing stuff. One day a book will be written about *World of Sport* and it will make great reading. It will be full of the memories that swept through those studios on that final Sunday morning two years ago. It was a day well summed up by Peter Coster in the *Herald* the following day:

> We are on the footpath outside the Channel Seven studios in South Melbourne and Ron, a mesomorph, and Ron, an endomorph, are together and opposite. Ron Barassi is muscular and defined and Ron Casey is round and ill-defined and such is *World of Sport*, the program they have come to praise and bury.
>
> *World of Sport* was sometimes fat and sometimes muscular and never thin in what it provided in 28 years of Sundays (there were a few Saturdays at the start). Barassi appeared as a coach on *World of Sport* on Sundays and carried off the giveaway goodies and Case devised *World of Sport* and gathered the sponsors who gave out the goodies. Inside the

building, a light blinks 'on air' and it is like... it is like it always is. Vast numbers of unshaven men, women without make-up, men in make-up are in Studio 1 which resembles what Central Casting might once have looked like.

Gordon Bennett, executive producer, says to Case, "You started all this." The smell of freshly poured hops is already drifting from the passage behind Studio I. It generally did, although this is the last day and people seem more inclined to start early. Were they ever disciplined? Ballantyne's Entertain Mints and Ballantyne's Vintage Tasty Cheddar Cheese are on the desk in front of Doug Elliott who does the live commercials and yells, on air, "Get out of here, Louie," when Lou Richards comes across to butt in.

The noise of conversation from the mob in the middle of the studio floor is more than a muted rumble as *World of Sport* is filmed around and in between and mostly in front of them, as it always is. "Case is walking around telling people to keep quiet and he doesn't realise he's not in charge any more," says Richards. "Case might end up as general manager somewhere else and give us a job," says Richards, and Elliot, 'Old Leatherlungs', rumbles, "Bloody oath." *World of Sport* was given to such expletives. Nothing more, of course. It was a family show. There is the whirr of pushbikes on rollers, and watchful, sad old crumpled faces.

'Leatherlungs' is upset. "Louie," he bellows, off camera but still on the set (the ability of directional microphones to pick up only the wanted is remarkable).

"Get the bastards to clap," he bellows, the old lungs puffing up like a square rigger in the roaring 1940s. "Get nicked," says Richards, who never took kindly to being told what to do.

Before the mob, on another set, the program turns on itself like a wheel. Bill Collins says, "The machine has jammed with the trots in it. No, it's alright."

All live, all action, no fuss, no recriminations. It was *World of Sport*. "It's the wrong bloody number," Lou Richards says to no one as he fishes around in the goodies trunk (this is an old tin trunk containing display boards, rolls of paper, with his live commercials written on them).

"It's not my bloody fault," he says to no one in particular as he finds the incorrect line and changes the number. "Club car badges are absolutely magnificent," he intones in what must be a Collingwood accent made resonant by 28 years of projection above the conversational roar in this studio.

"This is the only show I know in the world that has been going five minutes and is an hour behind time," he says. Big Don Scott, the former Hawthorn ruckman and captain, looks as if he has just ridden in from the high country. His taste in leather has turned to saddles, boots and suede coats.

"People who watch *World of Sport* might do a bit of gardening, go to church and then watch *World of Sport*," says Richards. "It's been described often as organised chaos, but everyone knows what to do. People have a go at each other but no one ever cracks the sulks. *World of Sport* put the Sunday roast in Melbourne out of business. When *World of Sport* was on (*World of Sport* has become past tense) Mum could put down a pie in front of them and they'd eat it."

Feminism has not been heard of at *World of Sport*. Occasionally women might appear as guests but the atmosphere is as redolent as a dressing room.

Richards is talking to Channel Seven finance director Gerry Carrington about some missed investment opportunity. "I didn't have the $10,000," Richards says. Carrington, with glass of red wine in hand rather than beer, although in a beer glass, says, "I'd like to be as broke as Lou."

'Crackers' Keenan, the former North Melbourne ruckman, asks Don Scott where he has parked his horse. 'Leatherlungs', with sails fit to burst yells, "Shut 'em up, Sam," at former Geelong ruckman Sam Newman, to the side, Jack Elliott, the *Herald*'s chief racing writer, is subdued as is a beer-gutted cameraman gazing into his screen, with fag drooping. There is an increasing conversational cacophony from the passage where the beer is flowing. Richards is heard to say (is this part of a commercial?), "We haven't got any balls."

Former VFL commissioner Jack Hamilton is here (most people here are 'former') and lifts a sockless foot on camera. It has something to do with a Lou Richards story about Hamilton wearing white shoes with socks. This time, the shoe is brown. 'Leatherlungs' is watching as Lou Richards does a live commercial. Off camera, Elliot hands his beer glass to someone to hold as he adjusts his flies.

"Don't do that, Doug," says Richards, while getting the telephone number right this time.

"Good on yer, Lou."

"Good on yer, Doug."

'Leatherlungs' would seem to be belligerent, but it was his last commercial. Other TV channels are in the studio, recording interviews while *World of Sport* is live around them. "I've got a few options," says Lou Richards. In the passageway, Bob Davis, the former Geelong coach who does not drink beer, is telling the one about the time his house was burgled and the burglar got away with 7000 neckties. They must have been free ties.

Case, red-eyed, is brought on to tell the one about the time he tried to telephone Jack Dyer ('Captain Blood' is not here today, having a previous engagement with a radio station).

"Jack told people he wasn't on the phone," says Case. "He really did have a phone but he kept it in a drawer so people wouldn't see it and ask to make a call. I decided he must have had the phone in the drawer and he couldn't hear me ringing, so I sent a telegram. I sent three telegrams and the last one was urgent, but he didn't ring back. He only lived over at Richmond, so I went around there and he answered the door. When I walked in I saw all the telegrams lined up on the mantlepiece, unopened. 'Why didn't you open the telegrams,' I asked. 'It's no good sending me telegrams, Case,' he said. 'I never open them. They might be bad news.'"

Yesterday the bad news finally came for *World of Sport*.

A RED-HOT 'TRIPEWRITER'

t's an odd thing that the birth notice informing the world that Lewis Thomas Charles, first born son of William and Irene Richards, did not appear in the classified pages of the *Sun* back in March 1923. This is odd because it seems that every moment in my life from that momentous occasion at the Bethesda Hospital in Richmond has been covered to the extreme by Australia's most read daily newspaper. The *Sun* in Flinders Street, Melbourne, houses one of the largest newspaper libraries in the world and the file on Richards, Lou is, if you don't mind me boasting, one of the biggest. It fills a floor in fact!

Next to my family, and my love for all things black-and-white, comes a long-term love affair with this newspaper. Somehow it got into my blood back in the 1950s when I took over from Jack Dyer, and despite offers to work in different fields of the media, my burgeoning television interests and years on radio, the *Sun* has always held pride of place in my heart. Don't get me wrong; I love getting my head on television, I love hobnobbing with Brian Naylor, Tony Barber, Kenny Sutcliffe and my old china Graham Kennedy, but papers are different. When I set out in 1956, HB pencil and notebook in hand, I was expected to preview VFL matches. As I explained earlier, Harry Gordon, the sports editor of the Sun, had assigned me Rex Pullen, a senior sports writer, as my first ghost. Later Mike Courtney took over and they were followed by a veritable haunted house of ghostwriters—a real who's who of Australian sporting journalism including some of the finest writers ever to have graced the grey portals of the *Herald* and *Weekly Times*.

III

Alan Trengove didn't have a clue about football but it didn't matter. I knew the tricks of the footy trade and he knew how to get them across. From the late-1950s into the early-1960s Alan and I developed much of the style that was to set 'Louie the Lip' apart from the rest. Later he would publish his own magazine, *Tennis Australia*, write a series of sporting biographies and under the auspices of the International Tennis Federation write the history of the Davis Cup. He was and still is one of the doyens of Australian sporting journalism. Next came a former Geelong footballer named Barrie Bretland. Barrie played 15 games for the Cats in 1949-50 and never really set the world on fire. His biggest claim to fame down there with the Pussy Cats in Sleepy Hollow was that he wore the number-17 guernsey—the same number that Sam Newman would wear in 300 games. While he wasn't a world champion player, he was a bloody good writer and would take over from Kevin Hogan as the chief football and cricket writer for the Sun. Barrie was a painstaking and methodical operator who very nearly brought about my downfall. In 1964 he talked me into a footy dare on the back page of the *Sun* that had me climbing to the top of the T&G Building in Collins Street. All I had to do then was paint the flagpole with a nail polish brush—a relatively simple task, you'd agree, especially when you are petrified of heights. Mike Bingham came next and, despite the fact that he didn't have the sense of humour shown by his predecessors, was a thorough and efficient ghost.

The secret of being ghosted is relatively simple when I look back over 30 years: you need first and foremost someone who is a talented writer, you need someone with a good personality, and you have to be able to communicate. It helps, too, if you can laugh with the bloke or lass belting away on the typewriter alongside you. A succession of ghosts have woven their way through my life over the last four decades. These include George Wilson, Greg Baum, Neil Kearney (who went on to achieve fame as a seeker of odd-bods on Nine's *A Current Affair* with Mike Willisee), Gary Tippett, Penny Crisp and Linda Pierce.

III

One man who has stood out over the last 20 years is Tom Prior; we have been a great team. Occasionally Tom needs a spell away from me and vice versa but it would be hard to find a person with a better understanding of the Richards technique. Tom is one of those old-style crime reporters—the foot-in-the-door type who grew up in a different era of newspapers, during a time when you cultivated your contacts in seedy pubs around the waterfront and mixed with some of the town's less desirable types. Tom gives the impression of being a rough-and-tumble reporter who looks as if he'd rather have a fight than a feed. To me he's always been a big softy under that crusty exterior. Working with Tom is a bit of a Rodgers-and-Hammerstein exercise. In fact, it's just like writing a musical. You go backwards and forwards, tossing ideas around, bouncing off each other until you come up with a finished product that you both feel is perfect.

My brief for the *Sun* in the beginning was to write a football preview. By the time I settled in with Tom over his battered Remington I was churning out six previews every Friday, a match review on Monday morning and feature stories in the sports page a couple of days a week as well as major features when required. This explosion fell squarely on the shoulders of Tom Prior and we kept up with the workload and, in fact, pushed it harder. We'd fight. We'd laugh. We'd stop the whole reporters' room as we cried ourselves silly over the red-hot 'tripewriter' (as it was affectionately known), but the copy was always in the basket on time. Football, the matches, the personalities and occasionally the big news took up most of our time in winter. When the VFL announced it was transferring the Grand Final to VFL Park in the early-1980s, the *Sun* sent Tom and me out to confront Premier John Cain, which resulted in a back-page story the next day. Tom always wanted me to parachute out of a light plane. I think it was a death—with me doing the dying. He might have talked me into plunging into Port Phillip Bay in the depth of winter or rowing Billy Goggin across the Barwon in a bathtub but I always drew the line at that parachute stunt. The good thing about Tom was that he loved sporting involvement in our stories. I'd get involved and he'd stand back and look on, notebook in hand, with a smirk on that ugly dial of his. He was outside the cage when I did my lion-taming bit with Nero the King of the Beasts that day. He loved the story but had no thought of stepping into the ring; no sir, no siree. I recall us going out to Calder to meet up with touring-car champion Peter Brock to mark the announcement of his participation in the .05 drink-driving campaign. The idea was that I would drive Brock around the Calder layout in his souped-up

THE ULTIMATE LINE-UP *The Sunday Footy Show* on Nine in 1993. **Back row, from left:** Dermott Brereton minus mullet, Sam Newman before the facelifts, Simon Madden, Simon O'Donnell and Mal Brown. **Front row, from left:** Ted Whitten had a new suit, Max Walker was the only one with a moustache and yours truly was sartorial, as always.

FANS IN HIGH PLACES *The Kiss of Death* was launched on Channel Nine's Sunday morning *Wide World of Sports* show in 1989. The prime minister, Bob Hawke, happened to be in town that day and agreed to come on the show with the authors Stephen Phillips and yours truly.

CELEBRATION TIME
Edna and I toast my MBE,
or 'Mouth of the British Empire'
as some wisecrack wrote.
Granddaughter Lucy is
along for the ride.

THIS IS YOUR LIFE Channel Nine's *This is Your Life* caught me off guard as I was talking to the faithful at a function at Victoria Park. Mike Munro frightened the daylights out of me. Later in the studios at Channel Nine, Edna was alongside as a host of colleagues, including Eddie McGuire, Trevor Marmalade and Sam Newman, roasted me.

GREATNESS Inducted into the Sport Australia Hall of Fame in 2008 and escorted onto the stage by my old mate Bobby Skilton, a triple Brownlow medallist. I wowed the audience with a few jokes and afterwards, prime minister Kevin Rudd told me he'd always wanted to meet me.

AN ENDURING PAIR Collingwood and Richmond play for the Richards-Dyer trophy, honouring our great partnership, and this day we used Jack's car to do our lap of honour before the round 19 match at the Melbourne Cricket Ground on 7 August, 1999.

HAPPY FAMILY One of my all-time favourite shots. Edna, Nicole (back left) and Kim (back right) and our five grandkids.

THE MODERN ERA Into the new millennium and *The Sunday Footy Show* had kicked on. Tony Jones was the ringmaster and Sam had been replaced as the resident wit by Billy Brownless. **Back row, from left**: Dr Peter Larkins, Danny Frawley, Chris Jones. **Front row, from left**: Brian Taylor, yours truly, Tony Jones, Mark Bickley and Billy Brownless.

BROTHERS IN GLORY In 2011, brother Ron and I were on hand to help launch 'Jock' McHale's biography, written by Glenn McFarlane. By now, we had stopped calling him Mr McHale and just occasionally referred to him as 'Jock'. In the middle is the 1953 premiership cup; I was captain that day and Ron was best on ground. They didn't present cups in those days. This one was produced years later.

THE SWEETEST VICTORY
The 19th man from my 1953 premiership side, Murray Weideman, was on hand to give me a push—although I had offered to push him— as Collingwood showed 88,000 football fans its 2010 premiership flag before a match against Carlton at the MCG in April 2011. Murray, a member of the Australian Football Hall of Fame (with me of course), would captain the 1958 premiership team.

Holden. The organisers had even prepared a special crash helmet with 'Lou' blazoned across the front of it. I slammed the pedal to the metal and just about went through the back of the seat as the G forces hit me. I looked down and saw that I was thundering around the layout at 90 (kilometres an hour, that is).

"Sorry to scare you, Brocky," I said as we hit the pits. "It was terrifying," he said with a hint of sarcasm. "Jump in, and I'll take you for a spin."

The next few laps were the most horrific in my life. We must have hit 200 kilometres an hour on the back straight, not that I'd know since my eyes were firmly closed. The seat belt was hugging me and I was hugging the roll bar for dear life. We hit one corner so fast I thought I'd end up on his lap. Never in my life have I been so happy to walk away from a car. I vowed I'd never step inside a car again, a car driven by a lunatic, anyway. (Only jokin', Pete.)

III

People who walked into the old offices of the *Sun* would stop and watch as Tom and I laboured over our Friday-morning previews. We'd sit at the sub-editors' table surrounded by the tools of our trade. Tom would have his 'tripewriter' and I would sit with my head buried in one of the dozens of gag books we had accumulated over the years. It started with a tome called 2000 Insults. Then we came up with *2000 More Insults*, and it snowballed from there. Any books that are filled with insults are perfect. It delighted us to entertain our readers but we liked trying to get some of our gags past the eagle-eyed sub-editors, who looked after the copy and prepared it for publication. From 1966 to 1973 Collingwood had a pretty good player named Con Britt and invariably we'd call him Con 'Edgar' Britt in our previews; the Edgar Britt, of course, being rhyming slang for what all of us are forced by nature to do every day. It got past the subs for months until one smartie picked up on it.

"Hey, Louie, you can't call this bloke 'Edgar Britt'," he said. "It means to have a you-know-what."

"Oh, sorry about that," I said, already plotting ways to get round him. The next week we called him Con 'Jimmy' Britt and no one said a word. In my school days it didn't matter whether you were going for an Edgar or a Jimmy; they both meant the same thing.

We've heaped praise on players, rubbished them, pulled at their idiosyncrasies and taunted them but very few have ever been upset. Most see it as a great way of promoting their game and keeping their name in lights. Let me tell you it is hard to be original, to keep churning out football previews week after week, season after season. By the end of 1989 I will have been at the *Sun* for 34 seasons and will have previewed 4170 VFL matches and countless interstate and night games, and written close to 700 match reports and as many feature stories on the champs, the has-beens and those that never were. Just looking at those figures makes me sag with brain drain. I can admit it now: there was one player who did make me tread carefully. Carlton's John Nicholls was a massive ruckman. He was not a monster like those of today's beanpole crop of two-metre ruckmen but a lump of granite with legs like trunks of old red gum and crystal eyes that show no emotion. Thank God I was a rover. Tom Prior would insist on sliding in the odd dig about 'Big Nick', giving the Blues' most feared player a little hurry-up here and there. I blanched at the very thought of running into him in my job as a football commentator with Channel Seven or on *World of Sport* where he was a regular guest. Often as not I would agree to the story as written and watch Tom drop the copy in the sub-editors' basket. Later that day when all was quiet, I would sneak back across Exhibition Street, go up to the third floor and deftly remove the offending slips of copy. It was alright for Tom. He'd be watching Essendon from the safety of the outer with his mates. I had to go and confront 'Big Nick' and that, in itself, could be a terrifying ordeal.

III

Last year when Christopher Skase won the football rights for his Australian Television Network it absolutely floored me when I read that his heavies had declared war on nicknames. The commentators, Sandy Roberts, Peter Landy and Drew Morphett, were directed to call the players by their correct names. To me it ended one of the great delights of Australian football. Wayne Schimmelbusch, the North Melbourne skipper, had a mouthful of a moniker and it was only common sense to call him 'Schimma'; same with Bertie DiPierdomenico—the one and only 'Big Dipper'. From the earliest days of football nicknames have been around and have added colour. They've made the players more human. Some who come to mind from those days are 'Chicken' Smallhorn, 'Carji' Greeves, 'Banana legs' Hopkins, 'Captain Blood', 'Basher' Williams and 'Smokey' Clegg, to name but a few. Tom Prior and I delighted in naming players. We'd spend hours working out good nicknames and it's amazing how many stuck. When a particular young Hawthorn rover started making a name for himself we decided to call him 'Lethal Leigh'. 'Lethal Leigh' Matthews was politely called 'Barney' by his Hawthorn team-mates because of his resemblance of Fred Flintstone's nextdoor neighbour, but over 340 games, 'Lethal Leigh' was the one that stuck. His mother was furious. One day she confronted me and had quite a go at me about placing this most unwarranted tag on her young darling. "I tell you what, Mrs Matthews," I said, stretching up to my full five feet six-and-a-quarter inches, "he'll make a million bucks out of that name and one day he'll thank me." I don't think she believed me, and viewed me with some suspicion for years. Leigh hasn't actually come up and blessed me for it either, but it is a name that has become part of football folklore. If he didn't like it, why did he call his autobiography *Lethal?*

Among my favourites were the 'Galloping Gasometer' and the 'Flying Doormat'. North Melbourne recruited a ruckman in its quest for success in the mid-1970s, a bloke with a more-than-ample girth and a thirst that was without equal. His name was Mick Nolan and a nicer fellow you'd never meet. Mick was a terrific tap ruckman and, according to champion rover Barry Cable, one of the best, but he looked terrible. He was large and rotund and even at full stretch would be out-sprinted by a geriatric tortoise. Next to North's Arden Street headquarters were situated a couple of monstrous gasometers in the good old days and Tom and I couldn't have thought of a more fitting tribute. Come to think of it, the gasometers were probably quicker than Mick. The 'Flying Doormat' was probably less effusive in his thanks than Mick Nolan; in fact, I hardly said a word to Carlton's ultra-shy defender Bruce Doull in all his years at Carlton. The 'Doormat' was recruited to Princes Park from Jacana and went on to play 359 games—more than any other Blue in VFL history. He played in four premierships, won three best and fairest awards and gave away about as many kicks as interviews. He was a human clam. Early in his career he was awarded the number-four guernsey but requested a higher number (finally he got 11) because his locker was too close to captain-coach John Nicholls'. Bruce hated all the attention that came Big Nick's way. He liked the quiet life. He probably would have had it, too, but for his hair. It started receding early. As his forehead crept back Bruce tried to conceal the fact. He'd comb it forward and spray it. He'd wear a monogrammed Carlton sweatband. He'd do anything. Meanwhile the hair was growing furiously at the back of his head—hence the 'Flying Doormat' tag. I don't know if he liked it. I can only remember interviewing him a couple of times in nearly 20 years and even then he didn't say much.

There were the obvious nicknames, like 'Slamming' Sammy Kekovich, North Melbourne's tempestuous ruck-rover of the 1970s and 'Fabulous' Phil Carman, the white-booted warrior who kicked goals for Collingwood and butted a head or two for Essendon. There was the 'Flying Dutchman', Essendon's Paul Van Der Haar whose Dutch roots and high fliers made him an obvious. 'The Fish', alias Paul Salmon; 'Superboot' Bernie Quinlan; and the 'Leyland brothers', Geelong's Nankervis brothers, Ian and Bruce, were others. The latter both skippered the Cats and between them played 582 games (a record for brothers in the VFL). They were prolific kickgetters and mighty fine players, make no mistake about that. The problem was that they developed a short zig-zagging game that crisscrossed Kardinia Park all afternoon. They'd pick up a million kicks but cover more kilometres than TV's Leyland brothers, hence the tag.

One bloke who scared the daylights out of footballers for most of the mid-1960s was a big bruiser from Hawthorn called Des Dickson. Des was a ruckman who was all fists and elbows, forearms and knees. Crikey, he could mow down an opposition side at the opening bounce. I christened him 'Delicate' Des and it stuck like glue. Middle age has quietened him down somewhat and I hear he does a lot for junior football up Bendigo way these days but in those rough-and-tumble days at Glenferrie under John Kennedy he was real mean. Channel Seven put together a tape some years back called 'Violent Saturday', an hour of the worst imaginable biffs and brawls, and you wouldn't want to know who starred—the one and only 'Delicate' Des. The tape was so popular that the VFL had to step in and ban its use. The League claimed it gave football a bad name. You're not kidding it did!

Another favourite nickname was bestowed on Richmond's current coach Kevin Bartlett. You have only to look at his career statistics to know why I dubbed him 'Hungry'. In a VFL-record 403 games, the whispy-haired rover gathered 8329 kicks, took 1090 marks and kicked 778 goals, yet there is not one mention of him handballing to a team-mate. Amazing that! I've had many a chuckle with Kevin on the very subject and I can tell you that I'm proud of him. The rover's code is to kick goals yourself, not set up some other mug to finish off all your good work.

III

Over the past couple of seasons I've been ghosted by Peter Simunovich, my one-time boarder and a dyed-in-the-wool Collingwood supporter, and Brian Meldrum. 'The Drum', as he is known, was a member of the *Sun's* racing staff for many years and has thrived in his new paddock since winning his clearance to the footy department. He does have a skeleton in his cupboard. Brian is the brother of 'Molly' Meldrum, the former compere of *Countdown* on the ABC, a member of the hugely successful *Hey, Hey It's Saturday* team and the confidante of the world's top rock stars. Molly is flamboyant, always wears a hat and is a crazed and besotted St Kilda supporter. Brian thankfully can claim innocence to all three of the above.

With the Phoenix across the road and 33 years at the *Sun* I've got to know generations of journalists and many of them, like Tom Prior, Harry Gordon and John Fitzgerald, have become very close personal friends. Harry was the man who lured me to the *Sun* and later became my editor and ultimately the editor-in-chief. A fine writer and great company, Harry was with me on many fishing trips on Port Phillip Bay, one of which stands out. Harry, the *Sun* features editor Neil Moody, his assistant in features and I ventured down to Keefers' boat shed at Beaumaris to hire a boat and head out in search of dinner. It was a hot day and, as you can imagine, perfect weather to drown a worm and immerse ourselves in a sea of Carlton and United's best. By mid-afternoon we were all pretty much under the weather and, to make matters worse, we hadn't even had a nibble. Finally Neil's offsider got a bite; more than a bite, in fact— a gulp. After a fair tussel the youngster pulled in this huge barracouta about 70 centimetres long and fierce to boot. Neil was furious that he'd been shown up by this assistant and promptly grabbed the fish and hurled it overboard. "Too milky," he stated flatly and went on fishing. It would have fed all of us but, as you might have guessed, it was all we caught for the afternoon. It's strange what the sun will do to you.

There have been highlights in my newspaper career, especially as a former footballer turned card-holding member of the Australian Journalists' Association. For me it was the 1968 Mexico Olympic Games. It had been a long and hard football season with Ron Barassi coaching Carlton to its first VFL premiership in 23 years and I was utterly exhausted from my media work and with running the Phoenix. Edna suggested that I take a few weeks off and get away from everything. My very good mate Jack Cannon was chatting over a couple of beers one night, talking about his latest assignment. He was to head the *Herald* and *Weekly Times* pool coverage of the Olympic Games in Mexico City beginning in mid-October. "Why don't you come over?" Jack suggested. "I'm sure we can find some off-beat stories for you and you'll have a damned good time as well."

Mexico City conjured up visions of the Incas and Aztecs, of sun and Spanish señoritas, tacos and tortillas and, all up, a pretty good time. Jack headed off a few weeks later to do the groundwork for the newspapers and I busied myself preparing my Olympic wardrobe.

III

Mexico City wasn't quite what I'd expected. It was stinking hot, smoggy and filthy. The place was crawling with people and the traffic was a never-ending snarl. For a bloke reared in the backstreets of Collingwood and who walked down one flight of stairs to get to work each day, it was quite an eye-opener. I checked into my hotel, the Maria Isabella, and promptly rang Jack at the Olympic press centre.

"Where are you?" Jack asked. "I'll come over and pick you up." I looked around the bar I was in and saw the name.

"I'm in the Salida Bar at the Maria Isabella Hotel."

Jack said he'd be only 10 minutes but an hour later he still hadn't fronted. Finally he walked through the door and looked far from happy.

"Where have you been?" I asked.

"The Salida Bar, the Salida Bar. You told me you were in the Salida Bar," Jack said. "I asked at the desk and they told me that Salida in Spanish means exit. I thought you were sitting under an exit sign and I've been looking everywhere." After that slight hiccup we grabbed a cab because Jack said he wanted to go and look at the 'big shoot'. I immediately envisaged a trip to the Olympic rifle range.

Our driver was a student aged about 19 and he handled English with the same aplomb as he handled the big Ford station wagon that he manoeuvred through the bumper-to-bumper traffic. I couldn't help but notice the mass of tanks and armoured cars and the soldiers and military road blocks everywhere. Jack explained that the students had been revolting, venting their displeasure at the fact that the Mexican government was spending close to $250 million to stage a fortnight of the Olympics when there were millions of peasants starving. Jack had been covering this story and wanted to pop out to the university for a first-hand look. Our driver chipped in and told us some bloodcurdling stories about the army brutality, how hundreds of young kids had been butchered and their bodies burned. At this stage I was craving the saloon bar at the Phoenix and the soothing words of my adored wife. We kept on driving. As we neared the university we could see soldiers with machine guns, tanks and armoured personnel carriers everywhere. This was the 'big shoot'. Jack kept reassuring me but the driver did not.

Every time he'd see a soldier or a policeman he'd slow down, wind his window down and yell "*bastardo*" and then spit in that general direction. "Jack, you'd better do something about this bloke. He's going to get us shot," I whispered. Fortunately Jack was thinking along the same lines and we made a hasty retreat.

At the press centre Jack managed to get me accreditation and organised a billet for me in the most upmarket section of Mexico City—the Pedrogale. Mine was a very ritzy little mansion, too, with maids and a swimming pool. The owner, the boss of Canada Dry in southern and central America, had let it out to the ambassador of Iran and me. Very distinguished lessees, if you don't mind. There was only one problem. The Pedrogale, full of its rich inhabitants, is situated in a maze. Its own security force occupies little sentry boxes scattered throughout. I was given a map but, despite the fact that I was less than 10 minutes from the press centre, it never took less than an hour to find my way home. Even then I had to coerce one of the local security blokes to ride along and give instructions, and that was costly. They wouldn't move unless they were well tipped.

Jack had worked out some stories for me and soon after I arrived suggested that I run the marathon course. I reckon he was second only to Tom Prior for harebrained schemes. He'd arranged for me to wear an Australian outfit and my running partner would be our gold medal hope and future world champ Derek Clayton. It was incredibly hot and the smog made it difficult to breathe, but off we went through the traffic-clogged streets, the little 'Kiss of Death' whispering encouragement to the tall Australian distance champion. We certainly didn't run the full distance together but after a kilometre or so I noticed the crowd was urging us on. They were yelling out "Louie, Louie", and it kept me going. Jack Cannon and his photographer Bruce Howard were travelling in the back of a station wagon up ahead, taking photographs and they heard the chants too. When I finally collapsed into the car, I turned to Jack.

"It's incredible," I spluttered, still trying to get my wind back. "All these peasants must like the football. They all knew me and were yelling out my name."

"They were yelling alright," said Jack. "They were screaming out 'Loco, loco'. It means 'crazy'. They reckon you're mad running in the heat of the day."

III

Over two weeks I saw some of the greatest sporting performances in world athletics history, with the rarified atmosphere making a mockery of the old world records. I saw Bob Beamon become the first man to jump 29 feet (8.85 metres) and Dick Fosbury introduce the 'Flop' as he flipped himself seven feet four-and-a-quarter inches (2.24 metres) over the bar. It was great to see Maureen Caird win the hurdles and Ralph Doubell shock the world by taking the 800 metres, but to me the most memorable, and disturbing, moment came when we were waiting for Peter Norman to collect his silver medal in the 200 metres. Norman, the lay preacher, had split the black American pair of Tommie Smith and John Carlos and all three were standing waiting for the US national anthem. When it struck up, both the Americans directed their eyes at their feet and with black-gloved, clenched fists gave the Black Power salute. It stunned the packed stadium and made front-page news worldwide.

One of my most important missions in Mexico City was to stand as watchdog while Jack Cannon and his team prepared their dispatches. The press centre was packed with the greats of world sporting journalism, from American legend Red Smith down. It was tightly policed and unless you had the correct accreditation, you couldn't get past the armed guards. That didn't stop Percy Cerutty from sneaking in. The bloke who coached Herb Elliott in his mission to become the greatest middle-distance runner in history was also probably the most eccentric I've ever met. Jack was terrified of him. Percy would sneak in as these hundreds of distinguished writers were agonising over their typewriters and scream at the top of his voice, "Where is the greatest sports writer the world has seen? Where is Jack Cannon of the Melbourne *Herald*?" Jack would cower with embarrassment as the world's press ground to a halt, looked at this strange little bloke and wondered who the hell this Jack Cannon was. It got too much for Jack; finally he called me in as the lookout. When I saw Percy arriving and sneaking past the guards, I'd run over to Jack and we'd scarper out through another exit.

CHAPTER 12

THE KISS OF DEATH

I hate seeing grown men cry and I loathe seeing them on their hands and knees grovelling, but that's the effect the good old-fashioned 'Kiss of Death' has had on people over the years. People stop me in the street, others yell from car windows, the phone runs hot before big matches and football coaches with not a trace of superstition in their bodies plead to be spared.

Tipping a winner is big business to this football expert and, over 33 years with Melbourne's *Sun*, I've got it down to a fine art. The problem is that when I do honestly believe a team is unbeatable, and unbackable, things generally come unstuck. My footy predictions have graced the back page of Australia's widest read daily paper for over four decades but instead of being treated with the respect due to a former Collingwood premiership captain, I'm treated with derision. Back in the old days things got so bad that I managed only six winners over four rounds, out of a possible 24. It was so bad that my ghost writer Alan Trengove suggested I was putting a jinx on the teams I'd picked. That was the birth of the nickname 'Kiss of

Death'. Rather than fight it, I rolled with the blows and used the old smooch to my benefit.

I remembered an old movie I'd taken Edna to see back in the 1940s, a gangster-style movie starring my lookalike, the ruggedly handsome matinee idol Victor Mature. It was called *The Kiss of Death* and to be blatantly honest, I pinched it. There were times when I tried my hardest to work out a winner and there were times when my brain became so addled I figured it would be easier to pick six losers. Work that one out! I've been fearless in my support of the underdog, I've put in the body and taken the knocks, I've received truckloads of hate mail and never let sentiment rule, except when Collingwood was involved. (That's different of course.) Over 33 years I've done stupid things in the name of football, generally acts born in desperation over a blazing hot Remington tripewriter in the newsroom of the *Sun*. You see, my tips are a vital part of the day-to-day life of people who follow VFL football. Take my mates at GTV 9, for example. Each year they run footy sweeps. There's one in the newsroom, another down in the executive offices, another in sales, and so on. If you haven't put your tips in by five o'clock on Friday evening, you cop mine. In some cases you get mine, minus one. That really puts the pressure on. This goes on in offices and factories all over Victoria. People I haven't even heard of ring and abuse me about my tips at all hours of the day and night. So you can understand just how important they are.

While the 'Kiss of Death' has been the ultimate weapon in the complete football arsenal, some of my famous dares have left me in the most precarious positions. My big mouth has got me into heaps of trouble. I've been perched up a flag pole on top of a city skyscraper and half-drowned in Port Phillip Bay. I have cleaned a city street with a feather duster, rowed across a river in a bathtub and been smothered with everything from pasta to pizza. The cruel thing is that the 'Kiss of Death' lets me down at my moments of greatest need.

III

When I first started writing at the *Sun* after my premature retirement as captain of the Magpies, my main weekly mission was to provide an analytical and expert preview of the forthcoming VFL round. My ghostwriter was Rex Pullen, a senior sporting journalist and a great mate. We got along well, churning out our weekly pieces and employing his journalistic skills and the full range of the Richards thought processes. My good friend Harry Gordon was our sporting editor and, I might add, a good customer of mine at the Phoenix. One day he suggested that my personality wasn't coming through, that a little lightheartedness was needed. He introduced me to a baby-faced young bloke named Michael Courtney and our brief was to put a little humour into Saturday mornings. We hit it off like Abbott and Costello and never looked back. Mike was just what I needed and I am proud to say he's made a great success in his trade. These days he's the editor of the *Launceston Examiner*. The *Sun* readers loved it. They loved my cocky style, my Collingwood arrogance and we struggled to keep pace with them. In the 1961 preliminary final I was convinced that Melbourne was too strong and powerful for Footscray, a team of up and comers captained and coached by Mr Football himself, Teddy Whitten.

Melbourne had played in every Grand Final from 1954 through to 1960 and had won five premierships under coach Norm Smith. So positive was I about the outcome that in my Saturday morning preview I wrote that I would cut Ted Whitten's front lawn with a pair of nail scissors if the unthinkable occurred.

That Saturday afternoon I was walking into the Melbourne Cricket Ground for the final along with some 86,000 others, and who should I bump into but the prime minister, Mr Robert Menzies. "Good day there young Richards," the prime minister said with half a chuckle in that all-too-familiar voice. "All I want to see is Melbourne get beaten here this afternoon so you can cut that lawn."

You wouldn't want to know, Footscray won by 27 points. Come Monday, I piled Edna and the kids into *Sun* photographer Lloyd Brown's car and headed out to the Whitten residence in Yarraville. As we got closer I mentioned to Lloyd that there were people everywhere. The streets were blocked, cars were parked bumper to bumper as far as you could see.

"What on earth's going on?" I asked Lloyd. "Do you reckon there's a footy match on at the Yarraville ground?"

"Nah, Louie. I think they might be here to see you," Lloyd said half-joking as we drove along Hampshire Road.

Sure enough there were about 3000 ardent Footscray fans packed into Ted's street and there was even a temporary grandstand arrangement propped up outside his house. Down on my hands and knees I went with those bloody nail scissors, clipping away until the crowd had its fun and Lloyd had his photographs. I can tell you it was hard work. Old Mr Football might have been a sight to behold on the field but off the field he was no horticulturist. He hadn't mown his lawn in months. The mob lapped it up. The *Sun* loved it and the readers clamoured for more; and you don't think Little Louie, the emerging megastar, would let them down not on your life. Ted Whitten was the perfect bloke to be involved in a prank like that, too. He was the biggest name in football and vied with the great Melbourne skipper Ron Barassi for the title of Mr Football.

On sheer ability Ted won that hands down but when it came to charisma, things might have swung back Ronny's way.

III

I first bumped into Ted back in 1951. He was a rookie from local side Braybrook, a kid with champion and class stamped all over him. I was the 28-year-old captain of Collingwood, a veteran with finals and interstate honours behind me. This didn't bother Ted one bit. We were playing at Victoria Park and I didn't even see him whack me. A perfect backhander broke my nose and my cheekbone. They all told me later who did it. It didn't really bother me all that much. You hand them out and you cop them back; part of the football lore. We met Footscray next in the opening round of 1952 at Victoria Park. The umpire bounced the ball and I grabbed the knock-out. I could see Ted bearing down on me so I held the football up with my fist behind it and as he got to me I let him have it right between the eyes. He went down like a bag of spuds. His eyes were going blacker by the second. When he came to, I was standing there. "A monkey never forgets," I snarled and walked away. Over 19 years Ted was to play 321 games for Footscray, captain and coach the side, play in the club's only premiership and win five best and fairest awards. He was the most versatile footballer in the VFL, a great competitor and a fashion plate on the field as well. He looked every inch the champion he was.

I remember Ron Casey and I inviting Ted down to the Old Scotch oval near the new Flinders Park tennis centre in Melbourne for a kick-off against the touring All Blacks from New Zealand. We were filming a segment on these rugby union greats and out of interest put up a challenge between our VFL superstar kicker Ted Whitten and their man Don Clark, one of the all-time greats.

When Ted came out of the change rooms he looked a million dollars. The All Blacks looked like unmade beds in comparison. The boys warmed up and did a couple of laps to stretch the hamstrings and loosen the muscles. A little red-haired Kiwi called to Ted to pass the ball from about 36 metres. Ted kicked the most superb stab pass. It hit the Kiwi on the chest like a bullet, knocking the wind out of him and leaving him sprawled on the turf. I don't reckon he knew what hit him. When it came to kicking, Ted was far too good with the old-fashioned torpedo punt and the drop kick but Don Clarke placekicked the ball about 72 metres and there the contest ended.

It was on the interstate trips that we saw the best of Teddy Whitten. In 29 matches for Victoria he was the heart and soul of VFL football and they tell me he was the life of the party afterwards as well. When he was first made captain of Victoria in 1962 he was asking me about his media responsibilities. "Never do anything for nothing," I advised him. "You're captain of Victoria now, so you should be charging these blokes for the privilege of talking to you." Sure enough, Ted arrived at Adelaide airport for the match against South Australia and was confronted by cameras and microphones. I was standing in the wings waiting for the pearls of wisdom. Ted promptly put his hand up and said bluntly. "No interviews. Lou Richards, over there," he said pointing to me, skulking in the wings, "Lou has told me you have to pay first." I've never felt so bad in my whole life.

Later of course he would become a master of the media game, a superstar interviewee who could turn a minute of questions and answers into a performance that would rival Lord Olivier. As chairman of the VFL selectors and the first chosen on all interstate trips, Ted is a born ham when it comes to drumming up support for these mid-season matches. One year in Adelaide I caught him off-guard. I grabbed him and dragged him over to our *Wide World of Sports* camera. "Ted, if you get beaten tonight will you promise your viewers that you'll resign?" I asked him pointedly. Now, this is a job that Ted had lusted after. It was the plum job for a past player and Teddy had been waiting in the wings for years. He looked at me with pleading eyes, going redder by the second. For the first time in 50 years he was lost for words. It gave me my greatest delight to tell him that we hadn't loaded the camera.

III

There was a succession of pranks over the years as a result of foolhardy footy dares. One year in my more athletic past, my ghost of the time Barrie Bretland talked me into a dare; yet another loser, naturally. That was never in dispute with Barrie. Come Monday and I was climbing the tower of the T&G Building on the corner of Collins and Russell Streets in Melbourne. My mission: to paint the flagpole with a nail polish brush. I ask you! I get vertigo standing on the bath mat. Looking back that was one of the worst moments in my life; worse than facing Jack Dyer running at me at full tilt. It wasn't the most dangerous, I hasten to add, not by a long shot.

In 1976 I came out in print suggesting that Fitzroy had no hope of beating Essendon in their crucial Queen's Birthday match at VFL Park. So positive was I of my prediction that I offered to jump off St Kilda pier if I was wrong. At seven o'clock on the Wednesday morning I strode down St Kilda pier, rugged up against the wintery 9°C morning in my thickest overcoat. Three hundred howling sadists were there to greet me, along with a handful of Fitzroy footballers. One old granny, all of 84 if she was a day, asked me if I was going in naked. You'd be joking! I thought I had them beaten. Under the coat I was decked out in a full-length wetsuit, but even then I could feel monstrous goose pimples bursting through. In I jumped.

The 1.83 metres between the pier and the water felt like 10 but that was nothing compared with the shock waves that swept over me as I hit the water. I almost passed out. Somehow in my rush to get the whole thing over with, I'd forgotten to do up the press studs under my crutch. As I wallowed semiconscious in the water, the long arm of Fitzroy ruckman Ronny Alexander plucked me to safety. *Terra firma* has never felt so good. However, that was only half of the ordeal. Ever heard of the brass monkey? Well, I can tell you that my willy was non-existent for weeks. It looked counter sunk and Edna didn't help me thaw it out, I can assure you.

III

Water has played a big part in our famous dares over the years. In May 1969 I fearlessly predicted that North Melbourne would beat Hawthorn; and if they didn't I'd take a bath in the horse trough opposite the Phoenix in Flinders Street. Hawthorn won and on a rainy Monday the lunchtime crowds turned up in their droves to see 'Louie the Lip' pay his penalty. Just after noon I saw that the coast was clear. I called one of my barmen downstairs and told him to empty as many buckets of hot water into the horse trough as he could without being spotted. I watched him cross Flinders Street half a dozen times, preparing my bath. When the crowd called and the *Sun* photographer was positioned I made my appearance in a pair of old baggy shorts. The Hawks' greatest fullforward Peter Hudson was on hand to scrub my back as I lowered myself into the lukewarm water. As my toes went under I froze. There was something terribly wrong. The water was freezing. 'Huddo' was beside himself. He'd seen the buckets of hot water being tipped in so he went and bought a couple of blocks of ice. I felt like the Titanic after it had been hit by the iceberg.

The Barwon River in Geelong is the site of the annual public schools' Head of the River rowing regatta. It was also the site of my 1980 footy prediction gone wrong. Collingwood and Geelong were due to play at Kardinia Park in August and I told my faithful audience of *Sun* readers that if the Magpies lost I'd row Cats coach Billy Goggin across the Barwon in a bathtub. The Cats won by 18 points and everyone in Sleepy Hollow knew about the bet. More than 5000 of them lined the river bank and peered down from the bridge as I loaded Billy into the bathtub. I'd donned a light-blue wetsuit for the occasion. I've got a cupboard full of them at home for these kinds of days. Silly Billy turned up in an old moth-eaten football jumper, tracksuit and life vest, and he was carrying an umbrella. God knows what the umbrella was for. As we pushed off, Billy confessed he couldn't swim—a typical Cat. Supported by four four-gallon drums and armed with a paddle, we were going well until the half-way mark. Up ahead and closing fast was a motor boat manned by Bob Davis, my old mate from *League Teams*, and a bevy of Geelong players. "Pirates ahoy," Billy yelled. I wasn't listening. I just rowed like my life depended on it, ducking and weaving to avoid the hail of rotten eggs and tomatoes and a salvo of flour bombs. Then it dawned on me: Billy had been warned and had his umbrella up to protect himself. As soon as the bank was in sight, Goggin was off like a flash, slithering to safety and leaving me to get dumped into the river. "I wasn't going to be the last rat off the sinking ship," the coach told anyone who'd listen.

I've had the bucket tipped on me more times than I care to mention but, I modestly point out, there's always been a camera or two there to record the event. Grand Final day 1988 and I told my faithful throng that Melbourne would provide the upset of the season and beat the mighty Hawthorn, the undisputed odds-on favourite for the flag. Should Hawthorn win, I would cheerfully wash Dermott Brereton's red Ferrari with a cotton ball on the steps of the Hawthorn Town Hall. The history books will show Hawthorn winning by a record 16 goals and my diary will show that I dutifully turned up at lunchtime with bucket, car wash and cotton balls in hand. Ever tried washing a car with a cotton ball? It's bloody hard work. The crowd loved it. They loved seeing me in my adopted Hawthorn jumper and Dermie standing alongside like a cat who's just swallowed a mouse.

"Let's brighten things up, Dermie," I whispered to the Grand Final hero. "Tip the bucket over me as soon as that cameraman is ready."

"I couldn't do that," said the VFL toughie.

"Do it," I ordered, and he did. Lovely shots they were, too.

III

Carlton have been a bad result for me over the years. There's been something about the Blues that has irked me when it's come to picking them. On one occasion when I tipped against them I ended up with a bucket of spaghetti being tipped over my head by Mario Bortolotto. Steve Silvagni dropped a pizza on me after I tipped against them in the 1987 Grand Final and even back in 1982 Wow Jones had his moment at my expense. I had tipped Richmond; Carlton won and my sentence was a hefty one. I had to don a dinner suit and wheel the Carlton big man up Lygon Street in a wheelbarrow... the indignity of it all! Ruckmen have had a strange effect on me. In 1978 I was positive South Melbourne would beat North Melbourne. So sure was I that I offered to piggyback Mick Nolan up Errol Street to the North Melbourne Town Hall should I be wrong. You guessed it. Now Mick is a lovely bloke. He's about 114 kilograms and 1.96

metres and he's got what you'd call an accommodating figure. He'd look good dressed in a doona cover. This day Mick sidled up to me and whispered in my ear. "Don't worry, Louie, I'll keep the weight off you." He'd have to be a ruckman. On he jumped and my body groaned under the weight. When you're 1.68 metres and a shade over 69 kilograms, in these circumstances you find your knees buckling and the footpath coming up to meet you. By the time I'd finished I reckon I'd shrunk to 1.6 metres.

Call them corny, call them contrived, call them what you like, but these pranks have been great fun. They've shown the human face of the footballers involved and they've dragged people out in their thousands. And from a personal point of view, they've sold millions of newspapers.

CHAPTER 13

WHEN LIPS COLLIDE

It started as just another Friday. It ended as one of the classic sporting confrontations and a day I'll never forget. I was sitting back learning my numbers for an Escort Cup night match that evening between East Fremantle and St Kilda when the phone woke me. It was Geoff Jones, the deputy chief of staff of the *Sun*.

"Louie, we want you to drop everything and grab the one o'clock plane for Sydney. We want you to interview Muhammad Ali," Jones said.

"But it's 10 to 12 now."

"You'll make it," he reassured me. "We've already sent the cab."

So that autumn Friday back in 1979 I found myself at the Woolloomooloo Police Citizens' Boys club in Sydney with *Sun* photographer Alex Gall and reporter Peter Rees. The place was packed to the rafters with every TV, radio and newspaper reporter ever accredited by the Australian Journalists' Association in the last 50 years, and plenty of others, too. I took one look and knew our chances of getting an exclusive with the great man were about as slim as my chances of lasting 15 seconds in the ring with him.

"Let's get outside," I whispered to my team. We'd been walking to and fro along the footpath outside the club for about 20 minutes when a Rolls Royce glided to a halt alongside us. The door opened and out stepped the 'Louisville Lip'. Sometimes to colour this story I recount how he walked straight over to me and grabbed me by the hand, saying, "Louie, it's great to see you. I've heard all about you." In fact, he looked straight through me. I had one eye on my watch, knowing I had to be on the four o'clock flight back to Melbourne to call the football for HSV 7 and the minutes had been ticking away at an alarming rate. "Welcome to the club," I said as I held out my shaking paw. "Nice to be here," Mr Ali replied. In a second it dawned on me: he actually thought I was the welcoming committee, probably the president of the joint. 'The Lip' was in Sydney for an exhibition bout against a former foe, the European heavyweight champ of days past, Joe Bugner, and was on his way to a sparring session with another ex-champ, Jimmy Ellis.

"Don't wash your hand," I told him. "You can tell them all back in the States that this is the hand that shook Lou Richards' hand."

He looked at me with a touch of incredulity.

"I get paid for being a fool. What's your reason?" came back the reply.

"Okay, Ali, you've got the same old lip, but you've lost your zip."

He gave me that same look that he'd given Smoking Joe and, in the distant past, Sonny Liston, and to my great relief he walked away and started signing autographs for some young Aboriginal teenagers. We still needed a picture. Alex Gall had been snapping away as I conducted my in-depth interrogation but we needed that special snap. As he turned towards the door, he stopped, looking me up and down. Oh no, I've gone too far this time, I thought as he stepped up to me. Little Louie the quivering

coward was now toe to toe with his idol at last. He bent down and
wrapped those massive arms around me and gave me the biggest
bear hug in history. Gosh, he had smooth skin for a fighter. As my
feet hit the footpath he was off and so was I on the plane back to
Melbourne with a picture that graces my mantlepiece to this day.
It wasn't until we were on the plane that Alex Gall confided in
me. "We were very lucky, Louie," he said. "It was the last shot on
that roll of film." The next morning that bear hug was all over the
front page of the *Sun* and the story adorned the top of page three.
'Battle of the big mouths' screamed the posters. 'Lip to Lip' was the
front-page headline.

III

As for the football match that night, it was very forgettable but I can
tell you St Kilda lost. They lost everything in those days. A couple of
years ago, after I'd joined the Nine Network, our managing director
Gary Rice suggested that I fly to the States and set up an interview
with George Burns; after all, we looked so much alike. In November
1987 I flew out of Melbourne with Edna and our *Wide World of
Sports* producer Stephen Phillips and his wife Jill for the West
Coast of the USA. Now, all these stories sound easy in principle
but putting them into practice is a real pain in the backside. We had
a number in Hollywood for George and managed after many tries
to get in touch with his agent, one Irving Fein.

"Sure, Lou, George would love to do the interview with you
for Australia. He loves Australia. He loves Australians. Let's say
$5000," Irving said.

"Now hold on Irving. We only want a quick interview,
not a feature film. Can you cut back the price a thou or two?"

"No go, Louie. Five's the best we can do."

"What about a picture of the two of us, after all I am his dead ringer?"

"We'll think about that," Irving replied and then hung up. A week later Stephen and I had got to know Irving like a friendly uncle. We spoke to him every day, and every day he'd give us the same rundown.

"$5000 for the story, boys."

Finally we relented and settled for the black-and-white photograph, and Irving organised for us to come to the studios where George had his offices. About noon the next day we arrived at the studios off Sunset Boulevard and presented our credentials at the security gate. "Oh, you must be George's young son," the guard said to me. "Gosh, you look alike." Flattery always gets me and I was on cloud nine as he escorted us to George's office at the back of the lot. Ushered into the office, we finally stood face to face with the 91-year-old superstar.

"Mr Burns, it really is a great pleasure to meet you," I yelled. "Call me George," he replied. Modestly I suggested that he should call me Lou.

Now George is short. He's got big ears and wears glasses and smokes cigars the size of salamis, and at 91 he is still a very sharp old bloke.

"Lou, is that your own hair?" he asked as we settled back into our chairs. "Sure is, George. I'm the only man in the world with grey flannel hair."

"The problem with that," says George, "is that you're stuck with yours. I can change my hair whenever I like and to whatever colour I feel like." He offered me a cigar and I promptly pocketed it to show Edna later on.

"What age are you?" he enquired.

"I'm 65 next birthday," I replied, slightly taken aback at his audacity. With a puff of the cigar the old bloke was chuckling to himself. "When I was 65 I had gonorrhoea." Most youngsters think of George as God: after all, he has portrayed the almighty in a number of movies.

"You know, Lou, a lot of people think that I actually am God. They're forever writing letters to me with their problems. One woman wrote, 'Dear George, my husband and I are senior citizens and we still care about each other. Is it okay to make love in the 90s? Signed, Getting Up There.' I replied, 'Dear Getting, I think it's best around 70 or 75. If it gets any hotter than that, I turn on the air-conditioning.'"

III

The pad George had in Hollywood was nothing special. Filled with memorabilia and old movie posters, it was an office that could have been used by any old-time megastar. Every time George asked me a question I yelled and finally, after half an hour, it was getting him down.

"Lou, why are you yelling at me?"

"I thought you were deaf," I replied. "My mum's 87 and she has trouble hearing. I thought you'd be the same."

"She's 87 is she?" he said with that old familiar twinkle in his eye. It was wonderful to settle back and enjoy his humour, face-to-face.

"Open that door over there," he said.

I walked across the office and opened the door. It led nowhere. In fact, there in front of me was another door on which was stuck a large pin-up ripped from the pages of *Penthouse* or some such publication, He was rolling around laughing.

"Not bad, is she? Life begins at 90."

And the worst part is that you just had to believe him. When I met him he was writing his seventh book, *Gracie*, about his great love Gracie Allen who died back in 1964, and making a new movie.

As well as that, he was appearing regularly at Las Vegas with the likes of Frank Sinatra, Sammy Davis Junior and Wayne Newton. His was not a bad schedule. We swapped a few lines and then I asked him for his favourite joke.

"I don't tell jokes; Lou. I reminisce. I remember a story Walter Matthau often told. A school teacher was asking her young students about their fathers and the type of work they did:

'And what does your dad do, Lucy?'

'Well, Miss, my father is a lawyer.'

'Nice. And Mandy, what does your father do?'

'Well, he's a doctor.'

'That's great. And Johnny what about your dad?'

'Well, Miss, he's dead.'

Slightly taken aback, the teacher quickly regained her poise.

'And what did he do before he died?'

'Well Miss, he kind of went AGHHHHHHHHHHHHHH!'"

Before we took our leave we invited George to Australia to be our guests on the Nine Network.

"I've been down there twice and loved it and I hope to get down again. At the moment I'm working on my 100th birthday show. I've already booked the Palladium in London." Unbelievable.

III

On the same trip we took in a football match between the San Diego Chargers and the Los Angeles Raiders at the Jack Murphy stadium in San Diego. The highlight was the pre-match entertainment featuring the great Lou Rawls. A couple of nights later we were at the Forum to see the LA Lakers, the reigning world basketball champions, against the Clippers—and what a mismatch that turned out to be. The Lakers with 'Magic' Johnson, Kareem Abdul Jabbar and James Worthy were just too strong and had talent to burn. After the match we were invited down into the rooms and managed to organise a chat with Kareem. It turns out the Lakers love the VFL footy scene and are avid Hawthorn fans. "How's that 'Lethal Leigh' going? Man, he's tough," one seven-footer asked me. I invited Kareem to lunch the next day at our hotel on Rodeo Drive and organised a television interview for *Wide World of Sports*. To understand the magnitude of the Kareem name it was only necessary to look at the panic it caused back at the hotel when we asked to book a table. "Not *the* Kareem?" asked the startled bell-captain who had previously treated our party as a group of yokels from the back of beyond. "Why certainly, Mr Richards. Let's organise a private courtyard."

At 40 years of age and still pulling in a couple of million bucks a year Kareem was in the twilight of his superstar career. This man, who had played 18 seasons, scored 36,000 points, been on the court for 54,000 minutes, made 15,000 field goals and won six most valuable player awards is a living God in America. When he walked in I could see why. At 2.64 metres and with a shiny bald skull, the man tends to stand out in a crowd. I felt like a dwarf as I stared into his navel. George had been a laugh a minute, whereas Kareem was serious, caring and very particular with his answers. He was a thinking man's sportsman, like myself. Basketball took up little of our conversation. I happened to mention to him that he was one of my favourite actors and that certainly loosened him up. I remember him as Roger Roger, the co-pilot in that hilarious movie *Flying High*, and he told me that acting held a certain fascination for him. I felt like telling him to stick to his day job but when you're 81 kilograms lighter and 50 centimetres shorter, you tend to keep those subtle comments to yourself. He did tell me that in his previous 787 games over a 10-year streak he had reached double figures on the scoreboard and this was a record that he cherished. Well, you'll be pleased to know that the old 'Kiss of Death' worked with a vengeance. Within a week of our interview that magic streak came to a grinding halt when he scored 7 points in a match against the Milwaukee Bucks. I was glad I was out of town when I heard about it.

To be truthful it was far easier chatting to the great Kareem than it was to soccer superstar Pele. Back in the mid-1970s the world's greatest living round ball exponent was in Melbourne for an exhibition with his club side, Santos, and my ghost of the time, Tom Prior, had arranged an exclusive interview for the *Sun*. We hopped a cab down to the Queens Road hotel where the great man was booked in and prepared for our showdown. George Wallace, the long-serving secretary of the Victorian Soccer Federation, was on hand to do the introductions but came out with one note of warning. "Louie, you know he doesn't handle English very well? We'll have to work through an interpreter." Face to face with the 'Black Pearl' you got some idea of the man's charisma. It was like an audience with royalty and it took us only a few moments to realise what a genuinely wonderful bloke he was. Obviously Pele felt sorry for us because minutes into the interview he did away with the hired help and answered our questions in fluent English. The interpreter had been used as a blind. This man, who had grown up as a street urchin and become one of the richest and most powerful men in Brazil and who would be rated as the world's premier soccer player, chatted with us as equals. As a matter of fact, as we got up to leave he presented me with his Santos shirt, a memento I've treasured to this day.

III

My family and my friends know of my frustrations—my deep desire to hit show business. My desire has been only partially realised with television and the odd movie appearance over the years. Give me a microphone and I will sing, or try to any way. One of my favourite actors was the late Basil Rathbone and in the late-1950s I was asked if I could take him to a VFL match at the MCG. Ron Casey and I were broadcasting the game for 3DB and Basil was to be our special guest. He had come to Melbourne to star in the stage show *The Marriage Go Round* with the delectable Honni Freger at the Princess Theatre. Now Basil was getting on a bit and was no longer the athletic swordsman who had duelled at length with the great swashbucklers of the silver screen. He was a thoughtful and very dapper senior citizen, suave and immaculately presented, with that long nose overshadowing the pencil-thin moustache. Case and I were a bit overawed at first since it was our first meeting with such movie royalty. As the ice melted so too did my inhibitions.

"You know, Basil," I said in my very best and pucker Collingwood accent, "I've been feeling sorry for you for years."

"What on earth do you mean, Louis?"

"Well, first of all you had to fight Ronald Colman in all those movies and you always got skewered. Then when Ronald Colman died you bumped into Errol Flynn. You were the Sheriff of Nottingham and he was Robin Hood, and he got you in the end. And just when you looked like making it as the good guy, along came Stewart Grainger, and it started all over again."

To say he was flabbergasted would be an understatement. He didn't understand me. He didn't understand football, but he was very polite about it, anyway. The old human shish kebab... he was all style and all class.

If Basil was the arch-conservative on the screen, the epitome of everything pucker and English in the movies, Carol Channing was Hollywood to a tee. In the early-1970s, she flounced into Melbourne for a season of *Gentlemen Prefer Blondes* and won us all over with a flutter of her long eye lashes and those massive eyes. She may well have been past her peak but the old girl could certainly wow them. My mother-in-law Molly was with us at the Phoenix Hotel one day when I said that I'd seen Carol Channing over at the *Sun* office and had actually been introduced. "I'd love to meet her," Molly implored. Over I went and five minutes later was escorting Miss Channing along Flinders Street and up the stairs of the pub. Now the Phoenix was being renovated at the time and there were workmen everywhere. As we climbed the steep stairs to the lounge bar, Carol snagged her beautiful silk trousers on a piece of wood and ripped them from top to bottom. I was totally embarrassed but she just laughed it off, went upstairs and chatted to Molly before giving her, and everyone else in sight, an imitation diamond ring. Her current hit was *Diamonds are a Girl's Best Friend* and the phoney rings were part of the PR get-up. On the way out I asked her to sign our celebrity wall in the press bar and she was only too willing to oblige.

III

We decided to give the press bar on the new mezzanine floor of the Phoenix a bit of a newspaper flavour. We gathered some of the great front pages from Australian and overseas newspapers and had them mounted. On another wall we invited the superstars who frequented the pub to scrawl their signatures. Over the years we built up quite a collection. There was Marjorie Proops, the great columnist; Joe Levine, the Hollywood producer; Robin Nedwell from *Doctor in the House*; Hal Porter, the great Australian writer; plus a whole range of sporting greats. Herb Elliott had visited, as had Dawn Fraser, John Landy and many, many more. Visitors to the pub loved going in and having a beer and scanning the walls, picking out the great names and reading the old papers. It was something that Edna and I were very proud of.

The drinkers at the Phoenix would also notice a little bloke who darted about the place with a short-back-and-sides hair cut. He was a story unto himself. Gordon McMillrick worked for me for years and a more devoted member of staff you'd never meet. Impeccably polite to the women, impeccably rude, if you can understand that, to the male patrons, Gordie was unique. We rarely saw him upstairs where the journalists and their guests drank. He'd busy himself out of sight, cleaning the pipes, running the errands and doing the odd jobs about the place. One morning he woke me up at 7am.

"Boss," he whispered into my ear. "Boss, some bludger, some filthy rotten bludger has been drawing all over the walls in the bar."

As I rubbed the sleep out of my eyes I tried to work out what he was babbling about. When it was just dawning on me he started babbling again.

"But don't worry, Boss. I got a bucket of hot soapy water and scrubbed every bit off," he explained proudly.

Sure enough when I went down later the famous names had disappeared, the fruits of much convincing. At least we had the cleanest hotel wall in Melbourne.

CHAPTER 14

CALLING THE SHOTS

My old mate Ron Casey made some hard-nosed business decisions while running HSV 7 but there was one that stood out miles above the rest. In his wisdom, Ron negotiated with the VFL for the live television coverage of the 1977 VFL Grand Final, handing over a sum reported later to be $100,000 for the exclusive rights. The match was already a sell-out and 108,000 people packed into the Melbourne Cricket Ground on that last Saturday in September to see North Melbourne and Collingwood. It was a promoter's dream. Collingwood under its new coach Tommy Hafey had risen from last on the ladder in 1976 to top spot and beat reigning premiers Hawthorn in the second semifinal by just two points. North Melbourne was appearing in its fourth straight Grand Final and was coached by Ron Barassi. Magpie fans saw it as their best chance of winning the flag since they stunned Melbourne back in 1958, although they'd blown chances in 1960, 1964, 1966 and 1970. I'd been calling football for Seven since 1973 but never had I known tension quite like the build-up to this match. I had lost my long-time partner Mike Williamson and alongside me in the commentary box was a former ABC bloke named Peter Ewin. We were nervous, as you can imagine, because so many television sets in the country would be tuned in to us and secondly because the match was going out by satellite to a host of countries overseas. By three-quarter time I figured that Case had bought a dud. Collingwood were whipping North Melbourne and with half an hour to play led by 27 points. The black-and-white was racing in my veins. Somehow the Barassi magic worked and North Melbourne got back into the match, finally overtaking the shattered Magpies. With a minute or so left on the time-clock I thought that Collingwood had succumbed once again to the dreaded 'Colliewobbles'.

When 'Twiggy' Dunne marked within kicking distance I had my heart thumping in my throat. His goal levelled the scores and set the scene for one of the most remarkable and nailbiting finishes in football history. With seconds remaining Collingwood's Shane Bond, who'd come off the reserve bench, grabbed the ball and started sprinting round the outer wing. A few more metres and he could have scored but the siren beat him to it and for only the second time in 80 years a VFL Grand Final ended with the scores deadlocked. I thought to myself, "Shit, we've blown it." A moment later I realised that we had to come back and do the whole job all over again.

Good old Case had purchased a ratings blockbuster, achieving figures that were Australian TV records and you can bet your bottom dollar that he was back at VFL House bright and early the following Monday with his cheque book in hand. The replay was a better football match as a spectacle but North Melbourne, despite an arduous run of five finals matches in as many weeks, was perfectly tuned by Ron Barassi and won by 27 points. It was the start of live televised Grand Finals in Melbourne and despite the trepidation shown by the VFL in the years before, was a great winner with the sporting public. Looking back on that finals series I always recall with disappointment one aspect. I believe Collingwood was far and away the best team but we lost the flag when our star forward 'Fabulous' Phil Carman whacked Michael Tuck in the second semi-final. Carman had kicked only 40 goals for the season but he was the potential matchwinner in the big game. When he was suspended for two matches our chances of toppling North Melbourne slumped dramatically. That two-week suspension remains the most severe in the tribunal's history. How many players get rubbed out for two Grand Finals for one offence?

III

My radio partnership with Ron Casey at 3DB ended in 1973 when Ron was made station manager of HSV 7 and suggested I come across and call the football with Mike Williamson. Mike has been one of the great personalities on Australian TV and for more than a decade was the best footballer commentator by miles. He was loud and colourful and had the ability to generate excitement, therefore getting the best out of every situation. His breathless call of the 1966 Grand Final in which Barry Breen clinched St Kilda's first win by the merest of a point, is vintage television. He had the added advantage of working with Ted Whitten, Ron Barassi, 'Butch' Gale, Jack Edwards and Frank Adams before he teamed up with me in 1973. Mike was the boss and after the first couple of matches of the season I reckoned he was giving me a hard time. I couldn't get a word in. One Sunday down at *World of Sport* I was chatting to 'Uncle' Doug.

"How's the footy going, Louie?" Doug asked.

"I can't get a bloody word in. Mike never shuts up."

"He's got to come up for breath. When he pauses, you pounce," Doug said.

This was pretty good advice from the bloke who schooled me in the finer arts of football commentary all those years earlier. The following week Mike was calling the game at a thousand miles an hour and I was waiting for the break. He took a deep breath and I pounced. At quarter-time he suggested we alter the call. "Louie, how about we do two minutes on, two minutes off?" he said. From that moment on we never looked back. Mike knew everyone and was on first-name terms with everyone, from the pope down to the bloke at the gate. It was 'Newk' this and 'Muscles' that but the cruel thing was that he actually did know these sporting champs and was, in fact, good mates with all of them. It was a sad day for HSV 7 and for football when Mike decided to quit in 1976. His reasons were personal but many times over the years I wished that he was back calling because blokes of his calibre are hard to find. Generally the lot of a football commentator is a pretty happy one. The clubs like you to be at their games, they look after you, and the commentary positions have been improved enormously. This situation is a far cry from one of my first TV games for Seven at Subiaco in Perth in 1971.

Ron Casey and I called a simulcast of the state match between Victoria and Western Australia for 3DB and HSV 7. All was going well until Victoria's young rover Leigh Matthews earned his 'Lethal' nickname with a vengeance. He ran through Barry Cable, the golden-haired veteran of Western Australian football, knocking the little bloke flat. It was sickening to see. Can you imagine a diesel hitting a car at a level crossing? That's how it looked through my field glasses and I winced as I saw Matthews virtually carry Cable for about 20 metres. The thing I love about Leigh is that he just keeps on playing as if nothing has happened. It's a man's sport and you cop the knocks, as far as he's concerned, and I respect him for that opinion. In the commentary box, however, things were getting heated. The Western Australian crowd are parochial at the best of times but that afternoon they went mad. Ron and I were Victorian and that was enough for them. I was glad to get out of the joint and back on the plane. I told Ron that if that flight was delayed I'd swim home. On the subject of Leigh Matthews, I would like to make one point. He's one of the greatest footballers I've ever seen and an object lesson to kids. He never took his eye off the ball, whether while roving or resting in the forward pocket. You tend to overlook the fact that he was big for a rover-about 1.78 metres and close to 88.9 kilograms. Being hit by Leigh was like being hit by a truck but he would have been the first player chosen by VFL coaches in any side from the mid-1970s on. He played 340 games, kicked 915 goals and was Hawthorn's best and fairest eight times. Add four premierships and 14 state guernseys and you get some idea of his worth. To me the legend began that afternoon in Perth, all those years ago, when he made that shattering debut for Victoria. It's no mean feat to come close to starting a civil war in your first appearance.

III

All up I called football for 15 seasons on HSV 7; four with Mike Williamson, one with Peter Ewin and the last 10 with Peter Landy. People loved to knock Landy but to work with him was a joy. Although he loved being opinionated he was the consummate professional, never flustered and always totally prepared. It stuns me to see him left off big match coverages these days. Peter did have one major failing: he was a mad one-eyed Hawthorn supporter and though he tried his best to appear unbiased it often worked in reverse when he was calling a game. Hawthorn would be playing some mob and be trailing by three goals five minutes into the match. Peter would drop them, stone dead. "Well, Hawthorn are gone, they've folded," Landy would tell his tens of thousands of viewers. You couldn't say he was a man of great faith, our Peter.

I have always believed that the former player is the one whose job it should be to voice his opinion about football. It was a lesson I learned over many years with Doug Elliott, Ron Casey and Mike Williamson. Bob Skilton had won three Brownlow Medals and was possibly the best expert comments man I've worked with, and I had played 250 games. We have the credibility to make statements, to praise or criticise. Backing up the commentary team of Landy, Richards and Skilton was Alf Potter, the doyen of football directors and the man who did more to establish Seven as the football network than any other. Alf had started off Seven's live sports coverage in the 1950s and was with them, through the introduction of colour, to the 1980s. He was our pilot and guided us through some rough waters. I remember Alf's voice in my headset. I recall his voice in one ear and the crowd noise in the other. Alf would be pointing out incidents and telling us to prepare for a commercial break or merely saying "well done". He was always there. One night Bobby Skilton was summarising the match and had forgotten a very crucial point. "They beat them for the ball, were too strong in defence; that's right Alf, and they had a winning forward line," Skilton said.

We all broke up.

To Alf must go much of the credit for the technically superb coverage of League football. Seven have done for football what nine have done for cricket and to see both you realise how spoilt we are here in Australia. A few years ago a sporting producer was visiting from the USA. She sat in with Peter Landy and me as we called a VFL match and she was stunned. "Where are the cue cards? Where's the autocue?" she asked. In the United States the top sporting commentators don't ad lib. Here you'd be dead if you couldn't. Most Saturday afternoons Peter Landy would have to leave the match before time-on to beat the traffic and make his way back to Dorcas Street, South Melbourne, to read the sporting news and front 'The Big League' replay. That meant I would have to call the last five minutes of the game and then sum up for our live audience around Australia. For some reason one afternoon the game finished 14 minutes early and after a five-minute summary I was ready to say goodbye. Alf was onto me like a shot. "Keep going. Stretch it out," he said down the line. For 14 minutes I talked about bugger all and if you don't reckon that's hard give it a go some time.

III

The highlights for a football commentator are surely the VFL finals. The lowlights used to be the night football at VFL Park.

Back in 1977 the VFL launched the $200,000 Amco Herald Cup under the brand new lights at football's headquarters at VFL Park. Before that we had night football down at the Lakeside Oval at South Melbourne but the poor spectator facilities, the lack of interest by the clubs and the dreadful lighting combined to bring down the curtain in 1971. In the mid-1970s the National Football League, under Keith Webb, organised competitions that were Adelaide based so it was only a matter of time before the VFL jumped on the bandwagon. Fitzroy and North were scheduled to play the first game under the lights at Waverley in May 1977 and more than 8000 had trekked out to the Park to see this latest innovation. Peter Ewin and I had taken up our positions and all was in readiness. There was only one small problem: the lights hadn't come on. How embarrassing! After 20 minutes the red-faced chiefs of the VFL discovered that some person, unnamed to this day, had kicked out a plug, keeping the whole stadium in darkness. It was the first of a number of incidents at the Park at night which haunt me.

Years later Carlton were playing and as was our practice we were preparing to name our best player of the night. The prize was a portable colour television. I personally thought Peter Bosustow, the Blues' modest and self-effacing forward, was a lay down misere. He'd played well and caught my eye. Someone mentioned Robert Klomp, the South Australian half-back flanker. To be honest I couldn't recall him doing anything wrong all night, so like a fool I let myself be swayed. Bob Skilton and Peter Landy mentioned other names but finally Doug Wade on the ground gave the vote to Klomp too. In the rooms Klomp look delighted to win the prize. When they flashed his match statistics up on the screen I could see why. In four-quarters of football he'd accumulated no kicks, no marks and dispensed two handpasses. Doug Wade said later that he'd been a stout defender and that had swayed him. It reminded me of a certain *Herald* football writer who awarded a Fitzroy player three votes in the *Herald* award one Monday night. There were some red faces when the bloke was dropped from the team the following Thursday night. Talking of Peter Bosustow, I can't help but think what a wasted talent he was to Carlton. He flashed in, did some brilliant things and then promptly left and returned home to Perth. He took the screamer of the 1980s at Princes Park one day, standing on the shoulders of Justin Madden, the Blues' 2.08 metre ruckman. As he fell to the ground in front of the Robert Heatley stand he still managed a dig at big Justin, "Don't worry mate, you'll be on *World of Sport*'s Mark of the Day tomorrow," Bosustow said, omitting to mention that Justin would be appearing in strictly a support role.

III

Another night the 'Buzz' had played a blinder and as he walked into the dressing rooms after the game, our man on the spot, Stephen Phillips, grabbed him to tell him he'd won the TV as player of the night. "Stuff the TV. Give me a call when I've won the car as player of the series," Bosustow said and promptly headed for the showers. One night in 1982 the Sydney Swans were playing St Kilda at VFL Park and the fog rolled in—a real pea souper that was so thick that you could barely see the players as they ran onto the ground. I've never called football in conditions like it. Amazingly the cameras seemed to cut through the fog and we could just call the play from the monitors in front of us. Alf Potter explained to us technical dunderheads later that the cameras were fitted with special filters for such a problem.

The same season Richmond played Swan Districts, John Todd's team from Perth, and a paltry crowd of just over 2000 saw one of the most incredible sharpshooting performances ever. The Tigers' full-forward Michael Roach started the game on the bench and didn't make an appearance until the nine-minute mark of the third-quarter. His 10 kicks netted him 10 goals and Richmond won by 186 points. I felt sorry for the Western Australians. It was like shooting sitting ducks. The poor old Sandgropers have always had miserable memories of VFL Park but nobody has worse than the Claremont boys who came over here under Graham Moss in 1979. They'd won their first-round match and were giving Hawthorn, the reigning VFL premiers, a nice touch along when all of a sudden the ground opened up and the sprinklers appeared. The Krakouers had been cutting Hawthorn to ribbons but with the ground suddenly slippery they and their team-mates faded and the Hawks moved towards yet another Grand Final.

There has always been something about VFL Park that has made it different from any other football stadium in the land. The fact that the bigwigs who bought the 212 acres of grazing land 30 years ago didn't realise that it was smack in the middle of a rain belt probably has something to do with it. Every year since 1977 when I started those night odysseys, Jack Edwards would pick me up in Toorak at six o'clock in the evening. It would be fine, with the first stars appearing on the horizon. By the time we got to Waverley it would be belting down and cold as well. Some nights it was so cold in the Channel Seven commentary box that I'd wear a pair of Edna's woollen tights under my slacks and be forced to wear gloves to stop my fingers freezing to my binoculars. I reckon if they built VFL Park in the middle of the Sahara Desert it would have become an oasis inside a year. Full marks to the VFL for having the initiative to move the series to a proper pre-season competition in 1989. The attendances boomed—up 13 per cent—and big crowds enjoyed watching their teams take part in fine, warm and dry conditions.

III

There was a time when I could be critical of the VFL but since they made me a life member in 1988 I've seen things their way more frequently. One thing that intrigues me is the rules review committee they formed a couple of years ago to look at changes to the laws of the game. Ron Casey was invited, as was Bobby Skilton, and I couldn't fault either appointment. It was the decision to include Ron Barassi that stumped me. Now, Ron has been one of the game's greats. He's probably the most inspiring captain to grace a football field and with over 200 games and six premierships with Melbourne, one of the most successful. As a coach with Carlton and North Melbourne he had few equals, although his five years at Melbourne bought him right back to the field. The old saying "players make coaches" was never better illustrated. Anyway, Ron's appointment made me think back to one of his brainwaves a few years ago. In a further bid to speed up the game, Ron suggested that big nets be built at the back of the goals to stop the ball being kicked into the crowd and halt the time-wasting of its retrieval. Tom Prior and I came up with a state-of-the-art development that enraged the supercoach. We designed a system in which the ball would hit the net, be funnelled into an underground tunnel and then be whipped back to the centre by a conveyor belt. The umpire would push a button and the ball would be sent up for the ruckman to do battle. It sounded simple; Ron was furious.

"You guys are a couple of smart arses," Barassi said. "You can't come up with an idea yourself but you have to knock other people."

"That's the trouble with you Barass. You think you're a genius but you know stuff-all about anything," I replied with a touch of Collingwood Tech.

Ron is one of those people who loves an argument. He's become a bit of an intellectual these days and calls them debates, but that aside, he loves being toe to toe. Seriously, few people have put as much into football as Ronald Dale Barassi and I love him dearly for it. He will blue until he's red in the face, especially on camera, but the moment you're finished he's cool and level headed and best mates again.

There was one moment in my football commentating career when level heads didn't prevail—the 1982 VFL Grand Final. Carlton and Richmond were putting up a terrific battle when out of the corner of my eye I spotted a naked woman running onto the ground. This was our first VFL Grand Final streaker and a good sort at that. Now, I've got a degree in arse-ology from Collingwood Tech., and I can spot a good-looker even at my advanced age and this bouncing blonde or brunette or redhead was OK. Alf Potter was having apoplexy in the van and the instructions were hitting my left ear like machine gun bullets. "Ignore her. Keep calling the game," Alf barked down the line. Ignore her, my arse, I thought and noted that Peter Landy had swung his field glasses onto the cavorting maiden as she made a beeline for the reticent Bruce Doull. 'The Flying Doormat' wanted nothing to do with her but I got the feeling that a couple of the blokes out there on the MCG that day wouldn't have minded a private interview later in the evening. Alf kept his cameras trained on this most pleasant interruption until she was finally tackled by the police and led from the ground to the cheers of the 100,000-plus crowd. It turned out she was a professional dancer from Adelaide who regularly exhibited her ample wares at some establishment named The Crazy Horse or thereabouts.

CHAPTER 15

THREE WISE OLD MONKEYS

And it came to pass that a great pestilence descended
upon the ancient city of Melbourne, and none of its
inhabitants was untouched, and some were heard to
cry out in strange tongues!
And every seven days the young men of the city would
meet in combat.
And each Thursday three wise men would sit in judgement.
And the wise men were John, Robert and Louie!
And their judgement was delivered in *League Teams*!

To the strains of the Hallelujah chorus, these words were the
cue for one of the most remarkable and durable shows in television.
Every Thursday night for more than 15 years *League Teams* was
beamed out of HSV 7's South Melbourne studios.

It was the cheapest TV in Australian broadcasting history. There
were a couple of microphones, a desk and three ex-footballers who

generally saved the station a quid by applying their own makeup. John, of course, was the notorious 'Captain Blood', the one and only Jack Dyer. Robert was the 'Geelong Flyer', the former All Australian captain and Geelong premiership coach Bob Davis, and Louie, the 'Kiss of Death', was yours truly. Together we turned what might have been a run-of-the-mill selection night footy panel into 30 minutes of mayhem. The ratings books rarely mirrored our following but we reckon we built a massive specialist audience over the years which included blokes who'd just come home from the boozer after a 10-hour lunch, insomniacs, hippies, football freaks and fringe players who were desperate to know if they'd cracked the big-time. I'd always been dark on Seven's executive sporting producer of the early-1970s, one Gary Fenton, for cracking onto the three wise monkey theme—hear no evil, see no evil, and say no evil. Too many people had commented on my resemblance to those furry critters over the years as it was. We were given the latest time slot they could drag up, yet over the years our cult following grew to such an extent that Melbourne, Monash and Latrobe Universities all had their own *League Teams* fan clubs. Each year they'd write in, begging for seats in the audience. That's how thick some of them were: they thought the canned laughter was the real thing.

Over the years we played to an empty studio, two cameramen and our long-time floor manager Wayne Fosternelli. Wayne was probably the most sartorial floor manager I'd ever worked with. He wore bell-bottom trousers and then flairs before they became a recognised fashion accessory. Jack used to look at him and say, "Take a look at those flairs. He looks like Rudolph Valentino tango dancing." Nothing fazed Wayne. He had the job of shutting us up so they could squeeze in the commercials, and occasionally he would. Basically the show was designed to announce the 12 teams for Saturday's round of VFL matches. By the time we pulled down the curtain at the end of the 1986 season, we were telling gags, reciting poetry, reading out recipes and indulging in non-stop banter and namedropping. It got so bad that the chairman of HSV 7 Dick Sampson, a committed Essendon supporter, finally rang Ron Casey, the general manager, and complained that his side was up and down so quickly that he couldn't read the team. The following day Case was onto us like a load of bricks. The gist of the message was to cut down on the rubbish and do the job we were paid to do, and that was to read out the teams. The next week we showed the Essendon team 16 times and Dick Sampson showed the white flag. There was no more executive interference.

III

League Teams had its birth many years ago on the wireless. It was a straightlaced announcement of the men to play that round of football. In 1959 I joined Ron Casey on 3DB's football team show at 8.30pm on Thursday nights. I tried to inject a little humour into the show but in those days people expected you to be serious. Ron recruited former VFL Grand Final umpire Allan Nash in 1960 and the three of us started turning the show around. I made it my job to upset the former man in white and he hated becoming flustered. Ron and he would drive in from Brighton to the studios in Flinders Lane and along the way Allan would vow not to get sucked in. "He won't get me tonight," Nashy would tell Ron as they drove along Point Nepean Road. Within 10 minutes he'd be gone, baited and caught.

The natural extension of *League Teams* on the radio was 3DJ3's excellent coverage of the Brownlow Medal count, live from Harrison House, the VFL headquarters in Spring Street. In those days, and right up to 1970, there was no televised count and the Brownlow Medal had not become the extravaganza it would be in the years ahead. Ron had the idea of sending his trusted emissaries out to the homes of the favoured players with the view of the scoop interview moments after the winner's name was announced. Rival radio stations and interlopers like Graham Kennedy and his *In Melbourne Tonight* were also in the race to get the winner on their shows first. In 1963 Essendon's Ken Fraser was highly fancied and I was dispatched to the Fraser home to be on standby in case the Bombers' champ took out the game's greatest individual honour. We were looked after magnificently and dined sumptuously on the cakes cooked by his mum. As the count got going it was obvious that Kenny wasn't going to win. Every time Bob Skilton polled votes, Ken would start clapping. I couldn't understand it. "Oh, Louie, he's a marvellous player—one of the best," Kenny would say as his hopes dwindled. After a few more votes went Skilton's way I realised that I was in the wrong spot. Embarrassed but with a job to do, I stood up, thanked Mrs Fraser for the cakes and took my leave, bolting out of the house and making a beeline for the Moorabbin home of Bobby Skilton, and I remember making it in the nick of time. Skilton won the medal; it was his second in five years while Kenny was to finish six votes behind in sixth place. I reckon his mum should have won the medal for her cakes that night.

A couple of years later Ross Smith was the favourite and Case sent me to St Kilda's Moorabbin ground. He had been told that arrangements had been made to smuggle Smith out of the ground and to a television studio, should he win. "Go down to Moorabbin, put on a hat and overcoat and stay out of sight," Case told me. I followed these managerial orders perfectly, donning my heaviest overcoat and pulling my old hat over my eyes. I found a quiet part of the car park and stood under a tree, listening to the count on my pocket radio. There was only one hitch: every time a car pulled up the occupants would get out, walk over and say, "G'day, Louie. He's a good thing tonight," or "Smithy's the one." My cover was blown but when Ross won the medal by a massive seven votes, he walked out amidst a bevy of St Kilda officials and I nabbed him: mission accomplished.

III

By 1970 Ron Casey was firmly entrenched at HSV 7, the Brownlow Medal was a massive ratings blockbuster on television and the coverage of football on radio was beginning to wane. Ron suggested that we move *League Teams* onto the television and he and I would team up with Jack Dyer. It wasn't long before Ron had to stand down as compere and he found the perfect replacement in Bob Davis. Over the years I've met a million blokes who reckon Bob's dumb. I don't subscribe to the popular theory. I always tell them, "Find 10 of your mates and put $100 in each of their pockets. Within an hour Bob will have found a way to dispossess them of the lot." A sharp, flashy footballer, he was one of the greats and a genuinely witty bloke on television. Bob has lived most of his life in Sleepy Hollow, as I like to call Geelong, and calls himself a "purveyor of classic pre-loved autos". In other words, he flogs second-hand cars. He remains to this day the only man who has ever coached Victoria to defeat on the Melbourne Cricket Ground and I'll rub that in as long as I live. All the same he was ideal to take over the compere's chair recently vacated by Casey.

One year the executive sporting producer Gordon Bennett had the bright idea of dressing up our set for the last show of the year in which we would introduce the Grand Final line-ups. We would dress up in dinner suits with black ties, have our desk immaculately decked out with shiny candelabras and have chandeliers glinting in the background. Bob announced proudly that the evening's show was coming live from the sumptuous surroundings of the Richards penthouse, offering viewers a rare insight into the living conditions of the rich and famous. The next day I bumped in North Melbourne's coach Ron Barassi.

"Crikey, Lou, that penthouse of yours looks fabulous," the master coach enthused. "You dummy. That was done in the studio," I informed him. (Coaches—they're all the same!)

The black ties almost cost Bob his job. Over the season Bob had built up his friendship with a South Yarra clothing retailer named Charles Lux. Bob was forever calling in and adding to his wardrobe. Finally Bob suggested that if Charles supplied the Yves St Laurent dinner suits, the 'Geelong Flyer' would do the rest. Well, Bob never let up. Despite the fact that we had a rival clothing mob advertising and paying handsomely for the rights, Bob wouldn't let up on Charles Lux. He must have mentioned the store 20 times. Twelve months later he was still at it and Casey and Bennett were pulling their hair out. Case read the riot act to him and Gordon Bennett suggested that one more mention would result in his TV demise. That Thursday night Bob looked anything but worried. We'd been going about a minute and a half when I said to Bob.

"No mention of 'you know who' tonight, Bob."

"No, Louie. No mention of Charles Lux," he said.

Well, he must have mentioned his name 15 times in 20 minutes and everyone was so exasperated that the matter just died a natural death.

Jack Dyer always arrived looking as though he'd just woken up. He'd walk into the make-up room, apply his own with the panache of a Red Indian chief and walk into the studio. Most of the time he looked as though he was sound asleep but during the ad breaks he'd wake up. Our major sponsor was Carlton and United Breweries and they flogged Carlton Draught mercilessly on the show. Out of the break I'd say to Jack, "You can't beat a long cold glass of Foster's." Jack would look vacantly at me and say, "Yes you can." I'd sit there and think that the big dummy was going to bugger it up. I was waiting for him to mention Courage, the rival brand. Like an old ham, Jack would lean into the microphone and drawl, "Give me a glass of Victoria Bitter any day."

Early on we did a commercial for the drag show 'My Bare Lady' or some such production and three of the blokes waltzed into the studio done up as women. Jack couldn't take his eyes off them. At one point we were sitting there with a 'lady' each on our knees. When they left Jack couldn't stop talking about them.

"The one on my knee was a ripper sort," Jack said.

"But, Jack, it was a bloke," I pleaded.

"I don't care if she was a bloke; she was a bloody good sort."

The one thing about Jack is that you can't beat him. For years he'd park his car out the front of the studios and come out hours later, after a few relaxing ales, and find it was gone. In fact, it hadn't moved. Jack had merely forgotten where he'd parked it. Things became so bad that Jack invested in a massive steering wheel lock and would sit there fiddling with the contraption for ages before and after the show. (It wasn't as if any self-respecting car thief would have hankered after Jack's old Holden.)

Jack always had trouble with names and found it nigh on impossible to decipher some of the more ethnic names that had snuck into football. The young Hawthorn winger Robert DiPierdomenico was a nightmare for him, and Robert just wouldn't go away. Jack started with Robert Domenico, then it became Robert Dipper-menico and he finally settled on Dipper. In real life he had the same problems. The story goes that Jack was called to the courts one day to give evidence about a fellow employee at the *Truth*. Jack was asked by the magistrate to identify one of his workmates.

"What's his name?" the magistrate enquired.

"Bongo," said Jack.

Jack didn't have a clue but had called this bloke 'Bongo' for years and to him that was close enough. Poor old Rollo Roylance, the racing editor of the *Sporting Globe*, had worked with Jack on *World of Sport* for more than 20 years. To the very last show Jack called him Roylo Rollo. Bob and I were lucky: it's hard to stuff up a three-lettered name.

III

Television has changed markedly since those early days of *League Teams*. I recall Bob Davis being hauled over the coals by Ron Casey for telling off-colour gags. "Why do Catholics have bigger balls than Protestants?" Bob asked me. I shook my head. Jack, always the prude, buried his in his massive gnarled hands. "Because they sell more tickets." Bob shrieked with laughter but wasn't so cocky when Case got through with him. Another time I was extolling the virtues of a hot dog at the footy and saying how nothing could be nicer washed down with a can or two of Fosters. "Yeah," said Jack nonchalantly. "I love a franger at the footy." While some people might believe there is some similarity in texture between a frankfurter and a condom, the majority of people who lit up the switchboard didn't see the joke.

Mrs Moon, a publican in Geelong, was also soured at the *League Teams* humour and hit us with a writ. We had a habit of sending cheerios. They were not sanctioned by the station and both Gordon Bennett and Ron Casey would repeatedly tell us off. Still, they persisted. We always said hello to Mrs Yabby, the wife of Hawthorn's coach Allan Jeans; to Maureen Hafey, wife of Tommy; to all Sam Newman's ex-wives and, of course, to Pauline Casey, which infuriated Ron. Mrs Moon was a favourite, however.

"Mrs Moon hasn't been too good," Bob announced one night.

"Oh," I said, "what's wrong?"

"She's had two plastic hips put in."

"That's bad luck."

"You're not wrong. The other night things go so hot, one melted."

If that didn't infuriate Mrs Moon the next exchange wouldn't have helped. "You know Mrs Moon's husband hasn't spoken to her for three weeks," Bob said. "Poor bloke didn't want to interrupt her." We settled out of court for costs and we had to apologise for holding her to public ridicule.

Talking of being held to public ridicule, we were preparing for the show one night when Case told us we all had to appear at the Plough Hotel in Footscray the next day to film six 30-second commercials for Courage beer. Jack Dyer, Bob Skilton, Peter Landy, Keith Greig, the North Melbourne winger, Footscray's Bernie Quinlan and I duly arrived the next morning at 9.30am. The idea was that each of us had to say a word or two in each of the advertisements and the end product would be shown the following Monday night in Seven's exclusive Brownlow Medal telecast, sponsored by Courage. The first couple of commercials went like a breeze but soon the constant sipping and the heavy pace started to tell. Bobby Skilton hadn't sipped anything stronger than lemonade until he turned 28 and was wishing he was back in those teetotal days when it was his turn to star. We had 10 takes and every time Bobby stumbled on the word 'integrity'. "Integ-etry," he'd say time and again and the crew kept filling up our glasses and starting all over again. In my starring role I had to carry a tray of drinks and lean across Jack to deliver my lines. By this time we were all nicely pissed. Jack was fed up and delivered one of those coaching addresses that would have boiled his players' blood three decades early. "No matter what happens this time, no one say nothing," was Jack's sage advice. This was pretty good advice in a bloody commercial in which we all had lines to deliver. As I leaned over Jack I hadn't realised but the beer was trickling down 'Captain Blood's neck, a stream becoming a torrent. 'The Captain' didn't flinch. He sat there silently. Sure enough I made a mistake, and then another and by the time we got onto the sixth take everyone was breaking up, all except Jack, who didn't say a word. It was possibly the longest and hardest day I have ever put in and one I couldn't repeat.

III

As *League Teams* came to its end, courtesy of the Fairfax shakeup, a large hunk of footballing folklore went down the drain. How many shows could send up people so mercilessly? Who, apart from Jack Dyer and Lou Richards, could ask the governor of Victoria over for a nip or two after work? Sir Henry Winneke lived across from HSV 7 in St Kilda Road at Government House and Jack often remarked to me that the lights were always on when he drove home on Thursday nights after the show. "Let's invite him to the Grand Final edition of the show. He can be our special guest," I suggested and sat down and wrote him a letter. "Dear Sir Henry," the letter started, "I know you're a mad Hawthorn supporter and a keen viewer of *League Teams*. Jack knows this because your lights are always on late on Thursday evenings." Well, we invited him over for a beer but alas, he had a prior engagement that night. He did reply and said that he was an avid viewer of the antics of the three wise monkeys and would love to have a beer at our convenience. Jack was delighted. He suggested that we go over to Government House and watch *League Teams* with the guv. Seeing we did the show live every week, I'm not quite sure how Jack was going to manage it.

CHAPTER 16

MY MATES BOB

The ballroom of the Southern Cross Hotel was hushed on the morning of Saturday 24 September, 1988 as the prime minister made his way to the podium. Bob Hawke and I had been regulars at North Melbourne's Grand Final breakfasts over the years. Bob would enjoy a free plate of bacon and eggs and a glass of orange juice while 'Louie the Lip' at the microphone would wow the crowd with brilliant repartee.

On this occasion Bob and I were sharing the top table along with every dignitary, major and minor, in town for the VFL Grand Final between Hawthorn and Melbourne. Bob softened them up with a bit of patter, the old Canberra soft-shoe shuffle, and then turned his attention to me. "You might not know this," the prime minister told the 1200-strong audience, "but Lou Richards is one of Australia's top conservationists. Yesterday we appeared together on a show (Ray Martin's *Midday Show* on Nine) and he told a couple of jokes that I first heard him tell 33 years ago. I've never met a man who can conserve a joke like him." How can you win? Sure enough, we'd shared the stage the previous day with Max Walker and Ray Martin and naturally enough I whipped out my Bob Hawke patter, and didn't the blue-rinse set in the studio at GTV 9 in Richmond lap it up. I wowed them with the one about Bob coming home after being elected to parliament for the first time.

"I've been elected to Parliament," Bob told Hazel.

"Honestly?" she said.

"Sh."

As they rolled about the aisles I hit him right between the eyes. "You know, Bob Hawke would do anything for the workers, except become one!" They loved it and the old silver fox just sat there and was, naturally, upstaged.

As a bloke who traded his dungarees and overalls for the imported Italian suits and silk shirts, and made the move from Collingwood to the upper limits of Toorak, I've also moved up in the social set. Over the years I've moved into that elite circle of people who manage to get on first-name terms with the leaders of industry, with the people who run our country. Way back in the early-1960s, HSV 7 had a show called *Meet the Press*. It was a high-brow intellectual free-for-all, just the opposite to *World of Sport*. As it happened the show was often taped on Sunday morning while our sports show was on live in another studio. One morning I spotted Bob Menzies heading into the make-up room followed by his horde of minders. I raced back into the studio and ran straight into Ron Casey.

"Ron, the prime minister just walked into make-up," I said.

"Go and ask him for an interview," Case said in his usual deadpan manner. (Fair dinkum, all producers are the same—full of bright ideas.) If I had a hat, I would have gone hat in hand but I didn't, so I walked into the make-up room and confronted the great man as he was having those monstrous eyebrows touched up and the jowls powdered.

"Sir," I stammered.

"Yes, what is it?"

"I, er, Ron Casey, er, was wondering if you'd like to come on *World of Sport* this morning, if you've got time?"

"You're rather cheeky, young Richards. Of course I'll come on the show. I'd be honoured," Mr Menzies replied.

Well, he was just fantastic talking sport with Case. He was a great orator, a great lover of cricket and a great fan of the Carlton Football Club. As it transpired, he was also an avid viewer of *World of Sport* and knew he'd be richly rewarded for his appearance. As the interview wound up, I made my appearance with arms laden with giveaways and goodies from our sponsors and old Bob didn't let us down. Without even the slightest hesitation he popped the Huttons' Gold Nugget Ham under his arm, grabbed the Hardy champagne and the tie and marched off to his next appointment.

III

Not long after this meeting I was at the MCG for a Test match between Australia and the West Indies and I was strolling through the member's reserve with my ghost writer of the time, Barrie Bretland.

"How are you, young Richards?" came a voice from the official enclosure. "Fine thank you," I replied and I kept walking.

Barrie Bretland was aghast. "That was the prime minister talking to you, Lou," Barrie managed.

"Yeah, I know. Bob and I are old friends."

In fact, I was too nervous to stop and chat. Bob Menzies, Harold Holt and John Gorton all made cameo appearances on *World of Sport* and were terrific sports, enjoying the ribbing of the blokes but lapping up the limelight. They were the top politicians of their day. Smooth, eloquent and utterly Liberal, they were completely the opposite to our resident sitting member, the one and only Douglas Elliott.

'Uncle' Doug was fiercely Labor and for 20 years the ALP member for Melbourne Province in the Legislative Council, under Jack Galbally. In later years he would become firmly ensconced as mayor of his beloved Essendon. They called Doug plenty of names over the years; some were kind, some respectful but there were many others that won't appear in print here or anywhere else. To generations of sports fans, however, he was plain old 'Uncle' Doug, the one-time host of the *SSB Club* and the front man for the *Mickey Mouse Club* in the formative years of children's TV. He was, as I mentioned earlier, the driving force behind *World of Sport*, the original owner of the show, its number-one salesman and for 30 years its resident spruiker. For close to 30 years the show would open with one of Doug's hastily scribbled poems which were alive and to the point:

Love our sport,
Love that sport,
The all-in blue with Lou,
The loud retort.
Where friendship counts
And tension mounts
One little slip and the boys will pounce.
That's *World of Sport*, an all-in cavort,
Now here's Casey with our first report,
SPORT!

'Uncle' Doug had his own corner of the studio, a meeting place where the greats of the sporting world would stop and chat with a bloke who'd seen it all and knew them all like old mates. He was a few steps away from the pie warmer and legend has it that Doug could actually eat two Four'N Twenty pies at the same time, with the sauce sandwiched between them. Australian Test wicket-keeper Rodney Marsh might have set a new record by downing 40 odd cans of beer on the flight to London for a Test series but when it came to pies, 'Uncle' Doug was the world champion. He could clean out a pie warmer full of our favourite product before the first segment of the show had gone to air. I would guess that most kids and certainly their parents as well had no idea that the portly gent with the booming laugh and endless repartee actually did anything else but flog stuff on *World of Sport*. Few would have guessed that he was a respected parliamentarian for two decades. Instead they saw him as the bloke selling shirts to the fatsos, Patra orange juice to an audience of committed beer drinkers and Italian smallgoods to an audience that lived for that next meat pie. The master of ad lib, the blusterer, the booming voice in the background—'Uncle' was all of that and more, but most importantly he became the heart of *World of Sport*. He was always on hand to prop up the youngster making his first appearance, to crack a gag with a grizzled VFL veteran or to put a rocket up one of the regulars if he felt that we were flagging. The live ad was Doug's domain, his bread and butter, and he was jealously possessive.

III

Sam Newman had played over 300 VFL games with Geelong and had been to the altar three times by the time he joined the *World of Sport* football panel in 1981. He was a man of the world, brash and confident and he moved with the conviction of a bloke who actually wore white boots to match his blond tips. Yes, Sam Newman was ready for television. After football and the sports night circuit, *World of Sport* was the natural progression. Early on Sam plucked a lucrative advertising job on the show that required a live read each Sunday—a piece of cake for our boy. In those days the copy was written in large letters on a piece of butchers' paper and held at eye level next to the camera. The secret was to read the ad without actually looking as though you were reading. Sam practised for hours before the show and actually had it word perfect. In fact he was foolish to even resort to the idiot sheet.

The time came and Sam began his ad, flogging his product through houses in Victoria, southern NSW and Tasmania. 'Uncle' Doug looked on, a more-than-interested bystander. Sam had moved past the halfway mark and was looking good. Doug sauntered past and whipped out his cigarette lighter. The look in Sam's eyes turned to pleading as Doug flicked the lighter into action and casually set the sheet with the magic words alight. No matter how fast Sam read, he couldn't beat the flames as they engulfed his 30 seconder.

That was the baptism of fire. The next week Sam prepared longer and harder and got 'Uncle' Doug to promise that the cigarette lighter would stay in his pocket. He looked a million dollars as he ambled through his script, using that carefully cultivated Geelong Grammar diction, pausing at the right breaks. From the corner of his eye he saw Doug move into view. Nonchalantly the parliamentarian turned, undid his belt buckle and dropped his strides to the studio floor, baring enormous white buttocks. Sam lost his place, fumbled and regained his composure, momentarily. When 'Uncle' Doug bent over to pick up his crumpled trousers, the view from Sam's position was monstrous and the former Geelong captain stumbled, spluttered and went to water. It was all over, a complete mismatch.

CHAPTER 17

SWITCHING CHANNELS

In the space of a week in March 1987 HSV 7 Melbourne self-destructed. *World of Sport* came to a tearful end, *League Teams* died without even a chance to bid farewell and our 30-year association with the VFL ended unceremoniously. It's hard to look back without bitterness at the way the events unfolded, and the singular lack of communication from the people who ran Seven in Melbourne. To be fair, I don't think they knew themselves. ATN 7 and the Fairfax push in Sydney had taken control and Melbourne was merely an outpost; football was a minor consideration.

To millions of viewers Seven's coverage of VFL football from live telecasts interstate on Saturday afternoons, through *World of Sport*, the Big League Replay, the *Junior Supporter's Club* and *League Teams*, had become part of the Melbourne lifestyle. Kids had grown up watching footy on Seven, blokes went to work and canned our commentary, old ladies rang and abused us for our parochial attitudes and tens of thousands more just sat back and enjoyed every moment of it.

Without being immodest, I felt that the least the hierarchy at Seven could have done was to have called and filled me in on what was happening in my particular sphere and to have perhaps saved me from the embarrassment of what was to loom one Tuesday night at VFL Park. On Tuesday 17 March Melbourne were drawn to play Hawthorn in the second quarter-final of the National Panasonic Cup. Under lights, this would be a match that would attract about 6000 diehards. Seven Sport had reintroduced night football back in 1977 and for 11 seasons I had been part of the main commentary team, first with Peter Ewin and then for a decade with Peter Landy. This particular night Pete Landy, Jack Edwards (the former North Melbourne full-back who covered the rooms) and I were enjoying our traditional pre-match dinner in the VFL members' dining room. A cameraman ambled over and casually announced that Seven had dropped its coverage of football and the rights had been picked up by the ABC. I was flabbergasted—absolutely shocked. Seven had controlled the football rights for the VFL telecasts for 30 years, sometimes in conjunction with the other commercial TV networks and hand-in-hand with the ABC.

III

At the end of 1986, just after Christmas to be precise, Ross Oakley, the chief commissioner of the League, had announced that Broadcom, a Sydney-based company, would manage the rights for the VFL. The murmur from the seventh floor at HSV 7 was strong. Seven would not work through a middle man for the rights. Through January and February negotiations continued and HSV 7 finally worked out an agreement with Broadcom. It was to be short-lived and, in footy parlance, Seven handballed the rights to the ABC on the eve of the season.

I have never been a bitter person but I feel the VFL made a big mistake when, in a bid to win more money, it farmed out the footy rights to an entrepreneurial mob. I felt the VFL had quickly forgotten the amount of work that Seven had put in to develop football in Victoria and to spread it nationwide. That night match between Melbourne and Hawthorn was one of the hardest I've ever called. Dermott Brereton wore a pair of bright green boots for the first time and even that failed to lift us. Melbourne won but in my mind footy was the biggest loser. The moment Seven dropped out of the VFL coverage the pack of cards came tumbling down.

The next afternoon I read with dismay in the *Herald* that the demise of *World of Sport* was imminent and that a national sports show would take over—out of Sydney, naturally. Ron Casey described the events as a tragedy and Premier John Cain rang John Fairfax headquarters in Sydney to lodge his personal complaint. He said, "Traditional programs which recognised the role of sport in Victoria should not be dropped by head offices in Sydney that treat this place as a branch office. I and thousands of others watch it every Sunday," he told Mr Fairfax. "It's a religion." That Thursday the editor of the *Sun* asked me to prepare an obituary on a show that was a major part of my life for nearly half a lifetime. I sat down with Tom Prior and compiled this report from my heart:

I am the wrong man to write an obituary for *World of Sport*. The program is too close to my heart. I'm not laughing on the outside and crying on the inside: I'm bleeding all over. I hope there will never be another *World of Sport*. How can anyone ever hope to recapture the fun and the triumph of creating a TV show which lasted a world-record 28 years? For many years

World of Sport was a raging success but, even if it had been a flop, it would have been memorable.

There was the time during one of our first football panels that my old mate Jack Dyer threatened to flatten me on air—and he wasn't joking either.

Then there was the time Bill Collins, a practical joker to this day, put a Playboy centrefold inside the door of a refrigerator which was used for an important advertisement. Poor old Ron Casey, the most staid of comperes, nearly fainted when the door was opened in all its revealing glory.

One of our football panellists went up to Sydney to cover an interstate game—and didn't come back for a week.

It was an oft-repeated joke that *World of Sport* was 'organised chaos', but the chaos seemed to have more point and urgency than a sleeping-bagful of ponderous talk shows elsewhere. Nobody could risk a minute away when Jack O'Toole was swinging a razor-sharp axe in the woodchop, or a couple of overweight tug-of-war teams from Werribee and Gippsland were risking heart attacks on the studio floor.

I'll never forget Case's instructions to the floor-crews, "If anyone dies, make sure it is off camera."

And how about the 'touch-ball' games when a young Kevin Sheedy and Francis Bourke threw themselves into action as though it was a Richmond Grand Final and there was no tomorrow. Incidentally, Case and I invented touch-ball over a very salubrious lunch in Bourke Street. I suppose I should mention that Bruce Andrew had a share in the invention of touch-ball but he was sober, so he didn't count.

But the on-camera happenings were merely the beginning. I played 250 games of VFL football but I probably made more friends in that famous backroom than I did in my entire League career. Sure, *World of Sport* was an old-fashioned show and probably had to go. The day of the national networks is here and the times are not a-changing; they have changed. Looking back in sorrow, I think it is fair to say that *World of Sport* gave a lot of enjoyment to a lot of people for a long, long time. There were some wonderful people involved over the years and I made some of my best friends in front of, and behind, those tired old *World of Sport* sets. I have some great memories and, as Jack Dyer would say, "No one, and I mean no one, can take them away."

With *World of Sport* gone, *League Teams* dead and buried and the football now with the ABC I suddenly found myself with plenty of time on my hands. I still had my job with the *Sun* but I had no intention of retiring from the electronic media at the very tender age of 64, an age when I felt I had plenty to offer. I had never bothered with contracts at Seven. I had dealt with Ron Casey as a mate and our handshake was a firm and unbreakable bond. With nothing to do I waited for the phone to ring. It rang and rang and kept on ringing.

Broadcom were interested in using me as one of their commentators on their national link up. My commentary would be heard everywhere but in Victoria. Morally, I couldn't work for them.

Tim Lane, the head of ABC Sport, rang and asked if I would be interested in working on ABC radio. He said he would have liked to work alongside me on television but doubted whether my personality would work with his. Thanks Tim, but no thanks.

David Johnston runs Ten's *Eyewitness News* and is one of the finest television newscasters this country has produced and when he rang I was all ears. He wanted me to appear on the news presenting a different look at Melbourne, a slant on the city seen through my eyes. I thought this was interesting and innovative but I asked him for a little more time to think it over.

The call from John Sorell, the gruff and bearlike news director at GTV 9, sat me back and made me think.

"You'd better come to us," Sorell said straightforwardly.

"Why?" I enquired.

"We'll make you look better."

"Why?"

"We've got better make-up artists."

Channel Seven turned up at my Toorak home. HSV 7 executive sporting producer Gordon Bennett and his Sydney counterpart Rick Jemison arrived with contract in hand and asked me to stay on. They offered me more money for what I gathered at the time to be quite a bit less work. Edna put her foot down.

"He's talking with John Sorell at Nine, David Johnston at Ten and Tim Lane at the ABC. He's not signing anything," Edna said in that voice that could kill any negotiation. My very good friend John Fitzgerald, a former editor of the *Herald* and now an executive with International Public Relations, the company that looks after Alan Bond, rang and suggested that I throw my lot in with Nine. I had people telling me what to do and people trying to help, all with the intention of getting me back on the road with the minimum of fuss.

III

Nine invited me down for a boardroom lunch with Sorell, the managing director Gary Rice and general manager Ian Johnson. It was like being with old friends. Sorell had been one of the most gifted journalists ever to work at the *Herald*. His 'On the Spot' column had been one of the most popular features of the newspaper and he'd won Walkley Awards for his stories on Red Adair, the US oil well trouble shooter, and the resignation of prime minister John Gorton. On top of that he'd been a good customer and a dear friend for close to 25 years. I'd known Gary Rice when he was with BTV 6 at Ballarat and had kept in touch socially, and Ian Johnson—well, he just looked familiar. It turned out that Ian had sat next to me years earlier in his capacity as secretary of the Box Hill Pioneers' footy club. Jack Dyer and I had been the star performers at one of his nights. The people at Nine were slick, professional and on the ball. They convinced me that this should be my new home. Jokingly, I suggested that they probably had a contract already drawn up. With that Ian Johnson whipped one out of his coat pocket. Seven have never paid their people well, and it had cost them some of the biggest names in the industry as a result. Nine, on the other hand, seem to know how to look after you—even an ageing superstar like me.

'Lou's lip lands new TV home' read the back-page headline in the *Sun* on Wednesday 25 March, and my association with Seven had come to an end. Alongside me in the picture were newsreader Brian Naylor, who had visited me as a customer at the Phoenix, worked with me at Seven and would work alongside me at Nine, and weathergirl Annie Peacock, whose mum Susan Rossiter had been a cadet on the *Sun* in my early days. The next day I visited Nine to work out some of the formalities and was stunned to see my own car park and a sign, 'Reserved, Lou Richards', in gleaming fresh paint. In 30 years at Seven, you parked where you could. There was a new *Wide World of Sports* blazer and my photo adorned the corridor. At Nine things are done quickly, very quickly.

III

I was amazed when the company executives told me that Edna was welcome to accompany me on any interstate or overseas trips that might bob up. How things had changed. I recalled one hectic March when Peter Landy and I had broadcast 14 matches in three weeks for Seven and in between I had compered the Moomba parade with Sandy Roberts. The following week we were supposed to fly to Sydney for a Swans match. I asked if Edna could go, too, and was told she could. A few weeks later I got the bill. In two years at Nine I was sent on assignments to Los Angeles, Toronto and London as well as to the Barrier Reef, Adelaide and Perth and on every occasion Nine sent us both first class. I can tell you, it is this sort of thinking that makes you put in that little extra for your employer. Nine made a play at getting the football rights in 1988 under our Sydney-based executive sporting producer David Hill. We won the rights for the Bicentennial Carnival in Adelaide but lost out to the Seven Network for the major package. The big money had come to Seven in the guise of Christopher Skase and deep down I was pleased for my old mates. I just hoped that the blokes who did all the hard work might be better rewarded.

Naturally, I was itching to call the football and felt as if a large chunk of my life had evaporated without it. That's not to say I wasn't busy. I'd never worked so hard in my life. On Sunday mornings I would co-host *Wide World of Sports* from 11am to 1pm. On Monday at 7.30am I would do a live cross into the *Today* show with George Negus and Liz Hayes. On Tuesday night and again on Thursday night I would do a roving report from one of the football grounds for the *National Nine News*. Some weeks I would do guest spots with Ray Martin on the *Midday Show* or on the *Cartoon Company* and on Friday night I would present my analytical and incisive preview on the coming round of football. On top of that there was a weekly story to prepare for *Sports Sunday* or *Wide World of Sports*. Throw in my columns for the *Sun*, which continue unabated, and my radio work with 3MMM every morning, and you can see that life is never dull around our part of Toorak.

III

My on-air relationship, or you might say partnership, with Jack Dyer had come to an end at Seven. Jack was in his mid-70s and looking forward to relaxing and catching a few fish. He'd had enough of football, after nearly 60 years as one of our greatest players and most loved commentators. I often wondered who might step in and fill the breach. Nine again came to the party. They found me a big log from Tasmania, another former VFL ruckman just like Jack, only this bloke was an intellectual. He used a fountain pen and preferred French champagne to cask wine. I'd worked with Max Walker many times over the years. We'd shared many a sports night and had worked together on HSV 7 in the old days at *World of Sport*. I can remember him now. He'd come in with that stupid big Cheshire-cat grin, smiling at everyone, his teeth chattering as he fought back the nerves. He was always perfectly prepared. He carried copious notes on which were squiggles and lines everywhere, coloured inks signifying the various points he meant to dwell on and every fact and figure underlined. Max was fastidious. He still is. *World of Sport* in those days was anything but that sort of show. Max would introduce the cricket segment and be running through his well-rehearsed patter only to find to his horror that the scores on the screen were a month old and the new cards had disappeared somewhere. He'd stammer and stutter and finally regain control. After some months he even learned how to ignore the bare buttocks of 'Uncle' Doug. Doug loved testing out the new talent with a bit of old-fashioned mooning when the newcomer was on live. Dreadful sight it was, too.

Maxie had an irritating fault in those days: he never quite figured out how to graciously finish his segment and throw back to the compere. He'd read the final score and look blankly at the monitor. No "goodbye". No "see you next week"; no nothing.

There'd be just a screenful of the top of Max's well-coiffed scone. By the time we caught up with each other on the set of *Wide World of Sports* for Nine, he was a transformed man. The onetime medium pacer who lapped up the limelight as a Test cricketer for Australia and who'd played close to 100 games for Melbourne in their blackest period in VFL history was a polished and articulate performer. He was a class act and loved by sports fans all over Australia. He was a joy to work with. Dumb, like all big blokes, and easy to throw, but like Jack Dyer, he just rolled with the punches.

We'd been working together only a few weeks when our producer Stephen Phillips suggested we look for a little publicity for the show. A circus was in town and Stephen suggested we dress up as a couple of lion tamers and go into the ring with these kings of the jungle. It sounded so easy. Max would stand on one side, I would be on the other and in between was a big hoop with *Wide World of Sports* emblazoned on the tissue paper. The idea, according to the ringmaster Lindsay Sole, was that the lion would jump through the hoop. Easy, eh! Now, Max has since written a bestseller called *How to Tame Lions*. In it he tells of his exploits in the lion's cage that fateful day in Parkville, Melbourne. Now it's my turn. Max was petrified. Like all fast bowlers he likes dishing it out but gets a bit nervous when facing the music himself. He was scared witless, which, I figured out later, wouldn't take much. His teeth were chattering, his moustache was twitching and he was babbling incoherently as we made our way through the packed stands, past the school holiday crowds and into the ring. I looked magnificent in the pith helmet, the jodhpurs, the elegant brown leather boots and leggings, the whole outfit. Max looked like a big ruckman dressed up as a lion tamer in his clobber. I had trouble focusing on his eyes, they were rolling that fast. Let me describe the ring. It was little and surrounded by huge steel bars and there lounging around the sides were three lionesses and a huge beast named Nero. Nero was your real lion: he was 300 kilograms of beast, with a huge mane, big teeth and might I just add, a fearful case of bad breath. I looked across at Max twice to make sure, but I did later ascertain that it was, in fact, Nero's breath which was on the pong.

"Come on, Louie, let's get this over with," Max stammered. "Grab the hoop so the flaming lion can jump through it and we can get the hell out of here."

"It's alright for you. You're only skin and bone since you went on that diet. And the studio can always find another fast bowler," I reminded him. "Where are they going to find another me?"

It wasn't Nero I was worried about. It was his girlfriends, slavering and growling behind my back, that had me the slightest bit edgy. The job completed, I helped my trembling mate to safety. "Good thing you had me in there," I told him as he mopped the sweat from his brow and we ambled over to talk to the waiting media. The next morning the *Sun* landed on my front step and there on the front page was Nero jumping through the hoop with the gallant and brave 'Kiss of Death' alongside him in all his splendour. There was no sign of Max. Evidently the artist at the *Sun* had realised there was only room for one megastar on the front page and they had painstakingly painted out Max.

III

My brief as a reporter on *Wide World of Sports* was to look at the funny side of the game and over the last couple of years we've had no trouble finding it. I'd always considered Hawthorn's great little rover Johnny Platten, with long unruly locks and that baby face, a dead ringer for that singing sensation of 20 years ago, Tiny Tim. For our preview of the 1987 Brownlow Medal we took Johnny up into the Dandenong Ranges to the Tulip Farm at Silvan. Johnny had no idea where we were going. When we arrived, I just handed him a ukulele and told him to tip toe through the tulips. He was staggered but co-operated and the sight of this Tiny Tim lookalike made for a great little story.

Naturally, he went on and shared the Brownlow Medal with St Kilda's Tony Lockett. 'Two Ton Tony', as I'd christened him a couple of years earlier, had been our host up at Ballarat a few months earlier as he motored towards his century of goals. On that occasion, football's most gargantuan eater and one of the game's most colourful and talented forwards insisted I go for a spin in his boat. I thought he wanted to take me for a gentle outing on the tranquil waters of Lake Learmonth. Anything but: he pushed the throttle down and took off like a maniac in search of the world water-speed record. It took my hairdresser weeks to get my distinguished grey locks back in order.

Hawthorn's strawberry blond Dermott Brereton was another feature. We ventured to his dress shop. That's right, the tough Hawk ran a dress shop at Somerville on the Mornington Peninsula. There was Dermie with a 'his' diamond ear stud and a mouthful of pins, hemming up a dress in the window. Crikey, times have changed. His mum says he's a wonderful son and I'm sure he is. If you reckon he might be a bit honky tonk, don't fear. His girlfriend Donna is Miss World material and a nice girl to boot. I loved chatting to Dermott and suggested he might like to take his St Bernard for a walk along the beach at Frankston, near his home. There would be great pictures of the waters of the bay gently lapping on the shore. All went well until we settled back for the interview. Now, I'm intense when I'm conducting an in-depther and this was no different. It was only the laughter booming across from the camera crew and my producer that alerted me. It seemed as if the dog had been relieving itself on my leg. I never really liked that dog.

III

Early one morning our team flew to Minyip in northern Victoria where they were shooting an episode for the highly successful *Flying Doctors* for the Nine Network. Our aim was to meet 'Big Bad Bruce', a renegade truckie played by Hawthorn's 'Italian Stallion', Bertie DiPierdomenico. Bertie has always been a favourite of mine. He's tough and rugged and goes non-stop for the ball all day, no matter who or what might be between his target and him. He's just like a player I see every morning when I shave, my favourite old superstar. 'The Dipper' had decided to try his hand at acting and had successfully auditioned for the role of the drug-crazed, lovelorn truckie. He really looked the part, too, and we were all keen to see the VFL's answer to Mel Gibson and Bryan Brown attack his lines. Liz Burch, who plays Dr Chris in the show, was a bit taken aback that this VFL player was getting so much publicity and said so. "Dipper who?" was her reaction. Poor old Bertie got flattened by the local doctor, a punch that wouldn't have knocked a mosquito sideways, and the Hawk strongman lay unconscious in the dust. Veteran comic Maurie Fields shrugged it off. "He's no Gregory Peck." Unbelievably, that episode of the *Flying Doctors* was a ratings blockbuster and the publicity generated by the appearance of 'The Big Dipper' was a real boost to the show. I believe that Liz Burch, to her credit, wrote Bertie a letter and said just as much. From what I've heard, the Hollywood talent scouts haven't exactly been battering down Bertie's door to get him onto the silver screen. Then again with his training and playing commitments he probably wouldn't have the time. Good news for Arnold Schwarzenegger and Sylvester Stallone.

As I approach my 50th year in sport and sports media, I am often asked about the future and I have the same stock reply. I plan to keep working for as long as I can. I love it—no, I thrive on it—and see no reason to stop doing something that gives me so much enjoyment. The secret is to mix with young people, to join in and have fun with them. Knock around with old people, and you start talking old and you get that way yourself. You get lazy and your brain starts to slow down and before you know it you're over the hill. As my old mate George Burns often says, "The trouble with people who turn 65 is that all they want to do is practise groaning when they sit down and talk about the soup stains on their ties." George may have the London Palladium booked for his 100th birthday. I'm not quite sure what little surprise Edna's got in store for mine. Whatever it is, I plan to sit back and enjoy it.

CHAPTER 18

STILL KISSING

Times have changed since that masterpiece, *The Kiss of Death, Memoirs of a Sporting Legend* became an international bestseller. Worst of all I am 20 years older and, sad to say, most of the wonderful people I wrote about back in 1989 have gone.

The toughest thing about growing old is saying those final goodbyes. On 8 March, 2008 I lost my wife and best mate, Edna. She was there for me and the family every step of the way. She was the footballer's wife, the business partner, the advisor, the mother of two, grandmother of five and the sounding board for the patter that would define my media career. I might have briefly been King of Moomba but in our palatial Toorak apartment she was always the one who handed out the orders, and to be honest that is the way I liked it.

For six years I watched her battle Alzheimer's and spent every day visiting her. I can't imagine a crueller way to lose the love of your life.

As Bobby Davis said at her funeral, "she was the perfect woman".

'Captain Blood', Bobby Davis, Ron Casey, Bill Collins and so many of the *World of Sport* gang are no longer with us. The biggest larrikin of all, my old mate Ted Whitten got the superstar send off he deserved with a state funeral that brought Melbourne to a standstill, while Jack filled St Ignatius, and the big church in Geelong was standing-room only for Bobby's farewell.

That's life, but the memories of these superstars and their contribution to life, sport and television will live on forever.

At the time of writing, I am still going strong. Well, not so strong—at 89 you don't order green bananas or firm mangoes.

The Mercedes has been superseded by the Ferrari (of wheelchairs) and the tripewriter has long since been replaced by my Apple MacBook Pro loaded with extra ram. Well, Stephen Phillips' Mac.

Now where was I when I was so rudely interrupted...

III

The prime minister Bob Hawke launched *The Kiss of Death, Memoirs of a Sporting Legend* on Nine's *Wide World of Sports* and for once that lumbering log Max Walker just looked on, tongue-tied. In a moment of unbound generosity the publisher produced a vinyl-bound edition to present to the prime minister. For once he held back the tears.

The reviews were astonishing. My favourite came from Denise Civelli in *The Geelong Advertiser* and on the front page—if you don't mind, umpire:

> The Ita Buttrose of football held court at the Collingwood
> Football Ground, better known I suspect as Victoria Park.
> Lou Richards, the shrunken, white-haired gnome-idol they
> like to call Louie The Lip and the Kiss of Death, was holding
> court in his home ground's social club.

And a parting shot, of sorts, at me and the prime minister:

The two mega-personalities came from nothing, their obscure
talents pushing through from bulbs sown in poor soil to
blossom into tall poppies.

Denise would be happy to know that the hair is whiter, I have
continued to shrink and Hawkey and I are still mega! I remain
puzzled by the obscure talents bit.

As that Irish poet Brendan Behan once wrote: "There is no bad
publicity unless it is an obituary."

III

As I have mentioned, the move to Channel Nine in March 1987
and Triple M the next year marked the beginning of a whole new
chapter in the life of this humble multimedia-megastar.

There were the morning appearances on Triple M with the
D Generation, a motley crew of solicitors, doctors and knockabout
types with a smattering of good sorts like Jane Kennedy to keep
us on our toes.

When I first went on the show I was asked to deliver a three-minute
slab of hard-hitting, robust footy news. I chucked in a few gags and
when no one laughed, let alone tittered, a new career was born.

I'd been mixed up in the radio caper for years but never had I been
treated with such ignorance by this pack of pimple-faced interlopers.
They mocked, taunted and refused to admit that my well-worn and
heavily rehearsed jokes were funny.

I was thrilled when asked to do a live broadcast. I was shocked
to find the location was the roof of the 7-Eleven store on the corner
of Toorak and Punt Roads at the height of peak period.

"Honk your horns if you want to hear Lou's joke," some idiot said on air. The place exploded with hundreds of car horns in unison.

III

Nine was a different story. They got their money's worth, I can tell you.

In 1990 I was dispatched to Auckland to commentate at the Commonwealth Games. Executive producer Jim Fitzmaurice looked at my bulging CV and decided that I was a natural for either the synchronised swimming or the lawn bowls. Although I was half keen to sit by the pool and watch a procession of young birds strolling around in Lycra with pegs on their noses, common sense (and Edna) prevailed. It would be the lawn bowls, and I suggested as expert commentator an old footy umpire and good mate, Ian Cleland. Not only was he good at the media caper, he was a man who knew the game backwards.

I gave him a call.

"Ian, Lou Richards here. We'd like you to join the Channel Nine commentary team for the Auckland Commonwealth Games. Will you come over?"

The next thing you know he's offering to pay his own fare.

"Shut up you silly old bastard," I whispered. "Someone might hear you and we'll all have to pay."

We had it all worked out. Ian would use his expertise and I would ask the dunno nothing about this game questions. "How do you get the jack? Who's kitty? Have you bowls for left-handers?"

It worked a treat but sadly I report that there were no further offers of Commonwealth or Olympic Games employment in the decades ahead.

I have two abiding memories of my time in Auckland, one pre-Games and one at the height of New Zealand's greatest sporting moment.

Max Walker and I had been sent to New Zealand to do some preview stories for Nine. We arrived on a Sunday evening and booked in at the Travelodge on the Auckland Harbour. We had a quick change of clothes and arranged to meet at 7pm in the lobby.

Those who know the shaky isles will know that it can be quiet and let me tell you Sunday night in Auckland is as quiet as it gets. The locals put five cent coins into parking meters just to see a little action. I jumped in the lift with our Nine production staff and as we descended the lift ground to a halt between floors. For 20 minutes we are stuck and the atmosphere is beginning to get a little on the steamy side.

"Why don't we ring for help?" asked one bright young thing.

I opened the little hatch and grabbed the phone.

The emergency line rang a couple of times and to my horror the voice that came on line was all to familiar.

"Hellooooo," boomed through the lift.

"Is that you, Max?"

"Yes, who's this?"

"It's Lou!"

"Lou Richards?"

"Yes, you blithering idiot, we're stuck in the lift and need help"

"Ohhhh. Which lift? In this hotel?" And so it went on.

When they managed to get us moving, there was the big dopey ruckman waiting at the desk. "Where have you been?" were his first words.

Ruckmen, you can't live without them; and you can't live with them.

At the height of the Games we were all tucked up soundly in bed and the fire alarm shattered the stillness at about 2am. Loudspeakers announced that we had to leave the building immediately.

It wasn't a pretty look in the foyer. The cream of Channel Nine's commentary team hanging about—from host Ray Martin down to the bowls commentator, yours truly, all decked out in an array of pyjamas. Fortunately I'd left the shortie pyjamas back in Toorak and had gone for the well-tailored longs. One man was missing. Norman May had been entrusted to deliver a bottle of Bollinger champagne to each Aussie gold medallist in Auckland and it was a job he handled with gusto. He did not let that Bollinger out of sight in his hotel room and occasionally, if he couldn't find the gold medallists, he would drink to their health in absentia. (He didn't look too hard, let me tell you.)

Staff went looking for him. Nine personnel banged on his door but no sign of 'Gold, Gold, Gold'.

Finally he was roused from his deep slumber and in no uncertain terms said he would rather burn to death in his bed than leave it at such an ungodly hour.

Needless to say it was a false alarm—Norman and the Bollinger— and the rest of the crew, would see out the Games.

III

Nine had this thing about danger. They revelled in it. Actually the producers loved it and we got to engage in it. Swimming with man-eating sharks for a feature off Great Keppel Island, fishing for barramundi in crocodile-infested waters in the Northern Territory, hitting 300 kilometres an hour in Peter Brock's Commodore, racing on the Grand Prix track in Adelaide or parasailing on the Great Barrier Reef.

My life meant nothing to these guys. While I diced with death Max was churning out bestsellers. A wicked variety of *Boy's Own* yarns with catchy titles like: *How To Kiss a Crocodile*; *How to*

Hypnotise Chooks; and *How to Puzzle a Python*. As we returned from each adventure I'd be sitting back in first class having a quiet heart-starter to settle my jangled nerves, while Max would be scribbling away on a big yellow legal pad with a Mont Blanc fountain pen the size of a small Mallee root.

He'd write a few words and then chuckle to himself. It must have worked because his books sold dozens; well tens of thousands, actually.

III

For more than 25 years at Seven my workload had been football, football and more football with a Sunday helping of *World of Sport*.

At Nine I found a whole new vocation and loved it. In 1993, Ian Johnson, then head of Nine, called me in and revealed, in strict confidence, that the network was considering a new Sunday morning football show; he asked whether I'd be interested in signing up.

It would be hard-hitting and provocative. It would feature the biggest names in football and knock Seven's coverage for six.

"Interested? Are you kidding?" I said. "I am ready to take charge."

It wasn't quite what he had in mind. Actually he wanted Max Walker to take the chair and insert a little sanity into an all-star panel.

He has a keen eye for talent, that Johnno, and he amazed me when he told me that he'd found a producer who had never really produced. It seems that John Sorell, the gruff news director, had decided to cut staff. A sports reporter would get the chop.

"How well do you get on with Harvey Silver?" he asked. Poor old Harvey was shunted into the job and the rest is history. Harvey would produce the show and do it so well that he was asked to produce a new Thursday night footy show in 1994; his career took on after-burners.

III

The first Sunday I arrived and looked at the motley collection of one-time superstars and worked out why Johnno had invited me.

I'd known Sam Newman for 30 years and watched him blossom into one of the great TV talents. Little did I realise that in the next 20 years he would become loved and hated but grow in stature to become one of the most talked about personalities in the history of Australian TV. One of the most, mind. Still has a long way to catch up with me, has Sam.

What you see with Sam isn't what you get. While he can be a pain in the bum, argumentative, opinionated, vain, arrogant and so on, he is highly intelligent and refuses to suffer fools gladly. And he holds his friendships dearly.

I remember visiting his home during one of his brief moments of domestic bliss. It was marriage number three I recall. We were playing tennis and I asked his wife Daisy if I could change into my gear.

I walked into the master bedroom and as I put my bag down I noticed a silver framed photo of Sam on the bedside table. The tanned muscles bulging, the moustache immaculate, the blond tips gleaming and couldn't help but enquire: "What a wonderful sight to wake up to each morning!" Daisy looked at me blankly. "That is his side of the bed," she said.

Sam was just one of a ruckmen-heavy panel alongside Max as Johnno had invited Essendon's Simon Madden to join us. To this day no one has matched his 378 games out Windy Hill way, nor his full-of-life personality. In that first year of *The Sunday Footy Show* he was a font of red-and-black knowledge as Kevin Sheedy's Baby Bombers took out the flag.

While Max was the star—in his own mind—the real stars were Mr Football, Ted Whitten and, in my humble opinion, yours truly.

Ted had been the mainstay of earlier shows at Nine, hosted the wrestling alongside 'Killer' Kowalski and spent so much time under the sun lamp he didn't even bother with make up.

Photos from that first season show the panel all dressed in sombre tones and Teddy in a slick silver suit. All a far cry from our first meeting when he ran a grocery store out west. In those days the apron was his suit of choice.

In that first winter of 1993 we had no idea of the health problems that would confront him.

III

In today's era of trial by video, Ted Whitten would have been fortunate to have played 20 games let alone 321 with the Bulldogs. He had every known dirty trick in his repertoire and was the master of the sly backhander and the tear-jerking squirrel grip.

As the AFL moved towards its centenary year in 1996 (actually its 100th season, but who's arguing) it was obvious that Mr Football was losing his fight with prostate cancer. To their eternal credit they sent him off in style. He had already been honoured for his contribution to State of Origin footy by having the EJ Whitten Medal struck and presented to Victoria's best in the toughest arena of all. He had made the catchcry "stick it up 'em" more famous than "up there Cazaly".

In 1995 the AFL was contemplating an Australian Football Hall of Fame. The first man to be inducted as a legend, at a special luncheon in his honour, hosted by League boss Ross Oakley, was EJ Whitten. In June he would do a lap of honour at the MCG, his head on the shoulder of his son Teddy junior. With his sight all but gone, he would sit in the Victorian rooms and have a private word with each of his lads before the Vics played South Australia.

To this day it was the most emotional moment I have witnessed on a sporting field.

He died two months later, aged 62, on 17 August.

Footscray named its oval after him and erected a massive statue of him in full flight and the Kennett government named a bridge in his honour on the Western Ring Road.

Channel Nine remains fiercely proud of its association with Teddy and televises the annual EJ Whitten Legends game featuring the old-timers as they raise money for prostate cancer research.

III

As the panel grew we added 'The Kid', Hawthorn's five-time premiership star Dermott Brereton for colour; and there wasn't much Dermie didn't know about football. In fact, there wasn't much Dermie reckoned he wasn't an expert on. As his premiership coach Allan Jeans once said: "Dermott knows the name of the unknown solider and the name of the bloke who shot him."

Simon O'Donnell had played footy for St Kilda and Test cricket for Australia so he and Max—the Melbourne ruckman, and Test fast bowler—got on famously and then there was Mal.

Malcolm Brown could make the Texas chainsaw massacre story look like a kid's picnic when he played football. He was a mighty player but tinged his game with an element of blood and guts that would have the tribunal working through the night.

If he didn't like you on the field, watch out. If he didn't like what he saw as a panellist, heaven help you.

III

So back to a Sunday morning footy panel for another 15 years.

My role would change as seniority—or more likely, the babblings of age—took hold. I would be given a throne as Harvey decided that a more regal bearing would help the look of the show. Actually I used to drive Max mad, butting in so often they moved me out the back and gave me my own floor manager.

There was one moment that stood out. Ian Johnson decided that we would do a Friday night special before the Grand Final in 1993. A preview show of the Essendon-Carlton blockbuster of the next day.

The studios at Nine were decked out in bits and pieces for drama shows, the panel had been polished up for the night and we had some big-name guests. Max was the host and Harvey Silver organised live crosses to the opposing coaches, Kevin Sheedy and David Parkin. We went live to the Blues' lanky bigman Justin Madden's place and dropped in on the Essendon champ Tim Watson.

They organised a bloke named Trevor Marmalade to stand at the bar and crack gags.

Sound familiar?

It produced massive ratings and would be the forerunner of Thursday night's *The Footy Show*. Born in 1994 it remains a marvel, and I'm proud to have been involved in two great, long-life footy shows that took things seriously and not so seriously, but had massive audiences all through.

I would be introduced to a bloke named Billy Brownless. I'd spent a lifetime teaching Jack Dyer and Sam Newman the rudiments of TV but Billy didn't need any help. He was naturally a big bumbling buffoon and tailormade for the medium. He was a darned good player and will always be remembered for kicking that goal that sunk the Bulldogs after the siren in the 1994 qualifying final at the MCG.

If you can't remember it, Billy will broadcast it to you off pat.

III

As I'd done for quarter of a century at Seven, I ran the handball competition with aplomb and handed out the prizes with gusto. I must admit after years of handing out Four'N Twenty pies, it came as a shock when I had to pronounce 'Telefunken'. I hate to think of the mess Graham Kennedy might have made of it.

Sam had moved on to the big time as the star of the Thursday night edition of *The Footy Show* alongside a kid who I'd bumped into over the years. From the moment you laid eyes on Eddie McGuire you had a feeling that he wasn't going to stop until he hit the heights.

He came to Nine with a big reputation as a hard-working, news-breaking football reporter from Channel Ten and put a few noses out of joint when he settled in to the chair as host of the new-fangled show.

"What a big week it's been in football," became his catchcry and since that opening salvo *The Footy Show* has knocked over every challenge thrown at it, continuing to flourish when Eddie handed over the host's job to Garry Lyon and James Brayshaw in 2006.

To my delight Eddie showed that he bled black-and-white and when Collingwood looked to be in dire straits he emerged as the club's powerbroker and saviour. His presidency has been the single most influential in my time in football.

His decision to move the club from Victoria Park to the old Olympic Pool in Swan Street met fierce opposition from narrow-minded supporters who couldn't see the big picture.

The results tell the story, with the club now boasting more than 70,000 members, a state of the art facility at the rebuilt pool and a premiership in 2010, Collingwood has regained its place as the biggest and best club in the land.

Not that it was all plain sailing.

III

In 1996 the AFL inducted 136 players, coaches, administrators, umpires and media men into the inaugural Hall of Fame. Twelve Legends were named, including my old mate Jack Dyer.

I was chuffed to be inducted in that first gathering and while some screamed blue murder that I had been overlooked for selection as a Legend, I learned to live with it. Sometimes you don't need a plaque on the wall to remind people of your contribution to the game.

Collingwood was filthy. The most famous football club in the country, and the dominant team of the first half of the game's history had not been seen to have produced one Legend! Gordon Coventry held the goalkicking record with 1299, no one could match Jock McHale's 714 games and eight flags as coach, Bob Rose was regarded as one of the all-time greats and the Collier brothers were megastars.

'Nuts' Coventry was elevated in 1998 and they changed the rules to let Jock in as the 2005 Legend.

It got to be embarrassing as Collingwood kept putting my name up for Legend status, and being told that I was ineligible. They did point out that when I retired in 1955 I had played 250 games (number nine on the all-time VFL list) and captained a premiership side. They added that I had been the most influential voice in the football media—in print, on television and on the radio— for another 50 years.

Collingwood do things in style. Perhaps not always but since Eddie has been the boss they haven't been afraid to slip the players into the fashionable fine label suits and serve up a bit of French champagne at functions. A damn sight better than the old Yakka overalls and the warm Foster's.

In March 2003 they put on an unbelievable birthday bash for my 80th at Crown. A black-tie dinner for the ages or should I say, aged. It was the club's way of saying thank you. It was also a little backhander at the blokes at AFL House.

The honours come along as you get on—I was named captain of the Greek team of the century in 2004 (a little Greek blood in the family bloodlines was enough to make you eligible) and looking at the line-up it was an obvious choice.

Brother Ronnie was coach of a side that included Anthony Koutoufides (v-c), Peter Daicos, Andrew Demetriou (to look after any administrative needs and statements to the media), Russell Morris (in for his blond, good looks) and a collection of Pannams ranging from grandfather Charlie to uncle Alby.

I was honoured to be selected but as I was 81 at the time, I felt that it was unlikely that I would be able to play for more than a quarter. Unless we were playing the Italian team of the century. In that case I would make myself available to play on Robert DiPierdomenico, who I always felt would be unable to handle my aggression and pace.

III

As the years roll on, so do the honours! In October 2008, my daughter Nicole escorted me to Crown, when I was inducted into the Sport Australia Hall of Fame, with the prime minister Kevin Rudd as the guest of honour. It wasn't a bad line-up of inductees either. Ian Thorpe, Todd Woodbridge and Mark Woodforde (the Woodies), baseballer Dave Nilsson, rugby great 'Alfie' Langer, Olympic winter gold medallist Alisa Camplin (who just happens to be a good Collingwood girl and board member) and swimming coach John Carew.

My old mate Bart Cummings was named the Legend.

When they introduced me the crowd went wild! Triple Brownlow medallist Bobby Skilton was on hand to give me the gong and then

I wowed them with a few oldies but goodies. I got back to my seat and Rudd was sitting there.

"Hey Louie," he said shaking me vigorously by the paw. "I've always wanted to meet you. I am a big fan."

I didn't like to deflate him by mentioning that he was the ninth prime minister, since Bob Menzies, to be part of Louie's fan club.

III

In 2009, the AFL contacted the family and said that they wanted to present me with a lifetime achievement award. The family talked about it and decided that if I wasn't up for Legend status in the Hall Of Fame it would be pointless taking second prize.

They had proposed that award be made at the Hall of Fame dinner, which actually added a little salt to some raw wounds for some at home and at the football club. AFL boss Andrew Demetriou said I'd been a "giant" and the "largest media figure in the history of the game" for more than 50 years. Spot on! In a statement he said:

> The Hall of Fame criteria for Legend status is extremely strict, based only around playing and/or coaching record, but the AFL wishes to state for the record that the contribution of Lou Richards to the media coverage and promotion of our game over the last 50 years is matched by few people in the history of our sport.
>
> The AFL Commission proposed that the selection criteria be changed so that Richards could be named as a Legend, but the Hall of Fame Selection Committee did not support the proposal. The AFL Commission then accepted that view.

I still make an annual trip into *The Footy Show* to present the Lou Richards Medal for the player of the year as awarded by the voting on *The Sunday Footy Show*.

One of the great moments came in 2010 when Collingwood won the AFL flag. It was long overdue and a credit to Mick Malthouse and his boys. Early in the next season I was asked to join 2010 skipper Nick Maxwell, with the other two living Magpie premiership captains, the suave Murray Weideman, who belted the daylights out of Melbourne in 1958, and Tony Shaw, another small, brave and talented onballer like yours truly who was best on ground in the 1990 win over Essendon that ended the 'Colliwobbles' after 32 years.

For me it had been 57 years. They didn't even have a cup in those days and the players went back to work the following Monday. There was no TV replay, no DVD from Australian Football Video on the Sunday morning—and no Sunday papers. No matter, it seems like yesterday.

It was part of what has been an amazing journey. I'm so glad to have had you along for part the ride, and I'm looking forward to the next volume, whatever it might bring to me.

THANKS

The Kiss of Death, Memoirs of a Sporting Legend wouldn't have been written without the generous help of many people with better memories than the central character. Ron Casey, Jack Dyer and 'Uncle' Doug Elliott, who feature prominently in the book, played a large part in shaping this footballer-turned-multimedia-megastar.

Past champs who gave up their time include Ron Barassi, Ted Whitten, Bobby Skilton, Leigh Matthews, Sam Newman, Kevin Bartlett, Bob Rose, Neil Roberts, Lou's uncle Alby Pannam and Bill Lawry. Thanks go to Mike Sheahan and Geoff Isles of the Victorian Football League.

The years at Channel Seven's *World of Sport* and *League Teams* came to life thanks to the help of many of those players already mentioned as well as Gary Fenton, Gordon Bennett, Sally Ricca, Sally Flynn, Colin Vickery, Paul Shire, Peter Landy, Sandy Roberts, Drew Morphett and Bill Cannon.

The move to Channel Nine was aided by John Sorell, Mary Hennessy, Lyn Elford, Robyn Smith and Barrie Bell, who also supplied the photographs. Also thanks to Michelle Stamper at

Channel Nine publicity for supplying photos. Special thanks must be reserved for Ian Johnson, David Leckie and Gary Rice in the front offices, who gave the project their support. Sir Eric Pearce dusted some memories from the radio days at 3DB and Phil Gibbs delved back even further.

No one has kept a better record of the Richards career, in print and photographs, than the *Herald* and *Weekly Times*. Colin Duck, editor of the *Sun*, gave us permission to cull the files and Don Richards put together a fantastic sample of photographs, many of which have adorned the front pages of Australia's most-read daily. Thanks go to Lou's long-time ghost at the *Sun*, Tom Prior, and to the *Herald* and Peter Coster for their articles.

Keith Hillier and Bernie O'Brien recounted the stories of Lou's horse-racing past and some dark memories of the 'after-hours' activities at the Phoenix Hotel.

At *Wide World of Sports* the book was helped in its prenatal stages by Annie Denton, Tonina Zekic and producers John Murray and Mark Fennessy.

Lou's daughters Nicole and Kim had a wealth of anecdotes and I am particularly grateful to Kim for keeping voluminous scrapbooks on her famous dad. To our wives Edna and Jill go our heartfelt thanks for putting up with our workload over the past 12 months.

Finally to Lou: my personal gratitude for devoting so many hours of so many weeks to a project that has become so dear to both our hearts.

To the team at the Slattery Media Group—Geoff Slattery, Olivia Hudson and Helen Alexander—the decision to update a great football success story came as something of a surprise. After talking to Lou it all made sense. It is a story of one man's rise from humble beginnings to be one of the most loved and recognised people in this country.

The second time round I am grateful for the support of Ian Johnson, Lou's mentor at Nine and now the boss at Seven, and to Gordon Bennett for his incredible memory and collection of archival photos from Seven.

Sam Newman recalled the early days at *The Footy Show* along with producer Harvey Silver.

And finally to Eddie McGuire who as a multimedia performer of great note himself, has kept reminding us that Lou was not only a Collingwood icon but the footballer who became the trailblazer for the many who have made their fortunes in the media.

Stephen Phillips
September, 2012